antam/Britannica Books

nique, authoritative guides
acquiring human knowledge

hat motivates people and nations? What
akes things work? What laws and history lie
ehind the strivings and conflicts of
ontemporary man?

ne of mankind's greatest natural endowments
the urge to learn. Bantam/Britannica books
ere created to help make that goal a reality.
Distilled and edited from the vast Britannica
iles, these compact introductory volumes offer
uniquely accessible summaries of human
knowledge. Oceanography, politics, natural
disasters, world events—just about everything
that the inquisitive person wants to know about
is fully explained and explored.

Disaster!

When Nature Strikes Back

**Prepared by
the Editors of
Encyclopaedia
Britannica**

DISASTER! WHEN NATURE STRIKES BACK
Bantam edition/November 1978

Bantam Books are published by Bantam Books, Inc. Its trademark, consisting of the
words "Bantam Books" and the portrayal of a bantam, is registered in the United
States Patent Office and in other countries. Marca Registrada. Bantam Books, Inc.,
666 Fifth Avenue, New York, New York 10019.

Printed in the United States of America

Foreword:
Knowledge for Today's World

One of mankind's greatest natural endowments is the urge to learn. Whether we call it knowledge-seeking, intellectual curiosity, or plain nosiness, most people feel a need to get behind the newspaper page or the TV newscast and seek out the background events: What motivates people and nations? What makes things work? How is science explained? What laws and history lie behind the strivings and conflicts of contemporary man? Yet the very richness of information that bombards us daily often makes it hard to acquire such knowledge, given with authority, about the forces and factors influencing our lives.

The editors at Britannica have spent a great deal of time, over the years, pondering this problem. Their ultimate answer, the 15th Edition of the *Encyclopaedia Britannica*, has been lauded not merely as a vast, comprehensive collection of information but also as a unique, informed summary of human knowledge in an orderly and innovative form. Besides this work, they have also thought to produce a series of compact introductory volumes providing essential information about a wide variety of peoples and problems, cultures, crafts, and disciplines. Hence the birth of these Bantam/Britannica books.

The Bantam/Britannica books, prepared under the guidance of the Britannica's Board of Editors, have been distilled and edited from the vast repository of information in the Britannica archives. The editors have also used the mine of material in the 14th Edition, a great work in its own right, which is no longer being published because much of its material did not fit the design imposed by the 15th. In addition to these sources, current Britannica files and reports— including those for annual yearbooks and for publications in other languages—were made available for this new series.

All of the Bantam/Britannica books are prepared by Britannica editors in our Chicago headquarters with the assistance of specialized subject editors for some volumes. The Bantam/Britannica books cover the widest possible range of topics. They are current and contemporary as well as cultural and historical. They are designed to provide *knowledge for today*—for students anxious to grasp the essentials of a subject, for concerned citizens who want to know more about how their world works, for the intellectually curious who like good reading in concise form. They are a stepping-stone to the thirty-volume *Encyclopaedia Britannica*, not a substitute for it. That is why references to the 15th Edition, also known as *Britannica 3* because of its three distinct parts, are included in the bibliographies. While additional research is always recommended, these books are complete unto themselves. Just about everything that the inquisitive person needs to catch up on a subject is contained within their pages. They make good companions, as well as good teachers. Read them.

The Editors,
Encyclopaedia Britannica

Contents

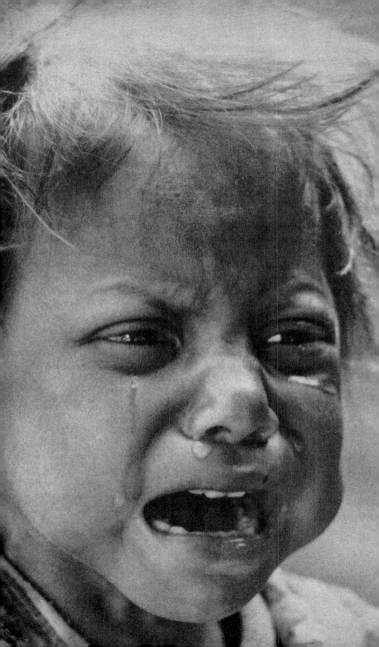

Introduction:
The Realities of Nature

In a matter of hours a Chinese city of a million people is reduced by earthquakes and fires to twenty square miles of rubble. Without warning a volcano erupts, and tons of molten lava entomb people in their homes. Torrential rains turn into floodwaters and inundate entire countries. A sudden avalanche of mountain snows destroys hundreds of sightseers. Drought devastates one-third of a continent. Forest fires and tornadoes, thunderbolts and dust storms continue to take their toll in the modern world. Parts of mountains give way, giant waves engulf entire islands, the earth trembles and shakes. Even an unusually severe winter or an epidemic of raging forest fires is enough to remind man that he remains half-helpless in the face of nature.

From the beginning of time, man has been both awed and terrorized by nature "in revolt"—the sudden disruptions of the Earth and its environment that often bring death and disaster with them. Our ancestors were totally at the mercy of these realities. Furthermore, they were dependent on the movements of nature for their normal livelihoods. If there were no wind, their ships did not sail, and if there were no rain, their crops failed. Premodern societies, which lived intimately with nature, tried to placate its powers with sacrifices, magic, or worship. But they rarely succeeded in turning nature to their needs or wishes.

The achievements of science have now freed us from much of the powerlessness that our forebears had to live with. Storms and other natural disasters, if no less dangerous, have at least become more predictable. Machines can perform many of the tasks that formerly depended on nature. Yet, possibly because of our very progress, contemporary society, with its mastery of many of nature's secrets, harbors a special fascination with the sudden catastrophe, the onrushing disaster, the awful shock of nature out of control. Our advances in predicting weather and catastrophes, and in controlling the environment, have made us all the more susceptible to the sudden freak of nature from which there is often no escape.

Besides, there is always the lurking fear that in making scientific advances we venture into areas where we have no

A contemporary lithograph shows the terrible effects of storm waves that struck the Gulf Coast of the United States in 1900.

right to be. What if nature should strike back? Mary Wollstonecraft Shelley gave expression to these fears as early as 1818 in her novel *Frankenstein*. Since then there have been a host of stories and films about obsessed scientists, seeking to harness the power of life and destroying themselves in the process. Indeed this danger began to become a reality with the development of nuclear weapons and with the discovery that industrial pollution can poison the air we breathe. Science, which has brought such benefits to mankind, has also made it possible to destroy civilization.

This book contains accounts of some of the most severe catastrophes of history—earthquakes, volcanic eruptions, tropical storms and tornadoes, floods, thunderbolts, and other natural phenomena dangerous to man. The book describes how they occur and explains the methods used today to collect information about them and to minimize the damage that they cause. It also relates such catastrophes to the mythologies of the past. Myths like that of the lost continent of Atlantis disappearing into the sea, as well as the many sacrificial and creation myths of diverse societies, suggest man's instinctive need to explain events over which he has no control.

Some of the catastrophes described in this book have become milestones of history. The sudden explosion of the Greek island of Thera destroyed the ancient Minoan civilization of Crete. The eruption of Krakatoa, the island volcano in Indonesia, produced a shock that was literally felt halfway around the world. A sudden earthquake destroyed Port Royal, the famous pirate capital of the Caribbean. These catastrophes are recorded here, as are more modern events such as the recent earthquakes in China and California and the real-life horror-story of the great Sahel droughts that had crept over Africa by 1974, leaving as many as 25 million persons in famine conditions. Was the latter yet another warning from nature that age-old ecological balances can change or easily be destroyed?

The new world of earth sciences has given us a unique perspective for examining these sudden transformations and what makes them happen. Yet for all the advances of present and past civilization, we have yet to master nature and doubtless never really will. It is perhaps not insignificant that in modern times cults and superstitions arise that are no more sophisticated—often less so—than the myths by which ancient and medieval people sought to placate the elements around them. In a culture that has tried to make everything predictable, nature's violence is the one variant, the one oddity, that no one can explain or prevent. We are all the more tantalized for our failures.

I. Catastrophes and Their Causes

"Even a slow catastrophe is quite fast."
—Gertrude Stein

"Everything in Nature contains all the powers of Nature."
—Ralph Waldo Emerson

"When men lose a sense of awe there will be disaster."
—Lao-tzu

1.
Earthquakes

As 1969 approached, a great many Californians were nervous. Scientists had been saying for years that a major earthquake might occur there at any time. During the 1960s, expectations of a coming disaster had built up rapidly, encouraged by predictions from the state's many astrologers, mystics, and religious prophets. For millions of Californians, earthquake study had become something of a fad.

Curt Gentry's book *The Last Days of the Late Great State of California*, a runaway best-seller, had provided the definitive description of the expected "Superquake": 20,000 square miles of land along the coast would break away from the continent; San Francisco would be reduced to piles of rubble; and Los Angeles, Santa Barbara, and San Diego would disappear beneath the waters of the Pacific Ocean. Thousands of people in the Bay Area had copies of a poster showing San Francisco being destroyed by such a cataclysm. Local clairvoyants had pinpointed April 1969 as the month when the quake would occur. As the time drew near, some pentecostal preachers—with talk of Divine retribution at hand—led their flocks out of the state. Some Los Angeles hippies, claiming that they had been warned by the Hopi Indians, fled into the desert.

April came and went, and nothing happened. The following year, in September 1970, a series of tremors did shake the Los Angeles area. The tremors sent thousands of residents rushing from their homes in the middle of the night. In February 1971 a second quake struck in the San Fernando Valley, north of Los Angeles, leaving sixty-five dead and more than a thousand injured and causing $1 billion in damage. Other tremors occurred later, but the expected Superquake has not yet materialized. The latest prediction, made by John R. Gribben and Stephen Plagemann in their book *The Jupiter Effect*, is that the quake will be triggered by an unusual alignment of the planets in 1982.

This contemporary concern with earthquakes is nothing new. The earth under our feet is ordinarily the most solid and dependable part of our environment. When its solidity vanishes, we are confronted with one of the most awesome of nature's phenomena. For this reason, earthquakes have always had a special significance for the human mind. In the eastern Mediterranean, where Western civilization was born, earthquakes were particularly frequent. The Bible speaks of them as an instrument of God's wrath and as a symbol of his power. According to the Gospels an earthquake marked the death of Jesus, and other quakes will precede his Second Coming.

The Study of Earthquakes

It has long been obvious that earthquakes are more likely to happen in some places—for example, the Japanese islands, southern Europe, and the western coast of North America— than in others. The reason for this had been a mystery until the recently developed theory known as plate tectonics. Scientists today believe that the Earth's crust is divided into

The San Andreas Fault is a line of slippage between two major plates of the Earth. Running along the western coasts of North and South America, the fault is responsible for the large number of earthquakes that occur in this area of the world.

large segments, or plates. They normally fit together some-what like the pieces of a jigsaw puzzle. Whatever movements they make are so gradual as to be imperceptible. Occasional-ly, however, the movement of the plates causes a sudden and violent motion at one of the "faults" where two of the plates come together. One such location is the San Andreas Fault, which divides the American Plate from the Pacific Plate and passes through the state of California.

The study of earthquakes is called seismology. A seismo-graph is an instrument used to measure the magnitude of an earthquake and to locate its point of origin (epicenter). Earthquakes are classified according to a scale devised by Charles Richter at the California Institute of Technology. The Richter scale measures the magnitude of an earthquake as a figure between 0 and 8.9. An earthquake of magnitude 2 is the smallest that would ordinarily be felt. Some of the most destructive quakes have had magnitudes of 8 or more. It has been estimated that such quakes are equivalent to the energy released by 10,000 or more World War II atomic bombs.

The Richter scale is logarithmic; each increase of one point on the scale indicates a seismic wave ten times larger than the preceding number. Each full step up the Richter scale indicates an energy release about thirty times greater than the preceding step. Although scientists studying earth-quakes have developed other scales that more accurately correlate the magnitude of an earthquake and its observed effects, the Richter scale is still the most widely used scale of measurement.

The intensity of an earthquake is the measurement of its effect over a given area. Intensity is usually measured by the Modified Mercalli scale. A quake of intensity 1 is felt by only a few people within the area. An earthquake with an intensi-ty of 12, the highest measurement, produces total damage within the area. In such a quake sight lines would be distort-ed and objects thrown into the air. The San Francisco quake had an intensity of 11.

The effects of earthquakes on the land and on water can be dramatic and devastating. Twenty-foot faults produced by earthquakes have been measured, indicating how far quakes can shift an area of land. Large fissures or surface breaks in land sometimes measure several feet across. It is not uncom-mon for objects such as fences to be displaced several feet. In mountainous areas, earthquakes often start destructive landslides. A *tsunami*, or seismic wave (sometimes mistakenly called a tidal wave), may be generated in the ocean by an earthquake that occurs under the sea or on land near a coastline. Some of the greatest damage and loss of life resulting from earthquakes have been caused by tsunamis hitting populated coastal areas. Two earthquakes and subsequent seismic waves killed as many as 20,000 persons in Agadir, Morocco, in 1960.

Every large earthquake is followed by a number of smaller quakes known as aftershocks. They begin immediately after the principal shock, and they may continue to occur for a few days or for as long as several years. Although individual tremors may last only a few seconds, or a minute or so at the most, the motions within the Earth that produce earthquakes may continue intermittently over a period of time.

The Ancient World and the Middle Ages

Ancient Greek and Roman authors mention earthquakes frequently, as does the Bible. Archaeologists have uncovered ample evidence to show that ancient cities often suffered from their effects. The great city of Antioch in northern Syria, for example, was struck by an earthquake during a visit by the Roman emperor Trajan in A.D. 115. Trajan himself escaped death only by crawling through a window to safety. Antioch was almost completely destroyed by another quake in A.D. 526, when approximately 250,000 persons lost their lives.

The physical remains found at archaeological sites are often revealing. One example is the Essene monastery at Qumran, not far from the caves where the Dead Sea Scrolls were found, that was laid in ruins by a quake in about 31 B.C. and rebuilt twenty years later. At some sites the actual cracks in the earth caused by the tremor can still be seen; in others there are inscriptions that record assistance given by the state or private donors to help rebuild devastated areas. More often, the evidence is confined to a sudden change of building materials, new methods of construction, or the removal of a settlement to a new site. The magnitude of an ancient earthquake can be determined from the extent of the area affected by it, the duration of its aftershocks, and the amount of damage found at its center. All of these factors can be estimated from the findings of archaeologists.

Certainly one of the most destructive earthquakes of Greco-Roman times was the quake that shook the entire eastern Mediterranean—Italy, Greece, Syria, Palestine, and Egypt—on July 21, A.D. 365. Alexandria, Egypt, one of the most important cities of the Roman Empire, was the hardest hit area. The famous 600-foot-high lighthouse at Alexandria whose beacon was visible from thirty miles out at sea—one of the Seven Wonders of the Ancient World—tumbled into the harbor. A great tsunami swept into the city, depositing boats on the roofs of houses and drowning thousands of Alexandrians. Two centuries later, the anniversary of the earthquake of 365 was still commemorated by special prayers for the protection of the city against natural calamities.

People in ancient and medieval times were as concerned as we are to predict the occurrence of earthquakes, and—just as today—astrologers and soothsayers to do the job were not lacking. Like their modern counterparts, they were no doubt often wrong. Even when their predictions were accurate, however, they had trouble making people heed their warnings. According to medieval chronicles, an astrologer foretold the quake that leveled Tabriz, Iran, in 1042, but no one paid attention to the prediction, and about 40,000 persons died as a result. Modern seismologists sometimes have the same difficulties. In Hawaii not long ago, people were advised to withdraw to higher ground because a tsunami was expected to strike the coast. The people did withdraw, but the tsunami did not come. Most people therefore ignored a later warning that proved correct, and many lives were lost.

What was probably the worst earthquake of all time took place in the Honan, Shansi, and Shensi provinces of northern China in 1556. Not many details survive in historical records, but from the size of the area affected modern scientists think that the estimate of 830,000 dead may not be exaggerated. This figure, if accurate, would make the 1556 quake not only the worst of its time but also the most destructive in all of recorded history.

Earthquakes of Modern Times

Port Royal, Jamaica, 1692. Today, Port Royal, Jamaica, is an unimportant suburb of Kingston, but in the late seventeenth century it was a major center of Caribbean trade, "the fairest town of all the English plantations." Founded in 1657, two years after England's seizure of the island, it was situated on a small point of land at what is now the entrance to Kingston's harbor. As a depot for the sugar, indigo, and cacao produced on the island, Port Royal quickly became Jamaica's main port. It was one of the world's chief slave marts and was frequently a resort of the buccaneers who infested Caribbean waters. Port Royal was known as a freewheeling, lawless place. As for its inhabitants, "there was not a more ungodly people on the face of the earth."

Port Royal seemed peaceful enough, however, as it sweltered in the tropical sun late in the morning of June 7, 1692. Ships at the dockside were being loaded for the long voyage across the Atlantic, while others were at anchor in the bay, waiting their turn to dock. Shortly before noon, the first tremor was felt, and people began running out of their houses into the streets. Minutes later came a second shock. This was followed by a third, which destroyed most of the town. At the same time seismic waves rolled in from the sea, engulfing the ruins.

Lewis Galdy, a merchant of the town, was walking along a street near the waterfront when the quake hit. The earth opened under his feet, and he disappeared into the sand and mud below. In a few seconds, the inrushing sea forced open the fissure that had swallowed Galdy. He shot up, still living, to the surface, where he was picked up by a boat. Galdy lived to old age, becoming something of a local celebrity because of the story of his marvelous deliverance.

The Reverend Emmanuel Heath, the rector of St. Paul's Church, was enjoying an early dinner and a glass of wormwood wine with the president of the governor's council when the quake struck. He described his experience in a letter to a friend in England:

> We had scarce dined before I felt the earth beginning to heave and role under me. Said I, "Lord, Sir! What's this?" He reply'd, composedly, "It is an earthquake, be not afraid, it will soon be over." But it increased and we heard the church and tower fall; upon which we ran to save ourselves. I quickly left him, and made towards Morgan's fort, which being a wide open place, I thought there to be more secure from the falling houses; but as I made towards it, I saw the earth open and swallow up a multitude of people, and the sea mounting in upon us over the fortifications.

Heath eventually made it out to one of the ships in the bay, the crews of which had stood and watched with horror as most of Port Royal with 1,600 of its inhabitants had vanished beneath the water before their eyes. He continued:

> . . . as soon as night came on, a company of lewd rogues, whom they call privateers, fell to breaking open warehouses, and houses deserted, to rifle their neighbours, while the earth trembled under them, and the houses fell on some of them in the end; and those audacious whores who still remain in the place, are as impudent and drunken as ever.

In another letter on June 28, Heath described the quake's terrible aftermath:

> It is a sad sight to see this harbour, one of the fairest I ever saw, covered with the dead bodies of people of all conditions, floating up and down without burial; for our burying-place was destroy'd by the earthquake which shaked to pieces the tombs, and the sea washed the carcasses of those who had been buried, out of their graves.

An attempt was made to rebuild Port Royal, but the town seemed to be jinxed. It was severely damaged by hurricanes in 1712 and 1722 and thereafter passed into insignificance, as nearby Kingston grew in size and importance. Old Port Royal became known as "the city beneath the sea." Many people claimed that they could see its houses at the bottom of the Kingston harbor or that they could hear the bells of its submerged church tower ringing during stormy weather. More recently, divers attracted by stories of pirate treasure have investigated the remains. No treasure has ever been found, but marine archaeologists have been able to identify the outlines of the old town and have found a great number of artifacts—including a watch with the hands stopped at 11:47, the exact time of the 1692 earthquake.

Lisbon, Portugal, 1755. By the mid-eighteenth century, Portugal's power had declined considerably from that of its golden age, two hundred years earlier. It was still the center of a worldwide empire, but most of its trade was controlled by Great Britain, its powerful ally. By the terms of a treaty between the two countries, a colony of British merchants in Lisbon had acquired a virtual monopoly over Portugal's exports and imports.

Much of Lisbon, Portugal, was destroyed by an earthquake in 1755. The earthquake itself was followed by a forty-foot seismic wave and then by fires that further ravaged the city.

Nevertheless, on the morning of All Saints' Day, November 1, 1755, Lisbon was still a city of great magnificence, with a population of nearly 300,000. The city had been largely reconstructed after an earthquake in 1531, and the wealth of the Indies had gone into the building of its many palaces, churches, and monasteries. On this day in 1755, however, the city was destined to be leveled anew by a second and even more devastating quake.

At 9:30 A.M. the churches were thronged with worshipers observing one of the principal feasts of the Roman Catholic Church year. In the great basilica the priests celebrating mass had just ascended the steps of the glittering high altar when the walls suddenly began to "rock and sway like an unsteady ship at sea." Three separate shocks occurred between 9:30 and 10:00, sending thousands of buildings crashing into the streets. Those who escaped death under the collapsing walls raced toward the open spaces along the Tagus River, only to be met there by a forty-foot seismic wave that came in from the sea to complete the work of destruction. About 60,000 persons died in this cataclysm and in the fires that broke out in its wake.

The earthquake itself was one of extreme violence, and although Lisbon was closest to its center, its effects were by no means limited to that area. Other Portuguese and Spanish cities also suffered damage, and thousands more were killed in Morocco and Algeria. The tremors were felt throughout

Europe, from England to Bohemia, and as far away as the West Indies. The ocean wave generated by the quake reached the coast of Holland in less than an hour, breaking the anchor cables of ships in the port of Amsterdam.

A disaster of this magnitude naturally made a strong impression on the imagination of contemporary Europe. Churchmen predictably interpreted it as God's judgment on sinners. The irreligious used it to ridicule the notion of divine providence; Voltaire, for example, made the earthquake the background for one of the episodes in his philosophical tale *Candide*.

In Portugal itself the earthquake was the occasion for the rise to supreme power of the Marques de Pombal, the man who was to be the effective ruler of the country for the next twenty-two years. The story goes that King Joseph I—who had been away during the quake and had thus escaped being destroyed in the royal palace—was approached by a delegation of the clergy, who urged him to order prayers to beseech forgiveness for the sins that had brought on the disaster. Uncertain about what action to take, the king turned to Pombal for advice. "Sire," Pombal said, "we must bury the dead and feed the living." Then armed with full powers, Pombal proceeded to do just that. He worked day and night, directing operations for the removal of thousands of corpses for burial at sea and supplying the survivors with the necessities of life.

Once the immediate emergency was over, Pombal set about rebuilding the city, laying out the Baixa district with broad, geometrically aligned streets and spacious squares and giving central Lisbon the appearance it retains to this day. Pombal also took this opportunity to abolish the privileges enjoyed by foreign merchants and to enact measures to revive native commerce.

Finally, Pombal conducted a systematic investigation into the facts of the disaster, sending detailed questionnaires to officials in every part of the country to collect data on all of the phenomena connected with the earthquake and to get exact figures on casualties and on damage to property. Thanks to Pombal's efforts, the Lisbon earthquake is the first for which we have anything like a complete scientific account.

San Francisco, 1906. The San Francisco earthquake is undoubtedly the quake most familiar to the majority of Americans. Along with the Chicago fire and the Johnstown flood, it has become one of the classic American disasters. It

The San Francisco earthquake of 1906 destroyed much of the city. Located on the San Andreas Fault, San Francisco has experienced many tremors, but nothing that can compare in destructiveness with the 1906 quake.

has been written about and sung about and portrayed on the screen, providing us with a dramatic and fearful image of what an earthquake can do to a large city.

It should be noted, however, that the San Francisco quake was not the strongest earthquake in American history. That distinction belongs to the Alaska earthquake of 1964. In addition, the New Madrid earthquakes of December 1811 and January 1812, which shook the entire Mississippi Valley, affected a greater area. The area around New Madrid, Mo., where the earthquake was centered, however, was sparsely inhabited at the time, and its effect was by no means as destructive as was the San Francisco quake.

San Francisco sits right on the San Andreas Fault, part of a crack in the surface of the Earth that runs along the entire coast of North and South America. Disturbances in the fault are the cause of California's frequent seismic tremors. San Francisco itself experienced minor shocks in 1868, 1892, and 1898, but nothing before or since that can be compared to the 1906 quake, which registered 8.3 on the Richter scale.

The city that was destroyed in 1906 bore little resemblance to the San Francisco of today. It was a boom town that had grown up during the Gold Rush of the 1850s. San Francisco had become the metropolis and financial center of the West, but it still retained much of its bawdy frontier character. The brothels, opium dens, and gambling establishments of its Chinatown and "Barbary Coast" districts were known the world over, but the city was also a thriving cultural center that attracted great names from the world of music, the theater, and the other arts.

The earthquake came at San Francisco from the sea at 5:14 in the morning of Wednesday, April 18, while most of the people were asleep. There were two shocks lasting only a little more than two minutes, but in that short time most of the cheap dwellings built on landfill near the waterfront—together with the city hall and several luxury hotels—were destroyed. Most of the gas and water lines burst, and the city's water supply was cut off. Lack of water, and the fact that fire chief Dennis T. Sullivan was killed in the first few minutes of the quake, crippled attempts to fight the numerous fires that broke out almost immediately. It was the fires, burning continuously for the following three days, that destroyed San Francisco.

There are many stories about people's experiences in the quake—of the famed singer Enrico Caruso fleeing from the Palace Hotel in a nightshirt, clutching an autographed picture of Theodore Roosevelt, and of actor John Barrymore wandering among the ruins in evening dress, gloriously drunk. Perhaps the most curious reaction was that of the psychologist William James, who was at nearby Stanford University. James had gone to California to experience "a touch of earthquake," and he greeted the tremors with elation:

> When I felt the bed begin to waggle, my first consciousness was one of gleeful recognition of the nature of the movement . . . glee at the vividness which such an abstract idea or verbal term as "earthquake" could put on when translated into sensible reality and verified concretely; and admiration at the way the little wooden house could hold itself together despite such a shaking. I felt no trace whatever of fear; it was pure delight and welcome.

Others found the experience less delightful. One pair of newlyweds escaped from their hotel room; when the husband returned to the burning building to rescue some of their belongings, he was killed. His body was found by a friend.

Not knowing about the man's marriage, the friend shipped the body back home for burial. It was weeks before the bride could find out what had happened to her husband.

Another husband, crazed after seeing his wife crushed under the walls of their house, put their two babies into suitcases and fled across the bay to Oakland. When he got there, he opened the suitcases to find that the children had suffocated.

A police officer found a man pinned under an iron girder in the wreckage of the St. Katherine Hotel. The girder could not be moved, and the man begged the officer to shoot him. The patrolman drew his revolver and fired but missed. Out of ammunition, the patrolman seized a passerby, gave him a knife, and asked him to cut the man's wrists. The passerby did as he was requested, and he and the policeman left, leaving the trapped man to die. Such grim scenes were repeated time and time again.

The fires spread rapidly. One of them, supposedly started by a woman trying to cook breakfast on her stove, was promptly dubbed the "Ham and Eggs Fire" by newsmen.

Damage to land and to buildings in the 1906 San Francisco earthquake was extensive. The rebuilding gave rise to a city much different in appearance.

Brigadier General Frederick Funston, the ranking military officer in the San Francisco area, received reports of looting soon after the earthquake struck, and he ordered troops into the city. Mayor Eugene Schmitz issued a proclamation announcing that the soldiers had orders to shoot looters on sight. Just how many looters and rapists were summarily executed is not known.

Meanwhile, the Navy took over the city's ferry services and began evacuating thousands of homeless people to the other side of the bay. Others, like Caruso, took refuge in the hills above the burning areas. Various methods were used to try to contain the fires on Wednesday, Thursday, and Friday. Buildings were dynamited to create firebreaks, and backfires were set. These measures helped, but for the most part the fires just had to burn themselves out. Their remnants were finally extinguished by rain on Saturday, April 21. The most effective firefighting action was taken by fireboats offshore, which trained their hoses on the wharves and kept them from destruction. The preservation of the port facilities was important in the city's recovery.

When the earthquake and its aftermath were over, approximately 500 square blocks had been razed. About 600 people were dead, and many thousands were homeless. The main business district was completely destroyed. Chinatown and

the Barbary Coast were gone, mourned by no one except the people who had lived in them. In an era of anti-Oriental prejudice, exultation at the destruction of Chinatown was open and unashamed.

Mayor Schmitz appointed a committee of fifty to supervise the work of relief and recovery. Aid poured in from the federal government, other states, other California cities, foreign governments, and private individuals. Makeshift shelters were set up for those whose homes had been demolished, and emergency food supplies were brought in to prevent famine. The main streets were usable again in a few days, and reconstruction began almost at once. San Francisco made a rapid comeback, but it never regained its preeminent position in the West. The center of growth shifted to southern California in the decades that followed.

Messina, Sicily, 1908. The Straits of Messina, between Sicily and the toe of the Italian boot, have long had a dangerous reputation. According to ancient Greek myths, the twin monsters Scylla and Charybdis—one on the Italian shore and one on the Sicilian—lay in wait to devour the unwary mariner who ventured too close. In historical times the straits and their adjacent areas were prey to repeated earthquakes. In 1169 a quake killed an estimated 15,000 people at Catania to the south on the Sicilian coast; then in 1509, on the Italian side, Reggio di Calabria was destroyed. At Nicastro, north of Reggio, about 10,000 died in the earthquake of 1638, and another 93,000 persons were killed in a quake that struck northern and eastern Sicily in 1693. And Messina, on the Sicilian side of the Straits, was devastated by a series of shocks between 1783 and 1786.

None of these quakes, however, compared with the great earthquake of December 28, 1908. Like the San Francisco quake, it occurred in the early morning, when most of the residents were in their houses. Aside from a slight tremor recorded at the Messina observatory at 5:10 A.M., there were no perceptible foreshocks. At 5:20 a deep, rumbling noise like thunder was heard, and then a rough, jolting movement began under the waters of the straits and spread rapidly to the east and west. By the time it was over, Messina, Reggio, and every other town and village on both shores lay in ruins. In the midst of the aftershocks the sea suddenly receded about fifty yards along the Sicilian coast from Messina to Catania. It then came back in a wave ten to twelve feet high, flooding the low-lying areas on the waterfront. On the Calabrian side the wave was higher, and the damage was worse. The intensity of the quake was greater around Reggio than it was anywhere in Sicily. The loss of life, however, was worse in the much larger city of Messina, which was also a tourist center with many luxury hotels and visitors and which therefore received most of the attention in the press.

In contrast to the Lisbon earthquake, which was felt throughout Europe, the Messina tremors affected only a relatively small area. In Taormina, for example, just a few miles south of the straits, only one major building was destroyed, and at Palermo, 125 miles away, the shock was barely felt. In the affected area, however, the death toll was enormous, estimated at more than 160,000. In Messina, the situation was worsened by the escape of hundreds of convicts from the city jail. Nearly all of the civilian authorities and the garrison charged with keeping order had been killed in the disaster. The convicts and others began looting stores and stripping valuables from the bodies of the dead and injured. The few policemen who tried to stop them were overwhelmed and either beaten to death or thrown into the sea to drown.

Help from the outside was delayed because of a general breakdown of communications between the area and the rest of the country, but on the next morning a Russian naval squadron anchored off Messina. The Russians landed medical personnel, who set up emergency facilities to care for the victims of the quake. Six hundred armed Russian sailors began to restore order. Units of the British Mediterranean fleet arrived later the same day, and with their help control was gradually reestablished.

The Swedish writer Axel Munthe, who was in Messina at the time, described the privations suffered by the survivors and the horrifying behavior of people without food and shelter:

> The biggest shark I have ever seen . . . was thrown up on the sand still alive. I watched with hungry eyes when he was being cut open, hoping to snatch a slice for myself . . . in his belly was the whole leg of a woman in a red woolen stocking and a thick boot amputated as by a surgeon's knife. It is quite possible that there were other than sharks that tasted human flesh during those days, the less said about it the better. Of course thousands of homeless dogs and cats sneaking about the ruins during the night, lived on nothing else,

until they were caught and devoured by the living
whenever there was a chance. I myself roasted a cat
over my spirit lamp.

The Great Kanto Earthquake of 1855, here depicted by a woodblock artist, was but one of many major Japanese quakes. Located on the Kanto Plain, Tokyo has experienced several major earthquakes followed by destructive fires.

In another incident recounted by Munthe, animals fared better:

> One evening in passing by the ruins of a palazzo I noticed a well-dressed man throwing down some pieces of bread and a bundle of carrots to two horses and a little donkey imprisoned in the underground stable. I could

> *just see the animals through a narrow chink in the wall. He told me he came there twice a day with whatever scraps of food he could get hold of, the sight of these poor animals dying . . . was so painful to him. . . .*

The homeless were settled in camps and had to endure great hardships during the remainder of a severe winter. When spring came, construction of a new city was begun south of the old Messina. Help was furnished by the U.S., Swiss, and German governments. A few years later, the old city itself was reconstructed on a concrete base spread with a layer of loose sand, which provided a "floating floor" for the rebuilt structures that required reinforced concrete frames. Such preventive measures helped to protect the city from later earthquake damage.

Tokyo, Japan, 1923. Japan in the early 1920s was a unique phenomenon in the non-Western world. In a little more than half a century, it had been transformed from an isolated and backward feudal state into a modern industrial country, the only Asian power that had been able to remain free of Western political control and the only country able to compete with the West on equal terms. The hub of the Japanese empire was the great Tokyo-Yokohama urban complex in the Kanto Plain on the east coast of the island of Honshu. The Kanto Plain, like the Messina Straits, is an especially earthquake-prone area, and Tokyo itself has also been repeatedly ravaged by fire as well. There were serious fires in 1657, 1668, and 1825, and major earthquakes in 1633, 1650, 1703, and 1855, but each time the city was rebuilt.

In the 1870s Tokyo began a process of modernization. It became the center of a nationwide railway system. Great department stores rose in the Ginza, the main shopping district, and business concentrated in the Marunouchi district. The eastern lowlands along the Sumida River became the first industrial area, and Yokohama developed as Tokyo's outer port. The achievements of five decades, however, were wiped out in a few minutes on Saturday, September 1, 1923.

The epicenter of the 1923 earthquake (known as *Kanto dai-shinsai*, the Great Kanto Earthquake) was near Oshima Island in Sagami Bay, about fifty miles south of Tokyo. As at Messina, there were no noticeable foreshocks. The main tremors began shortly before noon just as Tokyo was preparing to close down for the weekend. Thousands of housewives were cooking the midday meal on their charcoal stoves.

The city's ordinary private dwellings were made of light timber and paper and were packed closely together. They were well suited to a country where minor seismic disturbances were frequent. If the houses did collapse, they were easy to rebuild, and people caught inside had a better chance of escaping alive. But the houses were also extremely vulnerable to fire, a fatal weakness in this earthquake. In both Tokyo and Yokohama cooking fires and broken gas pipes fed flames in hundreds of different locations, eventually creating a general conflagration. Oil tanks at the naval base at Yokohama burst open, spilling thousands of gallons of burning oil into the streets and into Yokohama Bay. The oil turned the surface of the water into an inferno, incinerating many people who had jumped into the bay to escape the fires raging on shore.

With fire-fighting services immobilized, the fires burned for days, destroying three-quarters of Tokyo and four-fifths of Yokohama. The estimates of casualties varied considerably, but the dead probably numbered about 140,000 in the two cities alone, and perhaps as many as 200,000 in the Kanto Plain as a whole. A few major buildings survived in Tokyo, among them the "earthquake-proof" Imperial Hotel, designed by the U.S. architect Frank Lloyd Wright. Wright had specified the use of flexible steel frames sunk in bedrock with diagonal supports to counteract lateral movement so that the building would remain stationary while the earth moved under it. Also intact were the steel-reinforced headquarters of the *zaibatsu* ("great corporations") in the Marunouchi district and the Akasaka Palace, the residence of Prince Regent (later Emperor) Hirohito.

Hirohito himself had been scheduled to preside over the confirmation of Count Gompei Yamamoto as prime minister on September 1. The ceremony took place on the following day, but for the first forty-eight hours of the disaster little direction was available from the government in the Tokyo area. In the absence of newspapers or radio service, people had to rely on rumors for their information. When word spread that Koreans were responsible for the fires, panicky mobs took revenge by attacking the city's Korean population. Encouraged by extremist elements in the police, groups of vigilantes roamed through the streets and rounded up Koreans. At first they conducted summary trials and executed those they found guilty of looting or incendiarism, but before long the vigilantes simply began killing any Koreans they encountered. The exact number of Koreans killed is not known, but it was certainly in the hundreds before the army stopped the slaughter. Various Japanese leaders—including Rentaro Mizuno, the outgoing minister of the interior—have been blamed for inciting these riots, but the evidence for such participation is doubtful.

As help poured in from overseas, the work of relief and reconstruction got under way, and life gradually returned to normal. The Research Institute of Seismology was founded in Tokyo, which became a world center for the collection of data on earthquakes. Like the Americans and the Italians, the Japanese began to make increased use of reinforced concrete and steel frames to help protect their rebuilt cities from the devastations of future quakes. Stricter building codes were implemented after World War II that were given some credit for keeping the death toll for the 7.5-magnitude quakes of 1964 and 1978 to but 27 and 21 persons, respectively.

Masani Sugawara, a Japanese disaster specialist, warned, however, that another major earthquake in a strategic area could kill more persons in Tokyo alone than were killed in the entire 1923 quake. He claimed that Japan's wooden houses, though theoretically built to withstand earthquakes, offer "little resistance" against fires. He also said that food supplies would run short because there were insufficient stockpiles.

Anchorage, Alaska, 1964. The most violent earthquake ever recorded in the United States (about 8.5 on the Richter scale) occurred along the coast of Alaska on Good Friday, March 27, 1964. Its epicenter was about eighty miles east of Anchorage, and most of the damage done was in Anchorage and in the communities around Prince William Sound. North of a line passing through the epicenter the level of the earth subsided by as much as eight feet. South of the line, it rose as much as six feet. The quake generated a *tsunami* that destroyed port facilities and forest areas near the coast in Alaska, British Columbia, Oregon, and northern California and swept across the Pacific to Antarctica. On shore, much of the damage to property was caused by snowslides, landslides, and rockfalls. The main reason for the comparatively low death toll of 131 was the sparse population of the affected area, but other factors also helped. The quake struck at 5:36 P.M. on the eve of a holiday weekend when schools and offices were empty, and there were few destructive fires. Moreover, because the tide was low, the effect of the seismic wave was not as bad as it might have been.

The 1964 Alaska earthquake is the strongest ever recorded in the United States. The area affected was sparsely populated, but the quake caused extensive damage to buildings.

As always, however, the quake was a traumatic experience for those who experienced it. Huge gaps suddenly appeared in the streets of Anchorage. Robert Atwood, the editor of the *Anchorage Daily Times*, was practicing the trumpet in his home when the tremors began. As he rushed out of the house, he fell into a giant fissure that opened underneath him. He struggled to climb out again before the crevice closed, but he was unable to free his right arm. Looking down, he saw that he was still holding on to his trumpet, which was pinned under a rock. Releasing the trumpet, he managed to scramble out just in time.

Others were less fortunate. The facade of the J. C. Penney store came crashing down, raining large slabs of concrete onto the street below. One slab landed on a parked car, flattening it to within three feet of the ground and trapping a woman inside. The woman was rescued alive, but she later died of her injuries. The town of Kodiak on Kodiak Island in the Gulf of Alaska was flooded by a seventeen-foot sea wave, which carried William Cuthbert's fishing boat, and him with it, into the center of town. Landing unharmed, Cuthbert received a radio query asking for his boat's position. He replied that it seemed to be behind the Kodiak schoolhouse, five blocks from the shore.

The earthquake caused more than three hundred million dollars worth of damage and crippled Alaska's economy, which depends on transport facilities in the coastal area. Recovery was made easier and more rapid by assistance from the federal government, which also set up a special committee of scientists to study the disaster. The committee's 500-page report, which was published in 1970, made the Anchorage earthquake the most thoroughly documented seismic disturbance in history.

Central and South America, 1970s. Because of the relatively young and unsettled mountains in the area, Central and South America is a region especially prone to earthquakes. Within less than six years in the 1970s, the region suffered three of the most devastating quakes in its history. Perhaps never within such a short time had a series of earthquakes done so much damage to the area.

On May 31, 1970, an earthquake that measured 7.75 on the Richter scale shook hundreds of square miles of Peru, from its coastline to its inland mountains. The quake came at 3:24 P.M. on a Sunday, at a time when many people were inside their houses listening to a World Soccer Cup match being broadcast on the radio. Because the Peruvian team was in the finals of the soccer competition, the interest in the matches was intense.

The earthquake was centered in northern Peru. Many dams burst, and valleys became raging rivers. Llanguanuca Lake high in the Andes Mountains burst and carried away the towns of Yungay and Caras, with a combined population of 80,000. The 2,500 survivors of Yungay were later spotted clinging to the side of a mountain. An aerial inspection of the countryside shortly after the quake showed that many villages and small towns no longer existed. Miles of roads were buried under tons of debris.

The distribution of the international aid sent to Peru was

hampered by bad weather and impassable roads. Peruvian Indians poured into the cities to receive relief supplies. Many Indians suffered from the lack of alcohol and drugs to which they were addicted, and some hid the wounded and orphaned from the Spanish-speaking Peruvians, whom they had long distrusted.

The U.S. Geological Survey called the quake "the most destructive historic earthquake in the Western hemisphere." There were 66,794 people killed or missing and as many as 200,000 injured and 800,000 homeless. The long-term damage to the country's economy, however, was remarkably minor. Another quake, registering 7.6 on the Richter scale, struck the Andes border between Peru and Ecuador a few months later in December. At least twenty-eight people were killed and an estimated 600 were injured, but the damage to property was slight.

Managua, the capital city of Nicaragua, had been destroyed twice by earthquakes in its history before the quake of December 23-24, 1972. The 1972 earthquake, which measured 6.25 on the Richter scale, was centered on the city. The quake virtually destroyed the business, financial, and government districts, but the outlying and suburban areas were less hard hit. Relatively little damage occurred in the rural countryside.

The first tremor occurred at 11:10 P.M. on the 23rd and

A mother waves away a doctor who tries to help her small child at the Retiro Hospital in Managua, Nicaragua, after the 1972 earthquake. During the quake the hospital collapsed, killing 72 persons.

the strongest at 1:30 A.M. on the 24th. There were more than two hundred tremors on the morning of the 24th, and aftershocks continued for several days. Buildings in the heart of the city collapsed, and gas lines exploded, causing extensive fires. The electricity and water supplies were cut off, and the city of more than 300,000 persons was ordered evacuated in order to prevent epidemics. For a time hundreds of bodies lay in the streets. The reclusive American businessman Howard Hughes was living in Managua at the time but was evacuated.

The military headed by Gen. Anastasio Somoza Debayle, a former ruler of Nicaragua, assumed virtual control. Within a week services were being restored to the outlying parts of the city. Nicaragua received international aid, but there were charges that it was poorly distributed. General Somoza's generally efficient management probably helped the city recover from the destruction of the earthquake, but it also created internal political dissension.

It was estimated that between 6,000 and 7,000 persons died, 20,000 were injured, and 300,000 homeless. Recovery was hampered by a severe drought that had already threatened the country's food supply and by the destruction of the city's main hospital. Little of the country's industry was destroyed, however, and both the workweek and taxes were increased to aid in the recovery effort.

On February 4, 1976, Guatemala and Honduras suffered a severe earthquake that measured 7.5 on the Richter scale. The quake was also felt in El Salvador and in parts of Mexico. The center of the earthquake was about thirty miles north of Guatemala City. It struck at 3:00 A.M., and there were more than fifty tremors during the remainder of the day. Aftershocks continued for several days, but they caused little additional damage.

A city of one million persons, Guatemala City was severely damaged. The large slums in the old part of the city were among the hardest-hit areas, and reports were that the slums received the least recovery aid. The capital became a "camp city" for a time, with even the wealthy sleeping in tents or in their automobiles. The city was without electricity or safe water, and food prices quickly doubled. The damage was also extensive in the provinces outside Guatemala City. Many villages and towns were blocked by landslides and were without food, water, and medicine.

More than 22,000 persons were killed in Guatemala. It was

A family searches for belongings (above) after the severe earthquake that struck Guatemala in 1976. It was charged that international relief efforts were ineffective because of the problems of distributing the aid (below).

estimated that at least 75,000 were injured and that 1.5 million were left homeless. Although the damage to property was extensive in Honduras, remarkably no deaths were attributed to the earthquake.

T'angshan, China, 1976. The T'angshan earthquakes did not equal the Alaska quake in intensity. They measured 8.2 and 7.9 on the Richter scale, but in terms of destructiveness they were among the worst on record. Although the exact number of people killed was not published by the Chinese government, it was later reliably estimated at 700,000, exceeded only by the Chinese earthquake of 1556. These staggering losses were, as always, related to the time of day the earthquakes struck and the number of people living in the area. The first major shock, which did most of the damage, came at 3:40 A.M. on July 28, when almost everyone was asleep. The second occurred later in the same day. The epicenter was at T'angshan, a city of about one million people in northeastern China. The region affected by the shocks is one of the most densely populated in the country, including even the great urban complex of Tientsin and Peking, the capital of China. T'angshan, a coal-mining center with major facilities for the manufacture of railroad engines and heavy machinery, was completely destroyed. Several months later visitors to the site found twenty square miles of ruins where

Bucharest, Romania, suffered extensive damage in the strongest earthquake to strike Europe in the twentieth century. Because a well-organized effort to clean up and repair the damage began immediately, the city soon recovered.

the city had been and compared the devastation to that of Hiroshima after the nuclear attack of 1945.

Some of the most interesting eyewitness accounts of the T'angshan earthquakes were published in 1977 by Cinna and Larissa Lomnitz of the National University of Mexico. According to their reports, just before the first tremors began the night sky was suddenly lit up for miles around. After the shocks had ended, trees and plants around T'angshan were found to have been flattened as if by a steamroller. Many bushes that were still standing looked as though they had been burned on one side.

Bucharest, Romania, 1977. The strongest earthquake to strike Europe in the twentieth century was centered in Bucharest, the capital of Romania, which suffered extensive damage. The quake measured 7.2 on the Richter scale and was felt throughout the continent, from Moscow to northern Greece. The quake struck at 9:22 P.M. on Friday, March 4, 1977, when most people were in their homes, and lasted for about 74 seconds.

Bucharest is a city of about two million people, a large proportion of whom live in large apartment buildings. More than 1,400 people were killed in the earthquake, between 7,000 and 11,000 were injured, and up to 80,000 were left homeless. More than 30,000 buildings in the city were damaged, many severely. Twenty-three apartment buildings collapsed, killing many of the residents. Several hundred apartment buildings later had to be torn down because their structural damage was too great to allow repairs. Many factory buildings were damaged. The total damage to property in Romania was estimated at $1 billion or more.

Food was brought to Bucharest from the surrounding countryside within forty-eight hours. In each neighborhood, work teams were quickly organized to begin cleanup and repair work. Workers paid a two percent tax for the relief program, and they worked on their days off to help in the reconstruction efforts. People who had lost their homes and belongings were given clothes and small cash grants and were settled as soon as possible in quickly constructed and furnished apartment buildings.

Within a year much of the damage from the earthquake had been repaired, and the recovery in Bucharest was indeed remarkable. Much of the credit for the city's quick recovery must be given to Romania's socialist society and to the authoritarian rule of President Nicolae Ceausescu. Although there is no reason to doubt the success of the rebuilding of Bucharest, the Romanian government does control information about its country. Some visitors to Romania have seen evidence of structural damage to buildings, particularly to factories, that may affect the economy of the country for years.

Predicting and Controlling Earthquakes

The probability of an earthquake can be predicted statistically. For example, if a major quake has occurred in a particular locality about once every twenty-five years for the past two centuries, it is probable that the same pattern will continue in the future. But this kind of predictability is not much help in determining the exact time when the quake will strike.

In China changes in animal behavior are regarded as significant. A 1973 government pamphlet warned peasants to prepare for an earthquake:

> When cattle, sheep, or horses refuse to get into the corral,
> When rats run out of their hiding place,
> When chickens fly up to the trees and pigs break out from their pens,
> When ducks refuse to go to the water and dogs bark for no reason at all,
> When snakes come out from their winter hibernation,
> When pigeons are frightened and will not return to their nests,
> When rabbits with their ears standing jump up or crash into things,
> When fish jump out of the water as if frightened.

Although Western scientists tend to be skeptical about such methods of predicting earthquakes, some scientists have suggested that animals with very sensitive hearing may indeed become aware of noises caused by vibrations preceding an earthquake, vibrations too faint to be picked up by the human ear. Chinese scientists did successfully predict a quake on the Liaoning Peninsula in 1975, and evacuation of the local population probably saved many lives. The T'angshan earthquakes were also predicted but not with enough precision and certainty to avert the terrible destruction they caused.

In recent years research into highly technical methods of predicting earthquakes has been conducted. Most research

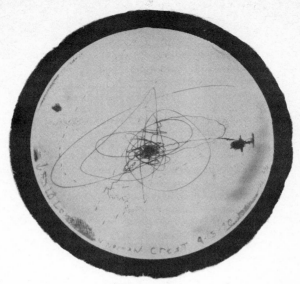

The accelerograph record above of the twelve-second San Fernando Valley earthquake in 1971 was made at the tremor's epicenter. A seismoscope recording (below) of the same quake was made at the Van Norman Dam that shows how the structure responded to the forces exerted on it by the movement of the Earth.

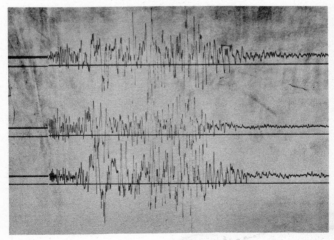

has concentrated on determining and measuring changes on or within the Earth that precede an earthquake. Scientists have learned, for example, how to measure changes in the magnetic properties of rocks that precede earthquakes within a few hours. Instruments have been used to measure minute tilting, shifting, and subsidence of land in active fault zones. (In some instances visible swelling, tilting, and other changes have been recorded.) Measurements have been made of even tiny displacements across fault lines.

Research has been conducted into the buildup of strain in the Earth's crust that precedes an earthquake. This buildup changes the density of rocks and alters the travel time of "artificial" seismic waves set off by controlled explosions. Other experiments have attempted to correlate the changes in the velocity of pressure waves (such as sound waves) in the Earth's crust with the occurrence of subsequent earthquakes. It has also been found that an increase in radon, a radioactive gas, in water may serve as an indication of an impending earthquake.

The ability to predict earthquakes has increased substantially over the past few years. Scientists have been able to predict some recent quakes with a high degree of accuracy. Additional research will undoubtedly improve prediction.

Perhaps the most promising method yet used to control earthquakes is known as the Rangely Project. The technique was discovered accidentally when it was found that fluid injected into a deep well produced a series of small earthquakes. When the fluid was withdrawn, the quakes stopped. It has been proposed that injections of fluid might relieve the buildup of stress in a fault area by acting as a lubricant on rocks at a deep level, producing a series of small, harmless earthquakes. Not enough is known at present about the safety of the procedure, however, to justify its use in densely populated areas.

Although effective control of earthquakes may not yet be possible, other developments may help minimize the damage and loss of life. One of the most important developments has been accurate measurements of the shaking of the ground during earthquakes. The measurements are made with an instrument called an accelerograph, which measures the motion of the ground in all dimensions. Better understanding of the movements produced by earthquakes, coupled with improved design of buildings, may help reduce the effects of earthquakes that cannot be predicted or controlled.

Surviving Earthquakes

The moving of the ground during an earthquake can indeed be frightening. Most of the deaths and injuries, however, are caused by falling debris. Knowing what action to take during an earthquake can save lives.

Persons inside a building, for example, should stay inside if possible. The safest position is under a heavy piece of furniture, away from walls, glass, and objects that may fall. If it is necessary to leave a building, people should avoid moving alongside buildings but should go to an open area. Those caught outside during an earthquake should stay outside, away from utility lines and from buildings. If caught in a moving automobile, people should stop but remain in the auto.

Avoiding panic is extremely important. Rushing toward the exit of a large building, for example, can cause panic, and death, in a crowd of people. Those in office buildings should not try to use elevators or stairways, which may well be blocked, in a frantic effort to get out.

Flooding and fires and explosions are often serious aftereffects of earthquakes. People should check for broken waterlines and for short-circuited electric wiring. If necessary, utilities should be turned off at the main source. Gas leaks are particularly serious. People should always avoid using open flames after an earthquake and should evacuate a building if they smell gas. Turning off the gas, if it is possible to do so, is advisable. Those living in low-lying coastal areas where tsunamis may occur should leave promptly for high ground.

Supplies of food and water are usually cut off in major earthquakes. Maintaining emergency supplies can be useful, or even lifesaving. Other emergency supplies, including basic medical supplies, and a knowledge of first aid are equally important.

For those who live in earthquake-prone areas, preventive measures are important. Measures such as strong supports for gas appliances, flexible gas connections, and secure foundations for objects like shelves can help minimize the damage from earthquakes. Modern knowledge about "earthquake-proof" construction should be applied to all new building in such areas.

2.
Volcanic Eruptions

In November 1963 the world witnessed the birth of Surtsey, a new island in the Atlantic Ocean off the southwestern coast of Iceland. Several days of volcanic eruptions beneath the water created a ridge that rose up from the ocean floor and reached the surface on November 15. Eruptions continued in the months that followed, sending clouds of ash thousands of feet into the air and forming an island a square mile in area, surmounted by a volcano several hundred feet high.

The appearance of Surtsey is an example of a process that has been going on throughout the Earth's history. Volcanic action has played a major part in the formation of our oceans and continents and continues to be an important mechanism in the geological changes that are taking place.

A volcano is defined as an opening in the Earth's crust, through which magma (molten rock and gases) reaches the surface, and the structure, usually a hill or a mountain, formed by the escape of these substances. This process is often extremely violent, accompanied by terrific explosions, and has frequently caused great destruction to nearby human communities. For this reason volcanoes have traditionally been regarded with awe and have even been worshiped as gods by many people. The word *volcano* is derived from Vulcan, the name of the ancient Roman god of fire. The Romans imagined Vulcan as a blacksmith who made weapons for the gods. They associated him with various volcanoes, especially with the smoking mountain of Vulcano off the coast of Italy, which they believed to be the chimney of his forge. Most volcanoes are classified as inactive (which simply means that they have not erupted within human memory). A volcano like Stromboli in Italy may erupt every few minutes for centuries; others may lie silent for a thousand years and then suddenly become active. There are more than five hundred known active volcanoes in the world today, and their history must occupy a prominent place in any catalog of natural catastrophes.

Great Volcanic Disasters of the Past

Thera. The volcanic eruption that may have had the greatest influence on the history of civilization took place seventy

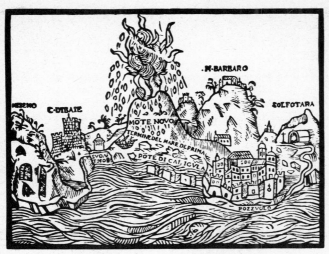

An early German woodcut (above) depicts the creation of a new mountain by volcanic action in the Bay of Naples, near the ancient city of Misenum. At Devil's Postpile National Monument in California (below), crystallized columns of basalt are remnants of a lava flow later exposed by glacial action. Active volcanoes are found throughout the world; Mount Spurr (right) is in the Alaska Range.

miles north of Crete in the Cyclades Islands in the fifteenth century before Christ. Today, the Greek island of Thera, also known as Santorini, is roughly the shape of a crescent. Thera encloses a bay on the north, east, and south, with the smaller island of Therasia on the western side and two volcanic islets, the Kameni or "Burnt Ones," in the middle of the bay. Scientists believe that where the bay is now there was once a volcanic mountain nearly five thousand feet high. The force of the eruption in the fifteenth century B.C. was so great that it completely destroyed the mountain, leaving in its place a huge crater, or caldera, thirteen hundred feet deep, most of which is now under water. Thera and Therasia are the remnants of islands that were left after the eruption. The Kameni were created by later volcanic activity.

The disaster was forgotten for more than three thousand years; evidence of it was rediscovered in the 1860s when workmen who were extracting pumice from the volcanic rock uncovered some ancient ruins on Therasia. These remains and others on Thera itself were investigated by Ferdinand Fouqué, a French geologist who recognized their significance and published the first scientific account of Thera in 1879. Further excavations beginning in 1896 on the main island by Baron Hiller von Gärtingen, a German archaeologist, unearthed buildings and wall paintings of a previously unknown ancient civilization. When more extensive ruins of the same type were also discovered at Knossos on Crete by Sir Arthur Evans, it became clear that the settlements on Thera had belonged to a highly sophisticated Bronze Age culture. It seemed that the culture had spread from Crete to the neighboring islands beginning in about 2500 B.C. and had suddenly and mysteriously disappeared in about 1500 B.C. Evans was unable to decipher the writings he found at Knossos, but he named the new culture "Minoan," after Minos, a Cretan king mentioned in ancient Greek legends.

In the 1930s Spyridon Marinatos, a Greek archaeologist, noted the presence of volcanic pumice among the ruins of Knossos. He also noted the huge stones that looked as though they had been knocked out of place by a powerful wave. In an article entitled "The Volcanic Destruction of Minoan Crete," Marinatos advanced the theory that the Thera eruption had been responsible for the devastation of Knossos and the final disappearance of Minoan civilization. The idea had been suggested before, but by demonstrating the magnitude of the eruption, Marinatos was able to show that it must have generated a tsunami up to two hundred feet high. A tsunami would have hit the northern coast of Crete with terrible effect, and the theory could well explain the demise of Crete's flourishing communities.

In the 1960s new interest was aroused in Thera by Angelos Galanopoulos, who resurrected the idea, first suggested in 1885 and revived in the 1930s, that the island was a remnant of the allegedly lost continent of Atlantis. As described by Plato in the fourth century B.C., Atlantis had been a powerful state located on an island in the Atlantic Ocean about ten thousand years earlier. Its armies had overrun all of the Mediterranean lands except Athens, which alone had been able to resist them. Atlantis had finally been destroyed by the sea, disappearing beneath the water in a single day and night. Galanopoulos maintained that the legend of Atlantis was an exaggerated and distorted version of the history of Minoan Crete as preserved in folk memory and that Thera was the island that had disappeared beneath the sea.

Galanopoulos also tried to connect the Thera disaster with the biblical story of the plague of darkness that God inflicted on Egypt and with the flight of the Israelites, events that he placed in the fifteenth century B.C. Exodus 10:22 relates that ". . . Moses stretched forth his hand toward heaven; and there was a thick darkness in all the land of Egypt three days." The ash from a volcanic eruption can certainly darken the sky in the daytime, and the cloud of ash from such a powerful eruption could have drifted as far as Egypt. Galanopoulos's further suggestion that the parting of the Red Sea could have been caused by a tsunami seems less plausible, but it should be remembered that all of this is guesswork. There is no way that such a theory can be proved either true or false.

In 1965 Bruce Heezin and Dragoslav Ninkovich, two scientists from Columbia University, published the results of their study of volcanic ash taken from the seafloor around Thera. Radiocarbon tests showed that the ash dated from between 1500 and 1300 B.C., coinciding approximately with previous estimates and with the end of the Minoan period. The scientists also calculated that ash from the eruption on Thera had drifted in a southeasterly direction for up to five hundred miles, thus giving support to the idea that Egypt may have been affected.

Ancient settlements destroyed by volcanic eruptions often provide the most accurate kind of information about the remote past. The volcanic ash that covers them has frequently preserved them exactly as they were when the disaster struck. For this reason Spyridon Marinatos, who had had a thirty-year fascination with Thera, eagerly took advantage of the interest stimulated by Galanopoulos to acquire backing for an archaeological dig there in 1967. He selected a site near the modern village of Akrotiri on the southern coast. Much of the volcanic ash that covers the island was eroded there, making it easier for Marinatos to get down to the level where he believed he would find what he was looking for—the ancient Minoan city of Thera.

Marinatos knew that Fouqué and others had made finds near Akrotiri in 1870. He also thought it likely that the ancient Therans would have built their city where Crete, their cultural motherland, could be seen across the water on a clear day. His guess proved correct—the remains of a magnificent palace were discovered during the first summer of work. Further digging showed evidence that a severe earthquake had accompanied the eruption. From the fact that no bodies or metal instruments were found, Marinatos concluded that the inhabitants had received sufficient warning of the disaster to escape before it had occurred. The full story of what happened to ancient Thera may never be known, but as the excavations continue, they promise to reveal a unique and fascinating picture of life in the islands of the Aegean Sea 3,500 years ago.

Mount Vesuvius. Located just outside Naples on the west coast of Italy, Vesuvius is probably the most famous volcano in the world. The natural beauties of the Bay of Naples have attracted visitors to the area since ancient times, and today Capri and Sorrento, within sight of the great mountain, constitute one of Europe's most fashionable playgrounds. Vesuvius has also been observed by more scientists than any other volcano. A bibliography compiled in 1918 listed more than two thousand books and articles on Vesuvius, and many more have been written since then. A special observatory, the first of its kind, was built near its slopes in 1845. From information collected there volcanologists were able to confirm the existence of patterns in volcanic activity that helped to make eruptions more predictable beginning in the 1870s.

Geological evidence indicates that Vesuvius has been active for ten thousand years or more. Before its eruption in the first century B.C., however, it had been inactive for several centuries, and the early Greeks and Romans did not think of it as a dangerous volcano. Greek colonists settled in the vicinity in the seventh century B.C., and in Roman times the area became a popular seaside resort where many people had summer homes. Writing in the first century B.C., the geographer Strabo reported terrace farming on the slopes of the mountain but described the summit as barren and covered with ash. Spartacus, the leader of a slave revolt during the same period, took refuge in the crater of Vesuvius when he and his followers were being pursued by the Romans.

No doubt the most familiar episode in the long history of Vesuvius was its eruption in A.D. 79, which destroyed Pompeii and Herculaneum. Like the San Francisco earthquake, this disaster has been a frequent subject of fictional treatment, beginning with Edward Bulwer-Lytton's romantic novel *The Last Days of Pompeii* in 1834. We are fortunate to have an eyewitness account of the event in two letters written by the Roman author Pliny the Younger. Eighteen years old at the time, Pliny was staying with his uncle and namesake at a villa in Misenum on the north side of the bay. The elder Pliny, who was a famous naturalist and also the commander of the local naval squadron, lost his life in the disaster. The historian Tacitus asked Pliny the Younger for the

As the people of Pompeii attempted to escape the eruption of Mount Vesuvius in A.D. 79, they were covered by volcanic ash. When the city was excavated many centuries later, plaster casts were made from the impressions formed by the bodies of the people.

details of the great man's tragic end. According to the nephew's account:

> On the 24th of August, about one in the afternoon, my mother desired him to observe a cloud which had appeared of a very unusual size and shape. He had just taken a turn in the sun, and after bathing himself in cold water, and making a light luncheon, gone back to his books; he immediately arose and went out upon a rising ground from whence he might get a better sight of this very uncommon appearance. A cloud, from which mountain was uncertain at this distance, was ascending, the form of which I cannot give you a more exact description of than by likening it to a pine tree, for it shot up to a great height in the form of a very tall trunk, which spread itself out at the top into a sort of branches. . . . It appeared sometimes bright and sometimes dark and spotted, according as it was either more or less impregnated with earth and cinders. This phenomenon seemed to a man of such learning and research as my uncle extraordinary, and worth further looking into. . . . As he was coming out of the house, he received a note from Rectina, the wife of Bassus, who was in the utmost alarm at the imminent danger which threatened her; for from her villa at the foot of Mount Vesuvius, there was no way to escape except by sea; she earnestly entreated him therefore to come to her assistance. He accordingly . . . ordered the galleys to put to sea, and went himself on board with an intention of assisting not only Rectina, but the several towns which lay thickly strewn along the beautiful coast.

The elder Pliny never returned from his rescue mission, perishing in the holocaust at Stabiae on the other side of the bay. Meanwhile, his nephew and sister stayed on at Misenum until the next day, when the narrative continues:

> Though it was now morning, the light was exceedingly faint and doubtful; the buildings all around us tottered, and though we stood on open ground, yet as the place was narrow and confined, there was no remaining without imminent danger; we therefore resolved to quit the town.
>
> A panic-stricken crowd followed us, and (as to a

*mind distracted with terror every suggestion seems
more prudent than its own) pressed on us in dense array to drive us forward as we came out. When we had
gotten away from the house, we stood still, in the midst
of a most dangerous and dreadful scene. The chariots,
which we had ordered to be drawn out, were so agitat-
ed backwards and forwards, though upon the most level
ground, that we could not keep them steady, not even
by supporting them with large stones. The sea seemed
to roll back upon itself, and to be driven from its banks
by the convulsive motion of the earth; it is certain at
least that the shore was considerably enlarged, and several sea animals were left upon it.*

*On the other side, a black and dreadful cloud, broken
with rapid, zigzag flashes, revealed behind it variously
shaped masses of flame. . . . Soon afterwards the cloud
began to descend and cover the sea. It had already surrounded and concealed the island of Capri and the
promontory of Misenum. . . . I looked back; a dense
dark mist seemed to be following us. "Let us turn off
the main road," I said, "while we can still see. If we
should fall down here, we might be pressed to death in
the dark by the crowds following us."*

*We had scarcely sat down when night came upon us,
not such as we have when the sky is cloudy, or when
there is no moon, but that of an enclosed room when
the lights are out. You might hear the shrieks of wom-
en, the screams of children, and the shouts of men;
some calling for their children, others for their parents,
others for their husbands, and seeking to recognize each
other by the voices that replied; one lamenting his own
fate, another that of his family; some wishing to die
from the very fear of dying; some lifting their hands to
the gods; but the greater part convinced that there were
now no gods at all, and that the final endless night of
which we have heard had come upon the world. . . . A
heavy shower of ashes rained upon us, which we were
obliged every now and then to stand up and shake off,
otherwise we should have been crushed and buried in
the heap.*

Pliny did not mention Pompeii and Herculaneum in his
letters to Tacitus, and although Dio Cassius included a rather
imaginative account of their destruction in his history of

Visitors to the restored city of Pompeii can walk through homes where the ancient Romans lived. This is the atrium of the House of the Vettii, one of the most beautiful residences in Pompeii.

Rome written a century and a half later, there are few other references to it in ancient literature.

Located near the mouth of the Sarnus River, Pompeii was probably founded by the Osci (early inhabitants of the Campania) in the eighth century B.C. It became a Roman colony in 80 B.C. and was soon romanized in its language, constitution, and architecture. By A.D. 79 it was the commercial, agricultural, and maritime center of the Sarnus Valley and had a population of about twenty thousand inhabitants. As had happened at Thera, the pumice that covered Pompeii preserved the city much as it was at the time of its burial. In contrast to Thera, however, many people were killed at Pompeii. About two thousand skeletons have been found in the excavated area of the city. Many of them had their hands or cloths in their mouths, indicating that they were trying to avoid breathing the harmful gases released by the pumice from the volcano and that they died of asphyxiation. Others were killed when the roofs of their houses collapsed, and some were trapped when the buildings they were in were sealed off. Still others were probably suffocated by the fine dust that filled the air as they tried to flee. Several of the dead were found clutching bags of coins and other valuables.

On the other side of the mountain Herculaneum was buried by a mudflow, probably a day or two after the initial eruption. The population had time to evacuate, and there seems not to have been as high a death toll as at Pompeii. Composed of fine ash and lava (molten rock), the mud not only covered the town but also filled in the buildings and every open space, in some places piling up sixty-five feet deep. Herculaneum simply disappeared without a trace. At Pompeii, on the other hand, the rooftops of many buildings were still above ground when the eruption ended, gradually being covered in the course of time.

The location of both towns was forgotten during the Middle Ages. Interest in the ancient sites revived during the Renaissance, but they were not rediscovered until 1738 when diggers trying to find antique art treasures for the king of Naples accidentally stumbled onto the remains of Herculaneum. Pompeii was located ten years later; its discovery created a sensation throughout Europe and had a strong influence on the Neoclassical art and architecture of the late eighteenth century. Systematic excavation began in 1860 under the direction of Giuseppe Fiorelli, an archaeologist. By pouring plaster of paris into hollows left in the ash by the bodies of the victims, he was able to form plaster casts of men, women, children, and domestic animals, looking exactly as they had at the moment of death. After 1895, paintings and other artworks were left in place as they were found, and today the resurrected cities of Pompeii and Herculaneum are seen by throngs of visitors every year.

Vesuvius remained relatively quiet for nearly a thousand years after the great eruption of 79, although records do mention another outburst in 472 that spread ash as far away as Constantinople. In the eleventh century Vesuvius entered into a new phase of activity, and there were periodic eruptions thereafter, the worst of which began in December 1631 and continued for nearly a month. On December 16 the mountain suddenly exploded, sending tons of ash into the air in the characteristic pine-shaped cloud described by Pliny centuries earlier. Soon the whole area was dark as night, and the peasants from nearby villages abandoned their homes and fled into Naples. The next day lava began to pour out of two fissures in the side of the cone, or outer layer of the volcano. The lava flowed to the bay, covering everything in its path. Violent rainstorms added to the damage later in the month, but the worst destruction occurred in the first two days. Fifteen towns and villages were obliterated by lava and mudflows, and about four thousand persons were killed.

Mount Vesuvius has continued to be an active volcano in modern times. Of its more recent eruptions, one of the most violent and destructive occurred in 1906.

Since 1631 Vesuvius has been in an almost constant state of activity. One of its best known observers was Sir William Hamilton, the British ambassador to Naples from 1764 to 1800. Hamilton, whose wife was famous as the mistress of Lord Nelson, was an amateur volcanologist who wrote a history of Vesuvius up to the year 1779, using as one of his main sources records kept by the Neapolitan clergy. Whenever an eruption threatened, the Roman Catholic archbishop would lead a procession to the foot of the mountain, carrying the relics of Saint Januarius, the patron saint of Naples, and imploring God's protection for the city. The Church authorities carefully recorded the miracles wrought by the saint, thus providing Hamilton with important data about the volcano's past activity.

The most violent eruptions in recent times were those of 1872, 1906, and 1944. In 1872 huge rocks forty-five feet in circumference were thrown down the mountain, and the cone split from top to bottom on the northern side. In 1906 more than eighteen hundred explosions were noted in a single day. Red-hot pieces of rock, some of them weighing two tons, shot hundreds of feet into the air and then exploded like bombs when they fell to earth. The eruption of 1944, killing at least 100 persons, is believed to have brought Vesuvius's most recent cycle of activity to an end. Since then it has been uncharacteristically silent, but volcanologists say that a resumption of activity is long overdue.

Krakatoa. Many of the islands in the Pacific Ocean have active volcanoes that have continued to cause destruction in the 19th and 20th centuries. The eruption of Tambora in Indonesia in 1815, along with the sea waves that it produced, killed about 12,000 persons. The eruption of Bandaisan in Japan in 1888 caused a mudflow that killed nearly 500. An eruption of Taal in the Philippines killed about 1,300 persons in 1911, and a mudflow caused by an eruption of Kelud in the Philippines in 1919 killed more than 5,000.

On the evening of May 26, 1883, the steamer *Gouverneur-General Loudon* left Batavia, the capital of the Netherlands East Indies (now Djakarta, Indonesia), and headed west toward the Sunda Strait. On board was A. L. Schuurman, a mining engineer who had been ordered by the Dutch governor to investigate reports of volcanic activity at Krakatoa—a small, uninhabited island group between Java and Sumatra.

The main island, for which the group was named, was five miles long and had three volcanic cones: Rakata (2,700 feet high), Danan (1,460 feet), and Perboewatan (400 feet). On the northern side of Krakatoa were three other islands—Verlaten, Lang, and Polish Hat. The volcanoes had long been considered extinct. There had been an eruption in 1680, but since that time Krakatoa had been mainly known to mariners as the first landfall for ships making the eastward voyage across the Indian Ocean. Compared to giants like its neighbors Karang and Pulosari, Krakatoa seemed like a small and harmless volcano. During the previous week, however, it had suddenly come to life, sending a column of smoke and fire seventeen miles into the air and covering the surrounding sea with layers of pumice.

At midnight the *Loudon* reached Anjer on the Java side of the strait, where Schuurman and the party of sightseers who had come along with him could plainly make out the glow of volcanic fires on the horizon. Next morning as they approached the islands, they saw a great cloud of ash rising out of the crater of Perboewatan. Schuurman noted that the lush vegetation that had formerly covered Krakatoa was gone:

> *Only the peak (Rakata) still showed some green, but the southern slope was smothered with a thick layer of grey ashes from which arose an occasional withered and twisted tree trunk bereft of branches or leaves, like naked spectres. . . . From the middle of this dark and desolate landscape, the epitome of total destruction, a powerful column of smoke of indescribable beauty drifted over the sea, several tens of metres in width at its base. The column was hurled into the sky with the crash of thunder to a height of 3,000 feet when it became paler and paler as it abandoned its cinders to the east wind, which let them fall in the form of a blanket.*

Schuurman and the others went ashore. Struggling through a layer of ash that in places came up to their knees, they laboriously climbed up the cone of Perboewatan. The heat grew more intense as they neared the top. Looking down into the crater, they were thrilled to see a mass of boiling red hot lava at the bottom. Schuurman collected samples of the pumice to take back to the laboratory for analysis before they returned to the *Loudon* later that afternoon.

The eruption continued in much the same way for the next few weeks. By the end of June the upper part of Perboewatan had fallen away, and the volcanic activity had moved to the center of the island. Violent explosions continued to occur throughout July, but there seemed to be no real threat to the surrounding area. People gradually lost interest, and life went on as usual. On August 10 a government engineer, H. J. G. Ferenzaar, reported smoke coming from both Rakata and Danan and from several other centers of activity on various parts of Krakatoa. His were the last reliable observations made before the eruption reached its spectacular climax two weeks later on August 26 and 27.

The chaos of those two days was so complete that it was months before anyone could piece together a full picture of the catastrophe. In October 1883 the Dutch government appointed a commission to conduct an inquiry into the eruption of Krakatoa. Its work was complicated by the fact that so few people in the coastal communities survived to give evidence, and those who did survive often told conflicting stories. Most observers agreed that the volcano's behavior grew more ominous in the days preceding Sunday, August 26, but no one actually saw what happened on Krakatoa after that. At 1:00 P.M. on the 26th the island began a series of mammoth blasts that plunged the Sunda Strait into darkness for three days.

There were several ships in or near the strait on that day. The *Berbice*, en route from New York City to Batavia with a cargo of petroleum, was approaching the western entrance to the strait in the early afternoon. Seeing darkness and intermittent flashes of light in the distance, Captain William Logan thought at first that he was heading into a tropical storm. When ash began to fall on the deck, he decided to lie off Princess Island (Panaitan) for the night. He remained there for a week, carrying in his hold five small rubber trees from Brazil that survived the wrath of Krakatoa to become the basis for Indonesia's great rubber industry.

The local steamer *Loudon* was again on the scene, making one of its regular runs from Batavia to Telukbetung, Sumatra, touching at Anjer on the way. The boat was docked at Anjer when the eruption began, but the master, Captain Lindemann, set out across the strait anyway, passing well to the east of Krakatoa and putting in at Telukbetung.

The British sailing barque *Charles Bal*, heading east through the strait, was only ten miles southwest of the island when the eruption began. At 2:30 P.M. Captain W. J. Watson noted in his ship's log that something was being "propelled from the northeastern point with great velocity." The "something" was probably what was left of Perboewatan. The log continues:

> At five the roaring noise continued and increased; wind moderate from southwest; darkness spread over the sky, and a hail of pumice stone fell on us, many pieces being of considerable size and quite warm. . . . About six o'clock the fall of larger stones ceased, but there continued a steady fall of a smaller kind, most blinding to the eyes, and covering the decks to three or four inches very speedily, while an intense blackness covered the sky and land and sea. . . . The blinding fall of sand and stones, the intense blackness above and around us, broken only by the incessant glare of varied kinds of lightning and the continued explosive roars of Krakatoa, made our situation a truly awful one. At 11 P.M., having stood off from the Java shore, wind strong from the southwest, the island west-northwest, eleven miles distant, became more visible, chains of fire appearing to ascend and descend between the sky and it, while on the southwest end there seemed to be a continued roll of balls of white fire; the wind, though strong, was hot and choking, sulphurous. . . .

Around midnight Krakatoa went into the last stage of paroxysmal eruption. The magma forcing its way up the vents from the subterranean reservoir was being exhausted. When there was no more magma, a void began to form beneath the surface, and Krakatoa, like Thera, started its collapse into the sea.

On the *Berbice*, Captain Logan noted at midnight that:

> Ashes increased, pieces of pumice stone, thunder and lightning increased, fire balls fell on deck and were scattered about, fearful roaring, copper at the helm got hot; helmsman, captain and several sailors were struck by electric discharges. . . . At 2 A.M. the ashes, three feet thick, were lying on the ship. . . .

The final collapse occurred in several stages between 5:00 and 11:00 A.M. on the 27th. The collapse was accompanied by explosions that were heard farther away from the point of origin than those of any other volcanic eruption on record. At Elsey Creek, South Australia, a distance of more than two thousand miles, people were awakened from their sleep by the explosions. On Rodriguez Island in the Indian Ocean, about three thousand miles away, the sounds were mistaken for gunfire. Three quarters of Krakatoa disappeared below the waters of Sunda Strait, creating a huge whirlpool and generating tsunamis more than one hundred feet high and shock waves that went around the Earth seven times. The tsunamis ravaged the coastal areas of Sumatra and Java, killing more than thirty-six thousand people.

The most powerful blast came at 10:02 A.M. on Monday. Heer Schruit, head of the telegraph office at Anjer, had gone inland to escape the tsunamis that had flooded the town earlier that morning. Thinking that the worst was over, he and some other refugees were on their way back when suddenly they heard a deafening roar from the direction of Krakatoa, and mud began to rain down out of the sky. They turned around again and took refuge in a village on higher ground. Anjer had been totally destroyed. Jan De Vries, a pilot who worked for the port office, rose early and went down to the beach to look after his boats. As he was returning to his house, he heard the Indonesian fishermen behind him shouting "Banjir datang!" ("A flood is coming!"). De Vries looked around to see an immense mountain of water coming at him. In another moment, he was swept away by the tsunami. Convinced that his end had come, De Vries commended his soul to God. As the minutes passed, however, he found that he was able to keep his head above water as he was carried along. He finally managed to catch hold of a tree and climbed up above the flood, where he stayed until the water subsided. From his perch, De Vries could see nothing but a few roofs where Anjer had been. At Merak, a few miles north along the coast, only two people survived. A number of residents fled to the top of a 130-foot hill behind the town, but even there they were engulfed by the wave.

At Telukbetung, on the other side of the strait, the dawn of the 27th was greeted with relief by those who had lived through the ordeals of the night before. Their hopes were dispelled, however, when they heard the noise of the great explosion at 10:00 and saw a terrifying column of fire appear in the sky. The resulting wave reached the town shortly after 11:00. Like Anjer and Merak, Telukbetung was completely devastated. All of its houses, both European and Indonesian, were washed away, and an estimated five thousand people were drowned. The *Loudon* was still in port at 10:00, but

Captain Lindemann, alarmed by the noise of the volcano, made haste to get under way and was steaming out into Lampung Bay when the tsunami came in. Chief Engineer Van Sandick related what happened:

> . . . the ship had just enough time to meet with the wave from the front. After a moment, full of anguish, we were lifted up with a dizzy rapidity. The ship made a formidable leap, and immediately afterwards we felt as though we had been plunged into the abyss. But the ship's blade went higher and we were safe. Like a high mountain, the monstrous wave precipitated its journey towards the land. Immediately afterwards another three waves of colossal size appeared. And before our eyes this terrifying upheaval of the sea, in a sweeping transit, consumed in one instant the ruin of the town; the lighthouse fell in one piece, and the whole town was swept away in one blow like a castle of cards. All was finished. There, where a few moments ago lived the town of Telukbetung, was nothing but the open sea.

The safest place to be was away from land. Although many smaller craft were destroyed, none of the larger vessels in the strait was lost as a result of the eruptions. The *Charles Bal* was never more than thirty miles away from Krakatoa during the whole time. When it finally became light enough to see, Captain Watson found that his entire ship looked as though it had been cemented with volcanic ash. The ship was still afloat, however, and was able to make it into Batavia on the 28th.

On that same day the *Loudon* finally left Lampung Bay, where she had been kept by the darkness after escaping from Telukbetung. On the morning of the 29th she sailed past Krakatoa, and the Chief Engineer noted:

> . . . there is not any doubt that this is the cursed volcano which is the cause of all the misfortune, because the crater which distributed so much smoke and ash two days previously is destroyed, and the waves of the sea pass peacefully where there had been dry land. No more than one-quarter of the island can be seen, and the part swallowed up was as though torn . . . from the remaining section. Only two reefs, terrible sights, now rose above the vanished area. The volcanic eruption

The eruption of Krakatoa in Indonesia in 1883 was one of the most destructive ever witnessed by man. The violent activity of the volcano both destroyed and created land, and the material released produced visible changes in the atmosphere for several months throughout much of the world.

had not completely ceased. At eight different points thick columns of smoke could be seen. . . .

Meanwhile, word of the disaster flashed around the world, and in the next few weeks investigators worked to establish the vital statistics of the eruption. It was calculated that Krakatoa had ejected thirteen cubic miles of material, two-thirds of which had fallen within a twenty-mile radius. The remainder, about four cubic miles, had risen into the atmosphere in the form of fine dust and had drifted for thousands of miles. The atmospheric dust produced spectacular red and green sunsets as far away as Europe and North America several months after the eruption.

All that remained of Krakatoa Island itself in the wake of the eruption was about half of the cone of Rakata. The islands of Lang and Verlaten had been enlarged, but Polish Hat

The eruption of Mount Pelée on the Caribbean island of Martinique in 1902, as shown in this contemporary drawing, destroyed the town of St. Pierre.

had disappeared altogether. As the years went by, life slowly returned to the islands. By the early 1900s a large population of birds and animals was living amid the dense vegetation that once again covered the islands. There was no further volcanic activity until June 1927, when local fishermen noticed gas bubbles rising out of the water between Verlaten and Rakata. A new volcanic island appeared early in 1928. All the activity remained underwater until a new two-hundred-foot cone, Anak Krakatoa (Child of Krakatoa), was formed in 1952. Its periodic rumbling has continued to give notice of the destructive force underneath the Sunda Strait.

Mount Pelée and Soufrière. At the beginning of the twentieth century St. Pierre was the largest town and principal port on the Caribbean island of Martinique. Settled by French colonists in the seventeenth century, Martinique was still a French territory, but the majority of its people were descendants of West African slaves who had been brought to the island to work on the sugar plantations. The days of slavery were over, but sugar remained the island's most important product. St. Pierre was a quiet little community with narrow, winding streets and picturesque old houses. Five miles to the north was Mount Pelée (Bald Mountain), a 4,500-foot-high volcano. Its main crater was a bowl-shaped depression containing a lake, L'Etang des Palmistes, the shores of which were often used as a picnic ground. On the southern slope overlooking St. Pierre was a crater called L'Etang Sec, which at one time had also contained a lake. On the southwestern side of L'Etang Sec was a ravine known as La Rivière Blanche.

Mount Pelée was known to be active, but its only recorded eruptions in 1792 and 1851 had caused little damage. Like Krakatoa, Mount Pelée was not considered dangerous. Consequently, there was no great alarm when signs of activity were noticed in the Rivière Blanche early in April 1902. On April 23, St. Pierre experienced some minor earth tremors, and two days later an explosion in L'Etang Sec released a shower of ash that fell on the town. Some local people who climbed up to have a look at the secondary crater reported that it was a lake once again and that a small cone had formed on one side. Explosions and ash showers continued, and as they grew worse in early May apprehension began to increase in St. Pierre. Many businesses closed, and a considerable number of people left the town. Seeking to prevent a panic, the authorities assured the public that there was no immediate danger. The governor and his wife made the gesture of coming from the capital to stay in St. Pierre.

On May 5 the accumulated water in L'Etang Sec, heated to the boiling point by volcanic action, burst through the side of the crater. The water poured down the Rivière Blanche, forming a mudflow that buried the Usine Guérin, a sugar factory on the coast. The boiling mud flowed on into the sea, swamping boats and generating a wave that flooded parts of St. Pierre. Perhaps influenced by political considerations (an election was scheduled for May 10) or by the harmlessness of previous eruptions, the government and the local newspaper still advised against flight, but people continued to leave all the same. On May 6 and 7 the explosions on Mount Pelée were loud enough to be heard on neighboring islands, and heavy rains caused further mudflows.

On the island of St. Vincent, south of Martinique, another volcano, La Soufrière, had also been making threatening noises. Steam began to rise out of its crater on May 6; the next day, the steam developed into a column thirty thousand feet high. On the afternoon of the 7th, the eruption culminated in the formation of a *nuée ardente* (burning cloud), a dense mass of flaming gases and ash particles. Prefiguring the Mount Pelée conflagration, it quickly expanded outward and downward, destroying everything in its way and killing about 1,500 persons. Oddly enough, this tragedy reassured the people on Martinique, who thought the St. Vincent eruption might alleviate the pressure on Mount Pelée. Many of those who had left St. Pierre returned to the town.

At 7:50 on the morning of the 8th, Pelée suddenly exploded, sending up a dark cloud streaked with flashes of lightning. The *nuée ardente* shot down the sides of the mountain and over the ground, covering St. Pierre and annihilating almost all of its inhabitants in just two minutes. It then spread into the harbor at an estimated speed of one hundred miles an hour. Every house in the town was destroyed. Stone walls were torn to pieces; trees were uprooted and stripped of their bark. The ruins burned for hours; even at noon the heat was too intense for any boat to approach from the sea.

All of the vessels in the port were capsized except two—the British steamer *Roddam*, which got away to sea although many on board were killed or injured, and the American ship *Roraima*, which also suffered many casualties. One of the survivors on the *Roraima*, Assistant Purser Thompson, described his experience:

Our boat arrived at St. Pierre early Thursday morning. Four hours before we entered the roadstead, we could see flames and smoke rising from Mt. Pelée. No one on board had any idea of danger. Capt. G. T. Muggah was on the bridge and all hands got on deck to see the show. The spectacle was magnificent. . . . It was like the biggest oil refinery in the world burning up on the mountain top. There was a tremendous explosion about 7:45 soon after we got in. The mountain was blown to pieces. There was no warning. The side of the volcano was ripped out, and there hurled straight towards us a solid wall of flame. It sounded like a thousand cannon. The wave of fire was on us and over us like a lightning flash. It was like a hurricane of fire, which rolled in mass straight down on St. Pierre and the shipping . . . the air grew stifling hot and we were in the thick of it. Wherever the mass of fire struck the sea, the water boiled and sent up great clouds of steam. I saved my life by running to my stateroom and burying myself in the bedding. The blast of fire from the volcano lasted only a few minutes. . . . Before the volcano burst, the landings at St. Pierre were crowded with people. After the explosion, not one living being was to be seen on land. Only 25 of those on the Roraima, out of 68, were left after the first flash.

Out of the estimated thirty thousand people in St. Pierre, almost no one survived the disaster. Some accounts say that there were two survivors; others say four. One of the survivors was Auguste Ciparis, a convict who was saved by the fact that he was imprisoned in an underground cell; he was still there when rescuers dug him out three days later. Although severely burned, Ciparis recovered and was later featured in a traveling circus as "The Prisoner of St. Pierre." Another survivor was Léon Compère-Léandre, who gave this account:

On May 8, about 8 o'clock in the morning, I was seated on the doorstep of my house. . . . All of a sudden, I felt a terrible wind blowing, the earth began to tremble, and the sky suddenly became dark. I turned to go into the house, made with great difficulty the 3 or 4 steps that separated me from my room, and felt my arms and legs burning, also my body. I dropped upon a table. At this moment, four others sought refuge in my room, crying and writhing with pain, although their garments showed no sign of having been touched by flame. At the end of ten minutes, one of these, the young Delevaud girl, aged 10, fell dead; the others left. . . . Crazed and almost overcome, I threw myself on a bed, inert and waiting death. My senses returned to me in perhaps an hour, when I beheld the roof burning. With sufficient strength left, my legs bleeding and covered with burns, I ran to Fonds-Saint-Denis, 6 kilometers from St. Pierre.

On the afternoon of the 8th, Abbé Parel, a French priest, arrived at St. Pierre by boat and described what he saw:

When, at about 3 o'clock in the afternoon we rounded the last promontory which separated us from what was once the magnificent panorama of St. Pierre, we suddenly perceived at the opposite extremity of the roadstead the Rivière Blanche with its crest of vapor, rushing madly into the sea. . . . The coast was strewn with wreckage, with the keels of the overturned boats, all that remains of the twenty to thirty ships which lay at anchor here the day before. All along the quays, for a distance of 200 metres, piles of lumber are burning. Here and there around the city . . . fires can be seen through the smoke. But St. Pierre, in the morning throbbing with life, thronged with people, is no more. Its ruins stretch before us, wrapped in their shroud of smoke and ashes, gloomy and silent, a city of the dead. Our eyes seek out the inhabitants fleeing distracted, or returning to look for the dead. Nothing to be seen. No living soul appears in this desert of desolation, encompassed by appalling silence.

The desolation was indeed complete. The *nuée ardente* (the temperature of which was about 2200° F. at the point of emission) killed most of its victims instantly. In most cases they simply died from inhaling the heated gases. This type of eruption had been unknown to scientists before the Soufrière and Mount Pelée disasters. The term *nuée ardente* was first used by A. Lacroix, a professor who published an account of the Pelée eruption in 1908. The phenomenon occurs when magma, charged with steam and under great pressure, reaches a weak point in the chimney of a volcano. When the wall of the cone becomes unable to withstand the pressure and bursts open with a violent explosion, the mixture of magma dust and steam shoots out as though from a gun. After the publication of Lacroix's study this phenomenon became known as the Pelean type of eruption and has since been noted in other locales.

Mount Pelée's activity continued throughout the rest of the year. Another great eruption on August 30 wiped out four villages on the eastern side of the mountain, claiming two thousand more victims. In October a mass of hardened lava began to collect in the L'Etang Sec Crater and gradually rose in the form of a spine or tower. By May 1903 the spine had attained a height of about a thousand feet above the floor of the crater. After that its size was reduced little by little until it eventually disappeared. Along with the spine, a more permanent lava dome, or tholoid, also formed in the crater and sealed up the chimney. The formation of this lava dome has been found to be characteristic of Pelean eruptions.

Plate Tectonics and Volcanic Activity

Like earthquake zones, volcanoes are usually located close to or under the ocean. They can be grouped into several distinct chainlike patterns in various parts of the world. One major group is called the Continental Margin Chain. It begins in Antarctica, runs along the coasts of South and North America, follows the arc of the Aleutian Islands across to Siberia, and then takes a winding path through Japan, Taiwan, the Philippines, Indonesia, and New Zealand. The Continental Margin Volcanoes, which make a nearly complete circle around the Pacific Ocean, are sometimes referred to as "The Ring of Fire." The so-called Midocean Volcanoes form a second important chain, beginning in the Arctic Ocean and passing from north to south through Iceland and down the middle of the Atlantic Ocean. The volcanoes on the islands in the Atlantic Ocean are part of a mostly submarine volcanic mountain range called the Mid-Atlantic Ridge. Such ridges lie under all of the world's oceans. They play a key part in the generation of volcanic activity and in the formation of the plates that compose the Earth's outer crust.

The Earth's crust is of two kinds—continental and oceanic. Continental crust is made up largely of granitelike rock with a high silica content. From twenty to forty miles in depth, it forms the surface not only of the continents but also of the Earth's shallow seas, which are extensions of continents.

More than half of the active volcanoes today are located around the margins of the Pacific Ocean. They include Paricutín in Mexico (above), Kilauea in Hawaii (below), and Irazú in Costa Rica (right).

Oceanic crust, which forms the floor of the world's oceans, is thinner, less than ten miles thick in most places. It is composed of basalt rock, which is darker, denser, and lower in silica content than the continental crust.

Below the crust is a layer called the mantle. Composed of peridotite, a silicate rock that is relatively soft, the mantle has many of the characteristics of a liquid. Close to the center of the Earth the temperature of the mantle is higher than the temperature near the crust. Because the material lower in the mantle is hotter, its tendency is to rise toward the surface. As it does so, however, the material cools off and begins to sink again, setting up a convection current like that in a pot of boiling water.

According to plate tectonic theory, this mantle convection current is what caused the formation of the oceanic ridges and the oceanic crust. The hot, semiliquid rock rises to the floor of the ocean, where it is erupted by volcanic action, increasing the height of the ridge, and then flowing down on either side to form more oceanic crust. In this way the ocean floor is continually spreading out on both sides of the mid-oceanic ridges and has been doing so ever since the oceans were first formed hundreds of millions of years ago. At this rate, the entire surface of our planet would have been covered by oceanic crust long ago if it were not for the fact that, as the spreading ocean crust comes up against the nearest layer of continental crust, it drops back down into the mantle again, completing the convective cycle. This process accounts for the division of the Earth's crust into segments, or plates.

The line along which two plates meet is known in plate tectonics terminology as a plate margin. If a margin occurs along a midoceanic ridge, it is called a constructive plate margin. If it occurs where the oceanic crust goes back down into the mantle, it is called a destructive plate margin. There are also passive plate margins, where crust is being neither produced nor destroyed. Most volcanic and seismic activity takes place along such margins. Thera and Vesuvius are on the margin between the Eurasian and the African plates. Krakatoa is on the line between the Indian and Eurasian plates; and Mount Pelée and Soufrière are on the edge of a subsection cut out of the American Plate.

The action that occurs at the meeting place of the East Pacific and American plates, along the western coast of South America, offers a good example of how volcanic activity is generated along a destructive plate margin. The East

Pacific oceanic crust meets the Continental Plate in the depths of the offshore Chile-Peru Trench. The area below the trench, where two plates actually slide over one another, is called the Benioff Zone. An enormous amount of heat energy is created by the friction of this sliding action. The immense heat generated melts the rock in the Benioff Zone, and the molten material, or magma, then rises and collects near the surface. When the pressure of this accumulation reaches a point at which it can no longer be contained, there are eruptions in the chain of volcanoes along the coast.

Forecasting Volcanic Eruptions

Scientists' ability to forecast volcanic activity is in a relatively early stage of development. Extensive research is still being done to determine how changes in temperature and other factors can be used to predict eruptions. It is known, for example, that the water temperature in a volcanic crater lake increases as molten rock begins its rise to the surface. Earth satellites are now being used to detect changes in the temperatures of volcanoes. When temperature changes can be more closely correlated with actual eruptions, they will undoubtedly become a useful tool for prediction.

Scientists are also now measuring the underground movements of molten rock, an indication that the changes necessary for an eruption may be taking place. The swelling and sagging of ground surfaces around a volcano also seem to be indications of impending activity. Measurements of changes in the magnetic, electrical, and gravitational fields around a volcano are useful indications of changes in rock composition and movement. Scientists still pay close attention to a series of small eruptions, since it is well documented that such occurrences often are followed by a major eruption.

Controlling volcanic eruptions in any practical sense will probably continue to remain an impossibility. It can be said, however, that science is reaching the stage at which it can reliably begin to predict the probability of eruptions.

Much more is known today about the mechanisms of volcanic activity than was known even twenty years ago. Current knowledge does not necessarily guarantee that people can always be protected from the destructive potential of volcanoes. As scientific knowledge of these phenomena has increased, however, the number of human lives lost in volcanic eruptions has been reduced. The loss of life will no doubt be reduced still further in the future.

3.
Tropical Storms and Tornadoes

In his account of Christopher Columbus's second voyage to the New World, the sixteenth-century historian Pietro Martire d'Anghiera tells of a violent storm that arose in June 1495 while the explorer's fleet was at anchor off what is now the port of Santo Domingo, Dominican Republic. The storm sank three ships and inflicted great damage on the island, where the Indians

> *muttered among themselves that our nation had troubled the elements and caused such portentous signs. These tempests of the air (which the Greeks call tiphones, that is, whirlwinds), they call furacanes; which, they say, do oftentimes chance in this island.*

This is the earliest reference to a hurricane in European literature.

Hurricanes are tropical storms that usually originate in the tropical zone of the Earth's oceans between the Tropic of Cancer (23° 30′ N) and the Tropic of Capricorn (23° 30′ S). The word *hurricane* most often refers to tropical storms originating in the Atlantic Ocean, whereas *typhoon* usually refers to those originating in the Pacific. Most tropical storms develop in an area known variously as the doldrums, the intertropical convergence zone, or the equatorial low-pressure trough, where the prevailing winds of the Northern and Southern hemispheres meet. The exact position of this zone changes from one season to another, but its maximum extent is from about 15° N to 15° S.

A tropical storm is a cyclone, or rotating wind system, which is called a hurricane or typhoon if its wind velocity is greater than seventy-five miles per hour. The precise combination of factors that creates such a storm is not fully known, but it develops from an interaction between the winds (usually the easterly trade winds) and the heated surface of the ocean. Normally, a surface temperature of about 80° F is required. The ascent of warm, moist air from the ocean is followed by the formation of rain clouds and a drop in the atmospheric pressure. Under the influence of the low-pressure center, the winds begin a circular motion and form a

Hurricane Betsy caused extensive destruction in the Bahamas, Florida, and Louisiana (left) in 1965. High winds (above) and heavy rains that cause flooding (below) are the most destructive characteristics of hurricanes.

vortex that rotates clockwise in the Southern Hemisphere and counterclockwise in the Northern Hemisphere. The clouds near the water gather into a series of narrow bands that spiral cyclonically from the outside toward the center, where there is an area of calm called the eye of the storm. The air rises in a whirling motion, and as it nears the top of the spiral, which may be as high as forty thousand feet, centrifugal force gradually draws it outward again. The diameter of the system varies from fifty to one hundred and fifty miles or more.

Once formed, the storm system drifts westward with the prevailing trade winds at an average speed of about fifteen miles per hour. At the same time, the system moves slowly north (if it is north of the equator) or south (if south of the equator) until it leaves the tropical zone. At this point contrary winds begin to carry the storm back in an easterly direction, and it gradually dissipates.

The high winds and heavy rains generated by tropical storms can cause enormous destruction in populated areas and can affect an area several miles in width. Even more dangerous are the storm waves that they sometimes cause. Like the seismic sea waves associated with earthquakes and volcanic eruptions, these storm waves may sweep in on coastal areas, taking a terrible toll in life and property.

The Atlantic Hurricanes

The hurricane season lasts roughly from June through October. In midseason, in August and September, the storms develop mainly on the ocean side of the West Indies, most often east of the Lesser Antilles. Early and late in the season, in June and from the latter part of September onward, the most frequent area of formation is the western Caribbean. The number of hurricanes occurring in a single year has varied from between two and twenty-one; seven is the average. The West Indies, Florida, and the coast along the Gulf of Mexico are the land areas most often hit by hurricanes, but storms moving up the Atlantic coast of the United States frequently cause devastation much farther north.

After Columbus's initial experience in 1495, the early Spanish settlers in the Caribbean soon accustomed themselves to the fact that hurricanes were one of the hazards of life there. Just as the Indians had done before them, the Spanish invoked supernatural protection against the destructive winds. Prayers to Saint Francis were thought to be particularly beneficial. The Cord of Saint Francis, a short length of knotted rope, was often hung in people's homes as a talisman during the hurricane season.

Such safeguards, however, did not always work. The folklore of the region is replete with stories of Spanish treasure ships sent to the bottom of the sea by hurricanes, and in fact there were a number of such wrecks. The most famous was the *Nuestra Señora de la Concepción*, which went down off the Bahamas in 1643. Its cargo, six tons of silver bullion that was salvaged by the New Englander Sir William Phips in 1686, was valued at three hundred thousand pounds. Another lost treasure galleon was the *Atocha*, which sunk off the Florida Keys in 1622. A portion of its cargo was recovered by the treasure hunter Mel Fisher in the 1970s.

The Caribbean, 1780. One of the worst hurricane seasons in history occurred in the Caribbean in 1780, during the time of the American Revolutionary War. Eight tropical storms ravaged the islands and the Gulf Coast in that year, three of them in the first three weeks of October. The storms were notable both for their intensity and for their influence on the course of military and naval operations. By 1780, France and Spain had joined the United States in the war against Great Britain. Spanish, French, and British naval squadrons were all operating in Caribbean and Gulf waters, and all were affected by the storms.

Louisiana had been under Spanish rule since 1763. Its governor, Bernardo de Gálvez, was planning an expedition to drive the British out of Pensacola, the last of their strongholds on the coast. His military activities in the preceding year had already been impeded by the weather. In August 1779, shortly after the outbreak of war betwen Spain and England, a fleet of gunboats Gálvez had assembled for an attack on British outposts at Natchez and Baton Rouge was destroyed by a hurricane before he could get out of New Orleans. Quickly reorganizing his forces, Gálvez was able to take the British forts in September. In February 1780 he captured Mobile, and he then went to Havana to try to get reinforcements for an assault on Pensacola. Gálvez was still in Havana in July when Don José Solano arrived from Spain with a fleet carrying several regiments of troops, but the authorities in Cuba continued to procrastinate throughout the summer.

Comte de Guichen, the French naval commander, fought an indecisive action with the British under Sir George Rodney off Martinique in April. Then, after escorting Solano to Havana, Guichen sailed for Europe with his squadron in August. Rodney withdrew to New York, leaving part of his command in the West Indies.

That was the situation at the time of the first October storm, known as the Savanna-la-Mar Hurricane because of the damage it did to the community by that name on the southwest coast of Jamaica. On the afternoon of October 3rd, the town's inhabitants watched as dark clouds approached across the sea from the south. As the wind rose to gale force, fishermen in the harbor rushed to secure their boats, and rain began to come down in torrents. According to a report in the *Royal Jamaica Gazette*:

> *The sea during the last period exhibited a most awful scene; the waves swelled to an amazing height, rushed with an impetuosity not to be described on the land, and in a few minutes determined the fate of all the houses in the Bay.*
>
> *Those whose strength or presence of mind enabled them to seek their safety in the Savannah, took refuge in the miserable remains of the habitations there, most of which were blown down, or so damaged by the storm, as to be hardly capable of affording a comfortable shelter to the wretched sufferers. In the Court-House, 40 persons, whites and of colour, sought an asylum, but miserably perished by the pressure of the roof and side which fell upon them. . . .*
>
> *About ten the water began to abate, and at that time a smart shock of an earthquake was felt. All the small vessels were driven ashore, and dashed to pieces. The ships . . . were forced from their anchors, and carried so far into the morass that they will never be got off. The earthquake lifted the* Princess Royal *from her beam-ends, righted her, and fixed her on a firm bed. This circumstance has been of great use to the surviving inhabitants, for whose accommodation she now serves as a house.*
>
> *The morning ushered in a scene too shocking for description—Bodies of the dead and dying scattered about the watery plains, where the town stood. . . . The number who have perished, is not yet precisely ascertained, but it is imagined 50 whites, and 150 persons of colour are lost.*

From Jamaica the storm moved across Cuba and the Bahamas and swept up the coast of the United States, mauling one British squadron off Florida and another off Virginia.

The "Great Hurricane" of October 10–18, 1780, was one of the most severe on record. It first struck at Barbados in the Windward Islands. The British commander there estimated that not ten houses were left standing on the island after the storm had passed. There were more than four thousand dead on Barbados alone. The storm moved northward, striking the islands of Saint Lucia, Saint Vincent, Martinique, Dominica, Saint Eustatius, and Saint Kitts and causing more than twenty thousand deaths in all. Before blowing out over the Atlantic, the Great Hurricane battered the ships of Admiral Joshua Rowley's command, which had still not recovered from their encounter with the Savanna-la-Mar Hurricane only ten days before.

In Havana, Gálvez and Solano were meanwhile preparing their long-delayed attack on Pensacola. They waited until the Great Hurricane had moved out of the area (it stayed well to the east of Cuba) and finally left port on October 16 with seven ships and forty-nine transports that carried a four-thousand-man expeditionary force. Two days out at sea, they were hit by yet another storm, known to history as Solano's Hurricane. Their fleet suffered extensive damage, and they had to abandon their project. Pensacola's reprieve was only temporary, however. Not to be put off by adversity, Gálvez mounted another expedition and captured the British fortress in May 1781.

Solano's Hurricane was not the last of 1780. A week later a new tropical storm descended on the already hard-hit island of Saint Lucia. As late as November 17th, Admiral Rodney's fleet that was blockading the coast of the United States was dispersed by "a violent gale of wind," bringing to an end a season that would long be remembered for its calamities.

Miami, Florida, 1926. Around the turn of the century, Miami was still a tiny village whose citizens derived much of their income from "wrecking," the salvaging of ship and cargo from wrecks on the Florida reefs. A quarter of a century later after the land boom of the early 1920s, Miami had grown into a thriving city with a population of nearly a hundred thousand people. It was part of a resort complex extending from Fort Lauderdale in the north to the southern end of Dade County.

By 1926 the Miami area had not experienced a hurricane

in more than two decades, and most of the newcomers who had swelled its population knew nothing about tropical storms. Consequently, the storm that blew in from the sea on the night of September 17–18 came as a complete surprise. Roofs and entire houses were demolished by winds in excess of one hundred miles per hour. People caught in the open were unable to walk and had to crawl to shelter on their hands and knees. Many were killed by falling trees and flying debris.

George Woollard, a representative of the Coral Gables Real Estate Company, was working late in his lavishly appointed Miami Beach office that night. Around 10:00 he went outside to move his automobile, but the wind was so strong that Woollard barely made it back inside again. When he did get into the office, he found it flooded by a foot of seawater. Suddenly the lights went out. Then the front door flew open, and all at once the water was up to his waist. Woollard felt something touch his leg; reaching down he discovered the still-living body of a policeman who had been overwhelmed by the storm wave. Woollard revived the man, and they both climbed onto a desk. They stood there until the water became so deep that they had to cling to a chandelier.

Most of the damage along the shore was done by the high waves; farther inland, the wind and heavy rains took their toll. At 6:00 on the morning of the 18th, the wind suddenly died down and the sun came out. Thinking that the storm was over, people emerged from their hiding places. Richard Gray, a local meteorologist, realized that the calm only meant that the area was temporarily in the eye of the hurricane. He ran through the streets urging everyone to take shelter again. Few paid any attention, but half an hour later the storm returned with all of its fury. When it finally did end, there were more than one hundred persons dead, and another 25,000 were homeless. Property damage was estimated to be in the hundreds of millions of dollars.

As disasters go, the death toll from this storm was not particularly high, but it was important for its shock value. It made Florida conscious of hurricanes in a way that it had not been before. People began to insist on the need for adequate storm warning procedures and for buildings that would afford greater protection against hurricane-force winds.

New England, 1938. Twelve years later, Floridians were much better prepared when a Cape Verde cyclone was reported three hundred and fifty miles northeast of Puerto

Rico. "Cape Verde" is the name given to tropical storms that originate near the islands of that name off the coast of western Africa. They are the fiercest of all hurricanes. The longer a storm travels over water before reaching land, the stronger it becomes. Cape Verde storms pass across the entire width of the Atlantic Ocean.

When the storm was reported to be heading straight for Miami on the morning of September 19th, residents along the Florida coast boarded up their windows, took shelter, and prepared for the worst. The next day they were surprised and happy to learn that the storm had changed direction and was moving north instead. Florida was spared.

The U.S. Weather Bureau predicted that the storm would turn northeast and head toward the ocean. That would have been the normal pattern, but on September 20th a high-pressure area in Nova Scotia moved down the United States coast, deflecting the storm's path to the northwest toward Long Island and the New England states. Forecasters remained unaware of the storm's new course until the afternoon of Wednesday the 21st, when it was already bearing down on the Long Island shore. The millions of people in the endangered area had no advance warning, and like the Miamians in 1926, most of them had never experienced a hurricane. No major tropical storm had hit New England for generations, and it was popularly believed that such storms never came so far north.

Preceded by an eighteen-foot hurricane wave that spread havoc everywhere, the vortex of the storm reached Long Island at about 3:30 P.M. Along one stretch of coastline, of 179 cottages only 26 remained standing. Whole villages were sucked into the sea when the storm tide receded, and Block Island lost its entire fishing fleet. Parts of Connecticut were screened from the worst effects of the storm by Long Island. But New London was devastated.

Fires were ignited by short-circuited electric wiring, and attempts to fight the fires were rendered ineffectual by winds of 120 miles an hour. A passenger train was stalled just outside Stonington, Conn., on a low causeway with water on both sides. The engineer was astonished to see a cabin cruiser and a house torn from its foundations on the track ahead of him. Looking back, he saw that the rear cars of his train were slowly sinking into the water along with part of the causeway. The trainmen crowded all of the passengers into the front car, which they managed to uncouple from the rest of the train. The locomotive then inched forward, pushing the boat and the house off the remaining section of the causeway, and succeeded in reaching Stonington safely.

Helen Lee, of Napatree Point, R.I., had seen hurricanes in Florida and realized what was happening when the storm broke outside her beach house. Nevertheless, she was quite surprised when she was swept off her front porch and into Little Narragansett Bay. Although one of her arms was broken, she was able to climb into an inverted floating rooftop, which protected her for a while; later she held onto a mattress and the wreckage of a boat. After spending two hours in the water, she was washed ashore at Osbrook Point on the opposite side of the bay.

In Providence the entire downtown business district was flooded within a few minutes. The noise of short-circuited horns from submerged automobiles could be heard throughout the city. Novelist F. Van Wyck Mason was in Providence at the time, en route from Nantucket to New York City with the manuscript of his latest book. A burning electric wire had fallen on top of his bus on the way into town, and as he stepped off the bus, he was nearly killed by a pile of falling bricks. Holding the attaché case containing his manuscript above his head for protection, he made his way to the main railroad station to see if he could get a train to New York City. He got there just in time to see the roof of the station carried off by the wind.

The shore of Buzzards Bay on the southern coast of Massachusetts was inundated by twenty-foot waves on Wednesday evening, but most of the worst damage in the state was farther west. Pushing inland, the storm cut a swath through central Massachusetts, Vermont, New Hampshire, and northern New York State and moved into Canada, where it eventually blew itself out. In Worcester, Mass., the storm took the steeples off five churches, started fires, and wrecked one of the local high schools. In the Green Mountains south of Burlington, Vt., a young couple was relaxing after dinner in their recently assembled prefabricated home, unaware that there was anything but an ordinary storm outside. Before they knew what was happening, the roof and walls of the house were wrenched loose and carried off, leaving them holding on to the exposed foundation for their lives. Elsewhere in Vermont, the bodies of tropical birds native to the Caribbean that had been trapped in the eye of the hurricane fell to earth.

The pattern of a cyclonic storm system is clearly shown in the photograph above, which was taken by an astronaut on the Apollo spaceflight in 1969. The cross section drawing of a hurricane, below, shows the relatively calm eye surrounded by a towering wall of clouds, within which occur spiral bands of rain and strong winds.

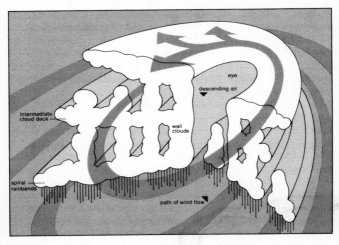

Like the couple in their prefabricated house, many people had no idea that they were going through a hurricane. One woman told reporters that she "was having the grandest time walking around town during the storm"; when she later found out that it was a hurricane, she fainted from the shock.

The highest state death toll from the storm—nearly 400—was in Rhode Island; there were nearly 700 dead over the entire affected area. Property damage was estimated at $382 million. Forty-five hundred homes and summer cottages were destroyed, and more than fifteen thousand others were damaged. Nearly six thousand boats were lost or disabled. Vermont lost two-thirds of its maple sugar trees, and New Hampshire lost half of its white pines. The New England apple crop was almost completely ruined.

Inevitably, there was widespread criticism of the U.S. Weather Bureau's failure to give warning of the hurricane's approach. It was generally agreed that weather forecasters had too easily discounted the possibility that the northeastern states might be threatened. Forecasters did not make that mistake again.

Hurricane Hazel, 1954. After World War II hurricane forecasting and hurricane tracking methods became more thorough and considerably more sophisticated. The story of Hurricane Hazel is a good example of how things changed. For one thing, Hazel had a name. Centuries ago, Caribbean storms were sometimes given the name of the saint's day on which they occurred (San Felipe, Santa Ana, and so on), and other ways of designating them had been tried at one time or another. But in the early 1950s it became the practice to use women's names for both hurricanes and typhoons. The first storm of the season receives a name beginning with the letter *A*, the second with *B*, and so on. A different set of names is used each year for ten years, after which names may be repeated. In 1978 it was announced that male names would alternate with female names.

This system of names is only one example of a more methodical approach to hurricane reporting. From the time when Hazel first began to form in the Windward Islands on October 3, 1954, it was kept under constant observation by U.S. naval aircraft and, whenever possible, by radar as well. By October 5th, a vortex had been formed, with a wind velocity of ninety-five miles per hour. Hazel first reached land at the small island of Carriacou, near Grenada, where it caused considerable damage to property. Reconnaissance planes, flying above the storm or within the eye, clocked the winds at 125 miles an hour on the 7th.

After passing over Carriacou, Hazel followed a zigzag course, moving west and west-northwest by turns and then northeast across the western part of Haiti on the 12th. The mountains on Haiti were high enough to disorganize the storm temporarily. Dame Marie, Anse d'Hainault, and other coastal settlements were destroyed, however, and heavy rains caused a landslide that buried the village of Berly near Port-au-Prince. At least 410, and possibly as many as one thousand, persons were killed in Haiti. The rain also caused flooding in Puerto Rico, although that island was spared the worst effects of the hurricane.

On the 13th Hazel left the Caribbean and drifted north into the Atlantic. Shortly after noon on the following day, the storm was one hundred miles east of Grand Bahama Island. The barometric pressure at its center was a low 28.70 inches, and the wind velocity, which had dropped off a bit, rose again to 150 miles an hour. According to Capt. William Harrell, a U.S. Air Force meteorologist, the eye of the storm was unusually narrow at this point—about eight miles across. He flew his plane down into the eye and had to maneuver carefully to avoid the surrounding wall of cloud.

Still moving north, Hazel reached the coast of North Carolina late in the morning of October 15th. Coastal residents had been warned by special emergency radio bulletins the night before. The local police, supplemented by Civil Defense and Red Cross workers, were standing by. Volunteers went from door to door to warn those who had no radios. The worst damage on the coast occurred between Georgetown, S.C., and Wilmington, N.C. At Garden City, S.C., near Myrtle Beach, the wind and abnormally high tides demolished the entire business district. Out of a total of nearly three hundred homes, only three remained habitable. Several beach communities lost all of their cottages. Long Beach, N.C., simply disappeared. No rubble or debris was left: concrete block houses, pavements, and everything else were washed away.

Instead of weakening as it moved inland, Hazel derived new energy from a pool of cold air over the continent and was transformed from a hurricane into an extratropical cyclone. On the afternoon and evening of the 15th, it moved rapidly through Virginia, Delaware, and Pennsylvania, reaching Toronto, Canada, at about 11:00 P.M. The storm produced the strongest winds ever recorded in Washington, D.C., and in New York City and produced record rainfalls in West Virginia. About eight inches of rain fell in the Toronto area on the night of October 15–16, causing the already swollen Humber and Credit rivers to overflow their banks and flood several suburban communities.

After leaving Ontario, Hazel steadily declined in force, slowly making its way eastward toward the Atlantic again. It had killed 99 persons in the United States and between 80 and 250 in Canada. Total property damage amounted to approximately $350 million.

Hurricane Agnes, 1972. Originating near Cozumel Island just off the Yucatan Peninsula of Mexico on June 15, Agnes slashed Cuba and raged for ten days along the eastern seaboard of the United States. The first hurricane of the 1972 season, it saturated the countryside with rain along a path 250 miles wide, killing 118 persons and causing an estimated $1.7 billion in damage. The rains brought flooding along the James, Potomac, Susquehanna, Ohio, and Genesee rivers. Robert M. White, director of the National Oceanic and Atmospheric Administration, called the floods "the most extensive in the country's history." Florida, Virginia, Pennsylvania, Maryland, and New York were declared disaster areas by the federal government.

In Virginia, the James River crested at thirty-six feet, breaking the previous record set in 1771. Seventeen persons were killed, and 8,000 were left homeless. Richmond had neither drinking water nor electricity for days. Gov. Linwood G. Holton had to prepare his appeal for federal assistance by candlelight. Two hundred blocks in the center of the city were flooded.

The worst devastation occurred in Pennsylvania. One hundred thousand people had to be evacuated from Kingston and Wilkes-Barre. Harrisburg, the capital, was cut off from the rest of the state, and the floodwaters rose to the first-floor ceiling of the governor's mansion. Sixty-four miles of the Pennsylvania Turnpike were closed to traffic. When delays were experienced in getting federal disaster relief, Milton Shapp, Pennsylvania's Democratic governor, led an angry delegation of his state's citizens to Washington, where they confronted George Romney, the Republican secretary of Health, Education and Welfare. The delegation demanded full compensation for all of the victims of the disaster, even the payment of the mortgages on their houses. The meeting

In 1972 Hurricane Agnes caused extensive damage in the eastern United States, including flooding on the Schuylkill River in Pottstown, Pa.

turned into a shouting match, with Romney calling Shapp a demagogue and accusing him of playing politics with a national tragedy.

In all, Agnes killed 134 persons, destroyed 128,000 homes and businesses, and caused more than $60 billion worth of damage. One unexpected casualty of Hurricane Agnes was the Erie-Lackawanna Railroad. Already in deep financial trouble, the Lackawanna filed for bankruptcy on June 26th, citing the damage caused by the storm as one of the main factors prompting its move.

Tropical Storms of Asia and the South Pacific

The typhoons of the Pacific Ocean area are distinguished from tropical storms in other parts of the world chiefly by their extent and their large number (an average of twenty a year in the North Pacific area alone). The peak season for typhoons is August, September, and October. South of the equator they are more likely to occur in February and March. In general, however, typhoons are rather unpredictable and have been known to occur in all months of the year. They occasionally grow to extreme size, and their area of influence may become as large as the entire eastern United States. Because of their size and frequency, typhoons cause widespread damage in all countries bordering the Western Pacific. A typhoon that struck southern India in late 1977 killed an estimated 20,000 persons.

Like hurricanes, typhoons have sometimes changed history. One especially famous example was the *kamikaze* ("divine wind") that saved Japan by destroying a Mongol invasion fleet in 1281. An example in more recent times occurred in the Samoan Islands in the late nineteenth century.

The Typhoon That Stopped a War. In 1889 empire-building fever was at its height, and the Polynesian kingdom of Samoa was one of the few out-of-the-way corners of the world that had not yet been taken over by one of the Western powers, In fact, Germany and the United States were on the verge of going to war to decide which country was to be Samoa's "protector." Both the Germans and the Americans were interested in exploiting the islands' copra and coconut oil, and the United States maintained a naval base on Samoan territory at Pago Pago.

In 1885 Samoa's King Laupepa tried to counteract German influence by inviting Great Britain to take control of his country. Germany reacted by deposing Laupepa and installing

Tamasese, a rival prince, in his place. Three years later, there was a rebellion against Tamasese's rule, but the Germans intervened to help him remain in power. The United States ordered a naval squadron to Apia, the Samoan capital on the island of Upolu, with orders to protect American property and to forestall a German takeover.

By March 1889 a tense situation had developed as three American warships—the *Trenton, Vandalia*, and *Nipsic*—faced three ships of the German Navy—the *Adler, Olga*, and *Eber*—in Apia's harbor. Each country resented the other's interference, and the least incident threatened to provoke hostilities. War hawks in the U.S. Senate were calling for action. To complicate matters a British man-of-war, the H.M.S. *Calliope*, was also at anchor in the crowded little port.

On March 14th the attention of the two opposing fleets was distracted by signs of an approaching storm. The respective commanders, Rear Adm. L. A. Kimberly on the *Trenton* and Capt. Fritze on the *Adler*, both grew uneasy as they watched the barometer fall. It was the typhoon season, and each knew that his chances of riding out a storm safely would be better on the open sea than in this particular harbor.

The harbor, actually nothing more than a shallow indentation in the coast, offered little protection for their vessels. In addition, a submerged coral reef extending out from the shore around the harbor was highly dangerous to shipping, especially in rough weather. Even the floor of the harbor was coral, and its thin covering of mud and vegetation did not provide a secure hold for an anchor. Nevertheless, neither Kimberly not Fritze wanted to be the first to pull out, so they both battened down and waited to see what would happen. At midnight, with rain falling and the wind velocity increasing, Kimberly gave the order to fire one of the *Trenton*'s boilers so that, if necessary, he could use steam power to counteract the force of the storm.

On the following afternoon a powerful typhoon passed just to the north of Apia. The ships had a difficult time, but no serious damage was done, and everyone breathed a sigh of relief when the barometer began to rise again. The weather continued stormy, however, and contrary to all expectation the typhoon returned that night with greater violence than ever. After passing Samoa, the storm had encountered a second tropical storm at sea, which had caused it to turn around and head back toward Apia again. Hours went by, and the fury of the typhoon intensified.

The *Calliope*, the newest and most powerful of the assembled warships, got up steam and slowly made its way out of the harbor over waves as high as houses, which tossed the ship around like a toy. The German and American ships remained, hoping that their anchors would hold and prevent them from being smashed against the jagged reefs. They were drifting dangerously, however, and several of them collided during the night.

The ships' peril increased in the early morning of the 16th, when the rushing current of the rain-swollen Singano River, which flowed into the harbor, began to scour the mud from the harbor floor. The ships' anchors slid across the smooth, treacherous coral bottom. The *Eber* sank with almost all of its crew at about 5:00 A.M. Two hours later, the *Nipsic* ran aground, and its commander, D. W. Mullan, gave the order to abandon ship; he and most of his men got ashore in boats. The *Adler* was thrown up on to the reef on its side shortly after 8:00.

The storm continued to rage all day long. Late in the morning, the *Vandalia* was wrecked on the point of the reef, and many of its crew, including the captain, were washed overboard. Survivors clung to the rigging and the side of the ship until the *Trenton* landed alongside several hours later. Many of the survivors were able to save themselves by climbing onto their sister ship. *Olga* escaped serious harm, avoiding the reefs and running aground on a mud flat.

The wind and rain finally died down that night, and the survivors were able to begin salvage operations on the morning of March 17th. The *Eber* and several merchant vessels that had been in the harbor had gone down. The *Adler*, *Vandalia*, and *Trenton* were wrecked beyond repair, but their cargoes were salvaged. One hundred and forty-six men—American, German, and Samoan—lost their lives.

The shock at the news of the disaster, called the worst ever suffered by the U.S. Navy in peacetime, ended all talk of war in the United States. At a three-power conference held in Berlin in the following month, the United States, Germany, and Great Britain agreed that King Laupepa should be restored to power and that the three countries would cooperate in exercising a joint protectorate over Samoa. This amicable arrangement continued until 1899, when the British withdrew and the United States and Germany divided the islands between them. Because of the way the typhoon seemed to dispel the tension that had existed between the rival powers, the great storm of March 1889 has been called "the typhoon that stopped a war."

Vera, the Super Typhoon, 1959. Considered one of the worst storms in Japan's history, Typhoon Vera struck the island of Honshu on September 26, 1959, spreading destruction over several provinces. The hardest hit area was Nagoya, the country's third largest city, which was almost completely ruined.

The Japanese are used to typhoons and do not usually panic when one is reported to be headed their way. Not many of the fifteen to twenty-five storms spawned every year in the northern Pacific actually reach the Japanese islands; but Vera, characterized by meteorologists as a "super typhoon," cut through the most densely populated area. The entire east coast of Honshu between Nagoya and Tokyo was flooded by a seventeen-foot storm wave. Tokyo itself was buffeted by ninety-mile-an-hour winds, which brought rail and air traffic to a standstill. The storm turned north in central Honshu, passing through the provinces of Toyama, Yamagata, Akita, and Niigata.

Nagoya, a busy industrial center with a population of well over one million, was the first point of impact. The winds reached a velocity of 135 miles per hour. The force of the winds and waves swept the *Changsha*, a seven-thousand-ton freighter, out of Iseo Bay onto the shore. Huge stores of logs that had been stacked up in the Nagoya lumberyards broke loose and were carried by rushing floodwaters through the streets, adding to the general chaos. Nearly six thousand houses were destroyed in the first few minutes of the typhoon. Eighty persons were trapped in the ruins of one apartment house, and many of them perished before rescue workers could reach them.

By the next day thousands of the city's residents were still perched on the roofs of buildings, and large numbers of them had to be removed by helicopters. To find food, some dived into the floodwaters and swam around trying to locate small kitchen gardens from which they could get a few vegetables. A considerable amount of looting was reported, and Nagoya police had to call for reinforcements to help restore order. Many survivors were stricken with tetanus and dysentery.

The casualty figures from Typhoon Vera—4,464 persons dead, about 2,000 missing, nearly 10,000 injured, and at least 400,000 homeless—offered shocking proof of the extent to which modern urban civilization, with all of its scientific safeguards, is still vulnerable to the destructive forces of nature.

A Cyclone That Spawned a Country, 1970. Tropical storms in the Bay of Bengal are usually known simply by their correct scientific name—cyclones. The coastal areas around the bay are periodically exposed to some of the most violent tropical storms in the world. They are especially frequent in Bangladesh, which lies at the head of the bay.

On November 12, 1970, this area—then part of Pakistan—was hit by the worst cyclone in living memory. It was the second storm to develop in the Bay of Bengal in less than a month. Both were located by weather satellite before they reached land, and advance warning was given of their approach. The first, on October 23rd, had done some damage but nothing out of the ordinary. Because radio warnings on November 12th did not indicate that the second storm was going to be worse, most people in the storm's path stayed where they were. Those most exposed were on the low-lying heavily populated islands off the coast, and for these people there was really nowhere to go even if they had wanted to. The mainland coastal settlements were only a little less exposed than the islands, and the main routes inland were by the many mouths of the Ganges River, which would be transformed into raging torrents by the cyclone.

On the night of the 12th, an immense sea wave swept across the islands, engulfing people, houses, animals, and trees. It then lashed against the coast and was followed by hurricane-force winds. Having spent itself, the wave receded, carrying thousands of people back into the sea with it. The official estimates of the number of persons killed reached a staggering total of 200,000; unofficial totals were even higher.

In the village of Dhali Gaurnager, farmer Nomohan Das and his family tried to get to a storm shelter, but the wind was so fierce they could not make it. Das formed a human chain with his wife and six children, and they crawled to a nearby house where they managed to get up onto the roof. They were safe there until the storm wave came, and they took refuge in the trees. Das told a reporter,

About dawn the water began to go down. I could see bodies, hundreds of them, floating out to sea. At about 9 in the morning the water finally went down all the way. My farm looked like a desert. There was nothing

left, but my family was all right. Only my aunt had been washed away with most of the old people. They were not strong enough to hold on to the trees.

Another man in the same village, Ginda Kumar Daz, lost two of his four children. He and his family were also on a roof when it was capsized by the wave. Two of the children were washed away immediately. Daz held on to his three-year-old son; his wife clung to their five-year-old daughter for a time but eventually lost hold of her, and the child disappeared in the flood. When morning came and the water subsided, Daz could see his wife on the other side of the river, naked and weeping, her body covered with blood; she had saved herself by clutching a thorny palm tree all night long. The river was so clogged with the bodies of the dead and dying that for several hours he was unable to get to her with his boat. Toward the end of the day one of their missing children, a nine-year-old girl, returned to the village with her aunt. They had been swept four miles downstream and had been so embarrassed by their nakedness that they had hid every time they saw a man. It had taken them all day to get back. "We wept with joy," Daz said. "Then we split open green coconuts and drank the milk."

Supplies for the relief of the cyclone victims were sped to East Pakistan from the United States, Great Britain, China, India, and many other countries. There were long delays, however, before these supplies reached the people for whom they were intended, when they reached them at all. East Pakistani leaders blamed the government in West Pakistan (a thousand miles away, on the other side of India) for not doing enough to help in the crisis and for having failed to implement the flood-control measures that had been promised for years. The eastern leaders saw this as only the latest instance in a long history of injustice and discrimination against their part of the divided country.

In reality, East and West Pakistan were united only by their common adherence to Islam, in opposition to India, their predominantly Hindu neighbor. The two parts of Pakistan differed in language, custom, and ethnic composition, and the dominant West Pakistanis often put their own interests before those of their Bengali brethren in the east. The cyclone occurred on the eve of a national election, and the indignation over the government's lack of concern about the disaster helped bring victory to Sheikh Mujibur Rahman's militant Awami League. The election eventually led to East Pakistan's breakaway from the west and to the establishment of Bangladesh as an independent country.

Tornadoes

A tornado, like a tropical storm, is a mass of whirling air, but one that develops over land rather than water. Also known as twisters or funnel clouds, tornadoes have a smaller diameter than tropical storms. The most violent tornadoes occur in the United States—especially in the Great Plains area—in the southern and middle U.S.S.R., and in southern Australia. In the United States alone they cause an estimated $50 million a year in damage. Like other storms their rotation is influenced by the direction of the prevailing winds and is usually clockwise south of the equator and counterclockwise north of it.

In the Northern Hemisphere, the tornado season generally lasts from March to October, but in the United States tornadoes are most frequent in April, May, and June. They normally occur in the afternoon and travel in an easterly direction. Tornadoes can be the most destructive of all windstorms. A tornado system in 1925 killed nearly 700 persons in Missouri, Illinois, and Indiana. The storms caused damage estimated at $17 million. In 1967 a string of tornadoes killed 56 persons in the Chicago area alone. Tornadoes that ripped through villages in northeastern India in 1978 killed nearly 500 persons and injured about 1,000. Tornadoes tend to be quite localized. Their paths are not normally more than about fifty miles long, and they rarely last for more than a couple of hours. The vortex, or funnel, has an average width of between three and four hundred yards. Sometimes people have stood within 150 feet of a passing funnel cloud and have not even felt a strong wind. The destruction can be complete in one place, while just a few feet away nothing is damaged.

As is the case with tropical storms, the exact mechanism that produces a tornado is something of a mystery, but the convection process is involved in the genesis of both types of storms. Just before the formation of a tornado the air temperature is usually a little above normal, but it then drops suddenly. The relative humidity is very high, and unusually colored clouds have been observed moving rapidly in the sky. Eyewitnesses often report seeing two masses of clouds moving toward each other and meeting with a loud noise like an explosion. The two formations break up, and the clouds shoot

The funnel cloud of a tornado is an awesome sight, and its wind velocities of 500 miles per hour or more make this kind of storm especially destructive.

down toward the ground and then back up again like rockets. After this, small segments of cloud begin to revolve around each other, and in this way the funnel cloud takes shape.

The funnel may be as much as a mile high and is wider at the top than at the bottom. It is sometimes compared to the tail of a huge kite or, because of the way it wiggles back and forth, to an enormous snake. Once formed, the funnel cloud begins to move horizontally at an average speed of between ten and fifty miles an hour. The funnel also moves vertically, sometimes seeming to hang from the sky, sometimes dropping down to touch the ground and churn up everything in its path. Its approach is signaled by a whistling sound, which changes to a loud roar as it gets closer. When the funnel actually strikes, the noise of buildings, trees, and other objects being torn to pieces drowns out everything else. Sometimes, instead of a single funnel cloud, there may be several that form an extremely dangerous "family" of twisters.

Tornadoes are often accompanied by electric storms with rain and hail. The sulfurous odor people occasionally notice in the vicinity of such a storm is probably from the lightning that often strikes around it, in some cases as frequently as twenty times a second. It has been calculated that the power in a small funnel cloud 350 feet in diameter is about 100 million kilowatts a second, greater than the capacity of all the generating stations in the United States. Wind velocities within a funnel are often as high as 500 or 600 miles per hour. Winds of that speed can make ordinarily harmless things into lethal objects, and sand and gravel borne on such winds penetrate the human body like bullets. After the St. Louis, Mo., tornado of 1896 a gardener's spade was found driven six inches into the trunk of a tree, and wheat straws were embedded at a depth of more than a half an inch.

Within a funnel cloud there is an updraft that is one of the storm's most destructive forces. When the funnel reaches ground level, it draws up into it whatever lies beneath. The story of Dorothy's house being carried into the air in L. Frank Baum's *The Wonderful Wizard of Oz* is no exaggeration. In one case, an entire church steeple was moved a distance of fifteen miles, and wooden houses have been blown as far as two miles. In 1919 a tornado collided with a railroad train, the Oriental Limited, near Fergus Falls, Minn. Seven passenger cars were thrown off the tracks, and the baggage car was hurled into the air and landed thirty feet away.

The immense damage caused by a tornado that struck Louisville, Ky., in 1890 is shown in this contemporary lithograph. The storm was followed by serious fires.

There are many stories about people being picked up by tornadoes and returning to earth unhurt. No doubt many of these are just stories. It is true, however, that objects drawn into a funnel cloud may be buoyed up by ascending air currents when they begin to fall back down again and may reach the ground slowly and gently. This phenomenon accounts for such oddities as mirrors flying through the air for miles and landing unbroken or kitchen cabinets being found blocks away with every dish inside still in perfect condition.

Other phenomena associated with tornadoes are caused by the partial vacuum created in the vortex by centrifugal force. The resultant fall in atmospheric pressure can be as great as fifty percent. When the funnel surrounds any object, the pressure of the air within the object suddenly becomes far greater than that of the air outside it, and this may cause the object to explode. This difference in air pressure may be what rips the surfaces from roads or tears people's clothes off in a tornado. Atmospheric pressure is certainly responsible for some of the worst damage done to buildings. Scientists have recently begun to investigate the possibility that sudden "downbursts" of wind of up to 150 miles an hour may create the apparently random destruction caused by tornadoes.

If the funnel is close to the earth but not actually in contact with it, only the roofs or upper stories of buildings may be affected. Houses, vehicles, or persons underneath the funnel may remain unscathed. On June 22, 1928, a man working on a farm in Kansas spotted a tornado in the distance. He was able to reach his cyclone cellar just in time. Looking up from the open cellar, he saw the lower end of the funnel cloud several feet above the ground. The flashes of lightning that accompanied the storm enabled him to get a good view of its center. He described it as a circular opening from about fifty to one hundred feet across, which seemed to extend at least a half mile upward. Smaller tornadoes were continually being formed around the main one, and they looked like tails attached to the end of a funnel.

On another occasion a husband and wife were driving along a road in their automobile and noticed what they thought was a dust storm ahead of them. They continued on their way and suddenly found themselves in the midst of a tornado, with debris of all kinds flying around the car. As they moved into the eye of the storm, everything became calm and quiet, and they were amazed to see a large boulder floating in the middle of the air. The next minute both were thrown out of the car as the winds closed around them once more.

A tornado in Louisville, Ky., in March 1890 was of this same type. Despite the fact that it never actually touched the ground, it caused an immense amount of damage. The storm originated about eight miles southwest of Louisville on the night of March 27th and quickly moved toward the city at a speed of forty miles an hour. It was described as balloon-shaped with a twisted, attenuated tail emitting "a constant fusillade of lightning" that made a noise like a thousand trains. After striking Louisville the storm leaped across the Ohio River to Jeffersonville, Ind., crossed back again, and raced along the Kentucky side of the river to the town of Eminence and into Carroll County, where it finally died out. It had travelled a distance of seventy-five miles.

In Louisville itself the tornado had cut an erratic 300-yard path through the city, tearing the roofs off hundreds of houses and demolishing the city hall, the main hotel, and the railroad station. The funnel cloud rose and fell and changed its course many times, giving the resulting devastation a hit-and-miss appearance. More than once it passed by a row of houses, then suddenly doubled back and leveled every one of them. Fires broke out in many places, and it took hours for volunteer firefighters to bring them under control. In all, the Louisville tornado left 106 persons dead, 235 injured, and property damage estimated at $3.5 million.

Protection from Storms

Much of the loss of life from tropical storms and tornadoes can be prevented. Improved detection and warning systems are now operating in many parts of the world; and people are generally receiving more accurate advance notices of such storms.

The damage from hurricanes is caused by the strong winds and by flooding. At the approach of a tropical storm, people living in low-lying areas should leave if possible. If not, they should take shelter in buildings that can withstand hurri-cane-force winds. Steel-frame and reinforced concrete buildings offer the best protection.

As protection for buildings, windows should be boarded up or shuttered if there is time. Criss-crossing windows with tape may help reinforce them. Bottled water, canned food, flashlights, and battery-operated radios help people maintain their lives until services disrupted by a hurricane can be restored.

Tornado winds moving across a body of water can create a waterspout in which water moves upward into the low-pressure area of the funnel cloud.

The principal damage from tornadoes is caused by high winds. At the approach of a tornado, a person outside should move at right angles away from the path of the storm. If caught outside in a tornado, a person should avoid open land and seek the nearest deep depression.

It is far safer, of course, to be inside a substantial building during a tornado. In large buildings a safe location is an interior hallway. In smaller buildings the best location is the lowest floor or space underground. Basements of houses generally offer good protection. A crouching position under a heavy piece of furniture is recommended. Wide-span roofs— such as those that cover many school gymnasiums—do not offer protection, since tornadoes often blow such roofs off. Because the normal supplies of water, food, and electricity may be disrupted, emergency supplies are valuable.

4.
Floods

Flooding often accompanies and contributes to the destructiveness of earthquakes, volcanic eruptions, and storms. Floods, however, particularly those of the world's large rivers, can by themselves be disastrous. The Huang Ho floods in China, for example, killed at least two million persons in 1887 and nearly four million in 1931. It is true that the death tolls produced by most floods are less than those associated with major pandemics and unusually severe famines. Deaths from the worst floods, however, far surpass the numbers of deaths for the bloodiest recorded battle—the First Battle of the Somme in 1916 in which about one million died—and for the worst recorded earthquake—that in China in 1556 in which an estimated 830,000 perished.

Floods can be classified as either accidental or recurrent. Both are considered natural, even the accidental when caused by such phenomena as landslides or excessive rainfall.

Accidental Floods

Accidental floods result mainly from the failure of natural or artificial dams. The sections of the Indus and Ganges rivers that flow through mountainous areas, for example, are especially liable to blockage by landslides and to sudden floods when the landslides give way. During the winter of 1840–41 a landslide from Nanga Parbat Mountain fell into the upper Indus. Water accumulated in a lake that reached a depth of more than three hundred yards and a length of forty miles. The lake overtopped its barrier the following June, causing it to fail abruptly and almost instantaneously release an estimated 2.5 billion yards of water. An army encamped near the channel about 250 miles downstream from the dam was overwhelmed by a muddy wave twenty-seven yards high.

The best-documented case of prehistoric floods is that of former Lake Bonneville in the Great Basin of the western United States. Originally without an outlet, its level was controlled by evaporation. After a tributary stream captured the Bear River, the lake began to rise. About thirty thousand years ago the water overtopped the lowest pass in the surrounding high ground. The water rapidly eroded a notch large enough to deliver, at its maximum flow, an estimated 2.5 billion cubic yards per second.

Some accidental floods are caused by the forces of nature acting on the very structures that have been built to control flooding. The dikes of the Netherlands, for example, were built to create habitable land by keeping back the sea from low-lying areas that would otherwise be under water. The dikes have given way several times throughout the history of the Netherlands, producing disastrous flooding that has killed a total of hundreds of thousands of persons.

Dams, of course, control flooding by regulating the flow of rivers. When a dam does not regulate its waters or is not strong enough to hold the water that accumulates behind it, the dam may collapse. In 1963 huge waves set off by an avalanche poured over the crest of the Vaiont Dam in Italy, killing more than 2,600 persons. The Teton Dam in Idaho collapsed in 1976, but the loss of life was low in the sparsely populated area.

Johnstown, Pa., Flood, 1889. Perhaps the best-known case of a disastrous flood caused by a dam failure occurred at Johnstown, Pa., on May 31, 1889. Like the San Francisco fire, the Johnstown flood has become an almost legendary catastrophe in American history.

Johnstown is situated in western Pennsylvania at the confluence of the Conemaugh River and Stony Creek. By the late 1800s the city had survived several relatively minor floods. About twelve miles upstream was the South Fork Dam, which was owned at the time by a wealthy private country club. The dam had apparently not been well constructed, and it was in poor repair. In addition, spillways—which ordinarily allow excess water to escape and relieve pressure on a dam itself—had been plugged so that fish would not escape from the reservoir. When heavy rains fell in late May the reservoir rose, and it became evident that the dam would not hold even though emergency spillways were dug.

A telegraph message of warning was sent to Johnstown. Some flooding from the rains had already occurred in the city, however, and the residents apparently did not take the warning seriously. In the middle of the afternoon on the 31st the dam broke, and a deluge of water inundated the Conemaugh Valley, obliterating several small towns. It was estimated that the wall of water was 125 feet high and that it moved at a speed of 50 miles an hour. Houses, factories, and people were swept away.

The Johnstown Flood in 1889 was the result of a dam failure in the Conemaugh Valley in western Pennsylvania. The wall of water that roared down the valley destroyed several towns in its path and killed an estimated 2,200 persons.

The deluge was documented by an eyewitness, a young train-engineer who alerted persons downstream of the impending disaster:

> *The big break took place at just three o'clock, and it was about ten feet wide at first and shallow; but when the opening was made the fearful rushing waters opened the gap with such increasing rapidity that soon after the entire lake leaped out and started on its fearful march of death down the Valley of the Conemaugh. It took but forty minutes to drain that three miles of water, and the downpour of millions of tons of water was irresistible. The big boulders and great rafters and logs that were in the bed of the river were picked up, like so much chaff, and carried down the torrent for miles. Trees that stood fully seventy-five feet in height and four feet through were snapped off like pipe-stems.*

As the cascading mass moved into the valley and gathered momentum it produced a sound "like incessant thunder" that forewarned the death and destruction for the people in its path. A passenger aboard a train stranded in the valley described the scene and his efforts to warn fellow passengers of the disaster:

> I put down my book and stepped out quickly to the rear platform, and was horrified at the sight that met my gaze up the valley. It seemed as if a forest was coming down upon us. There was a great wall of water roaring and grinding swiftly along, so thickly studded with the trees from along the mountain sides that it looked like a gigantic avalanche of trees . . . . In that instant I saw an engine lifted bodily off the track and thrown over backward into the whirlpool, where it disappeared, and houses crushed and broken up in the flash of an eye . . . .
>
> The rush of waters lasted three-quarters of an hour, while we stood rapt and spell-bound in the rain, looking at the ruin no human agency could avert. The scene was beyond the power of language to describe. You would see a building standing in apparent security above the swollen banks of the river, the people rushing about the doors, some seeming to think that safety lay indoors, while others rushed toward higher ground, stumbling and falling in the muddy streets, and then the flood rolled over them, crushing in the house with a crash like thunder, and burying house and people out of sight entirely. That, of course, was the scene of only an instant, for our range of vision was only over a small portion of the city.

With a population of about 12,000 persons, Johnstown was the largest city in the valley. Although many of its buildings were substantial—being built of stone rather than wood—they were destroyed by the rushing water. Some Johnstown residents who were picked up and carried by the raging water were rescued farther downstream. Debris was carried as far as Pittsburgh, seventy-five miles away. The number of deaths was officially estimated to be about 2,200, but the total may have been much higher. Even the first stages of the cleaning-up operations took months. And perhaps one of the most tragic aspects of the devastation was that it probably could have been prevented.

Grandview Cemetery contains the graves of 777 unidentified flood victims, and a national memorial, at the site of the old dam, commemorates the catastrophe. After another disastrous flood in 1936, the Conemaugh was tamed by a flood-control program that was completed in 1943. Yet, on July 20, 1977, an overnight, nine-inch rainfall again caused massive flooding, leaving Johnstown accessible only by helicopter. About 70 persons lost their lives in the rampaging water, and property damage was estimated at $200 million.

Recurrent Floods

Recurrent floods are peak discharges of water that are a part of the natural order. They must be taken into account by land-use planners and flood-control engineers. Such floods occur because stream discharges vary from one part of the year to another, because peak discharges vary from year to year, and because rivers do not fashion channels large enough to accommodate their largest flows. (Another type of flood occurs along sea coastal areas. Such flooding along the North Sea coastal areas of Europe in 1953 killed more than 2,000 persons. Flooding can also be caused by sudden excessive downpours. In Baguio, the Philippines, 46.7 inches of rain fell in a one-day period in 1911.)

A meandering river works and reworks the material in its valley bottom, developing a flood-prone area of low ground adjacent to the channel. This area, the floodplain, may be horizontal, or it may slope gently away from the channel. The river may also construct natural levees along the channel margins.

Rivers normally flow below their bank. At the full stage the channel is completely filled with water; at higher stages the floodplain is inundated. All peak flows are technically floods whether or not they cause inundation of the surrounding land. The main concern, of course, is with actual inundation.

China. For sheer destructiveness, China's Huang Ho and Yangtze probably have no equals among the world's rivers. Because of the devastating floods it causes, the Huang Ho, or Yellow River, is also known as "The Ungovernable" and "China's Sorrow." Rising in the Tibetan highlands, the Huang Ho flows through the North China Plain to the Yellow Sea. It is 2,900 miles long and has changed its course several times in the last four thousand years. One of the most dramatic shifts was in the middle of the nineteenth century, when its mouth moved northward by two hundred and fifty miles.

The river's name comes from the yellow earth (*huang t'u*), a mixture of clay and sand, that it picks up from deposits stretching across the middle part of its basin and carries downstream in suspension. The speed of its flow decreases as it crosses the North China Plain, causing much of this silt to drop down into the riverbed. As the bed rises, the stream has a tendency to overflow onto the surrounding countryside. When the rainfall is above average, extensive flooding often occurs.

That is what happened in 1887 when heavy rains in Honan Province precipitated what may have been the worst flood on record anywhere. The Huang Ho burst through its dikes at Cheng-chou, inundating the city within minutes. The water raced eastward to K'ai-feng, wiping out six hundred villages and towns on the way. In the plain below K'ai-feng, another fifteen hundred villages were flooded. From there, the water spread into the neighboring province of Anhwei. Farmers were unable to deal with the blanket of sediment deposited by the flood or with the standing floodwater that took as long as two years to vanish from some areas. Estimates of the number of persons drowned in this catastrophe ranged from two million to seven million. Another disaster occurred in 1931 when the Huang Ho again overspilled its banks. The eventual death toll was estimated at nearly four million.

In 1939, two years after the Japanese invasion of China preceding World War II, the Huang Ho went on another rampage, this time along its lower reaches in the northern provinces of Hopeh and Shantung. All crops and most housing were lost, and relief supplies were not able to reach the affected areas because of the war. Around 10 million persons were homeless and 200,000 died in the ensuing famine.

The Yangtze, or Ch'ang Chiang, is the longest river of China (3,400 miles) and the country's principal waterway. It meanders across the central part of the country from west to east. Flowing past the cities of Chungking, Wu-han, and Nanking to the East China Sea near Shanghai, the river links the interior of the country with the Pacific Ocean. Below I-ch'ang in Hupeh Province much of the river is diked. Nearly seven thousand square miles of lakes are connected to the Yangtze system, providing flood reservoir space in normal times. But as is the case with the Huang Ho, when torrential rains fall on the whole system at once, flooding results.

One of the worst of the Yangtze floods occurred in September 1911, when the country's "rice bowl" provinces of Hunan, Hupeh, and Anhwei were deluged, along with the city of Shanghai. Nearly a hundred thousand persons were drowned, and another hundred thousand died of hunger in the aftermath. Almost as bad were the floods of August 1954 when the Yangtze and the Huai Ho were swollen by what was called the heaviest rainfall in a hundred years. The rivers overflowed and devastated an area twice the size of Texas. The water crested at 96.06 feet, breaking the previous record set in 1931, when 140,000 persons were drowned and 22 million acres were inundated. The dams that had been built to contain such overflows began to give way. Hundreds of thousands of soldiers and peasants piled up sandbags and in some places formed human walls to hold back the floodwaters. Despite their frantic efforts, the dams crumbled, and the Yangtze spread over 27 millions acres (about ten percent of the country's total farmland), drowning 40,000 persons and obliterating hundreds of villages.

The Mississippi. The worst river floods in the United States are caused by the 3,800-mile long Mississippi-Missouri River system. From Cape Girardeau, Mo., south to the Gulf of Mexico, the Mississippi River is contained by a series of earthen levees or dikes. The levees were begun by French settlers in Louisiana in the early eighteenth century. Originally they were only about three feet high and were confined to the area around New Orleans, La. By the 1970s the levee system extended more than 3,500 miles along the river and had an average height of twenty-four feet.

After flash floods in 1882, the levees were raised and strengthened on the more vulnerable stretches of the river, but heavy snowfalls in the winter of 1889–90 threatened to raise the water level above the levees again in the spring of 1890. The first flooding hit Arkansas and Tennessee in March. In early April most of the ten thousand residents of Greenville, Miss., had to be evacuated to higher ground. The people of Madison Parish Front, La., worked for three days to build the levees higher to stave off disaster. They succeeded, but elsewhere in Louisiana fierce storms hampered attempts to keep back the rising floodwaters. When the levees gave way at Pointe Coupee, Concordia Parish, Nita, and Baton Rouge on April 24th, three thousand square miles were flooded. Timely warnings by the United States Signal Service kept the death toll to about one hundred persons, but fifty thousand were left homeless.

The great floods of the Mississippi and its tributary rivers in April–June 1927 were particularly bad. They were caused by an unusual coincidence of flood conditions in all parts of

Well-developed flood-control measures have not prevented flooding on the Mississippi River. Severe floods in 1973 inundated parts of St. Louis, Mo. (above), and other cities. Emergency sandbagging (right) could not prevent extensive flooding of agricultural land during the spring planting season.

the Mississippi system. The floods of the eastern tributaries normally reach their height between January and April, while the crests of the Missouri River enter the Mississippi in June. In 1927 the levees were breached in many places, and the floodwaters overflowed throughout the lower Mississippi Valley. An area of nearly 17 million acres was inundated, 313 persons were killed, and 700,000 were driven from their homes. Flooding was averted at New Orleans by cutting a gap in the levees a few miles below the city, thus allowing part of the floodwater to take a shorter course of about five miles to an arm of the sea instead of following the normal course of the river through the delta.

The 1927 floods caused $300 million in damage. The Red Cross collected $15 million for the relief of the stricken areas, and Secretary of Commerce Herbert Hoover personally directed emergency rescue operations, using forty river steamers and a vast number of smaller craft operated by Coast Guardsmen. He established tent towns to house the

In the worst flood in its history, the Ohio River poured over levees at Cincinnati, Ohio, in 1937. Several cities in the Ohio Valley suffered major damage from the Ohio and its tributaries.

refugees and, when the flood receded, helped move people back to their homes, providing tools, building materials, seed, and farm animals to aid their recovery.

In 1937 the Ohio River developed the largest flood in its history, but this time the lower Mississippi was able to receive and dispose of the unprecedented volume of water, which amounted to two million cubic feet per second. A system of channel cutoffs inaugurated in the early 1930s has reduced the danger of flooding by lowering the river stages as much as twelve feet in some places, and an improved levee system held the water within bounds everywhere except in the backwater areas of the tributaries. The record high flood of 1950 was also carried safely to the Gulf of Mexico within the levee system and control works. By the mid-1950s five reservoirs had been completed in the lower valley to draw off part of the discharge from the river.

A Mississippi flood in 1973, however, although it covered only 11 million acres, was disastrous to agriculture because water remained on farmland during the spring planting season. Flood-related accidents caused at least sixteen deaths.

Lynmouth, England, 1952. Toward the end of the summer season the seaside resort village of Lynmouth in North Devon was visited by a flash flood of tropical intensity. The rain gauge on the cliffs above the village registered 9.1 inches in twenty-four hours on August 15th—the equivalent of a million tons of rain per square mile. The area's thin soil with its rocky subsurface was completely waterlogged by nightfall. The normally shallow East and West Lyn rivers, which flow through narrow gorges from the top of the cliffs down to the sea, rose to a depth of forty feet, flooding Lynmouth and bringing huge rocks from the gorges down with them.

Trees, telephone poles, automobiles, and other kinds of debris were swept into the Bristol Channel. The following day, what looked like a forest of treetops floated above the waves half a mile offshore. The trees, rocks, and other heavy objects increased the destructive effects of the flood, demolishing buildings that might otherwise have withstood the force of the floodwaters. There were seventeen bridges across the East and West Lyn rivers between Lynmouth and the Exmoor tableland above it. As each bridge collapsed and was carried downstream, its wreckage smashed up against the next one, helping to bring it down in its turn.

Sixty-three-year-old Tom Floyd was in his house near the West Lyn Gorge with eight other members of his family on the night of the 15th. Ordinarily the river level was thirty feet below the road that ran past the Floyd home; around 9:30 one of Tom's sons looked out the window and saw that the water had reached the top of the gorge and was coming across the road. Tom Floyd remembered being "syphoned" upward and being carried along by the current until by an unexpected chance he was pulled from the flood by his daughter as he went by her house. All the other members of his family were lost.

On the morning of August 16th the flood had subsided, but Lynmouth and the surrounding area were a complete shambles. Mud and silt were piled twenty-five feet high in some places, and forty thousand tons of rocks (some weighing up to fifteen tons) had been deposited on the town. Ninety-three buildings had been destroyed, along with twenty-eight bridges. Thirty-four persons were dead. Lynmouth was rebuilt with contributions from throughout the world, and a new public hall was raised in memory of the flood victims.

Northern California, 1955. The twin communities of Yuba City and Marysville were founded during the California Gold Rush of 1849 on opposite sides of the Feather River, 120 miles north of San Francisco. Yuba City became the seat of Sutter County, which in the twentieth century developed into a prosperous fruit growing and dairy farming area. The Feather River, which rises in the foothills of the Sierra Nevada Mountains, thirty miles to the north, is joined by the Yuba River near Marysville. In December 1955, nine days of steady rain caused both rivers to rise dangerously, and Marysville in particular seemed to be threatened. Local authorities requested help from nearby Beale Air Force Base and from army installations in the area, while they tried desperately to shore up the earthen dikes along the Feather. Two thousand troops joined the civilians to stack up sandbags on top of the levees as the water continued to rise.

On December 23rd, nine thousand residents of the low-lying Linda and Olivehurst districts south of Marysville were evacuated. Later the same day the first break occurred in the dikes a few miles downstream, and thousands of acres of farmland were flooded, along with the towns of Nicolaus and Verona. When news of the break reached Marysville, six thousand of its residents were moved to Yuba City, or to Colusa, twenty-six miles away. But Yuba City itself was endangered as water began to seep through the dikes at Shanghai Bend, south of the city.

Around midnight the dikes gave way, and tons of water and silt poured through, sweeping north toward Yuba City and tearing to pieces everything in their path. The water spread out somewhat by the time it reached Yuba City itself, so the damage was not as bad as it might have been. But ninety percent of the city was flooded, and because there had been no warning, thousands of people were stranded and had to be rescued by boats and helicopters. Neighboring communities were filled with refugees by the evening of the 24th, and more than nine thousand were cared for in shelters set up by the Red Cross. With no telephone service, relief agencies often had to rely on local ham radio operators for communication with the outside world.

The next day was Christmas, and most of the flood victims spent a very uncomfortable holiday. In Marysville, where there had been no flooding, authorities allowed those who had been evacuated to return, but evacuees from Yuba City were not able to return to their homes—or what was left of them—until January 2. It took weeks to clear away the accumulated silt and debris. One of the main problems was created by the bodies of dead animals; more than six thousand cattle alone were drowned. The rebuilding of the levees was complicated when heavy rains returned in January. The river began to rise again, and there was another break in the dikes at Nicolaus. It was late February before the repair work was finally completed.

In all, eighty persons died as a result of the floods; 335 were hospitalized, more than four thousand were injured, and fifty thousand were at least temporarily homeless. The property damage was estimated at $225 million.

Italy, 1966. Probably the most widely publicized floods of recent memory were those that struck northern Italy in November 1966. Called the worst floods in the country's history, they caused enormous destruction in its most important industrial and agricultural areas and dealt a severe blow to the Italian economy. In the Tyrolean Alps a number of villages were badly damaged by landslides. The flooding was worst in the valleys of the Po, Adige, and Arno rivers. According to figures released by the Ministry of the Interior, at least 113 persons were killed in the disaster.

Along with the loss of life, irreparable damage was done to many valuable works of art, especially in the historic city of Florence. The city had been flooded by the Arno many times in the past, notably in 1333, 1577, 1666, and 1844. But the 1966 flood was the worst of all. On November 4th the water poured through the city like a torrent, depositing great quantities of mud and debris. Although the major collections in the Uffizi and Pitti galleries escaped harm, many churches and museums suffered severely. The most notable casualties were the Etruscan collections in the Museo Archeologico and Cimabue's "Crucifix" in the Museo di Santa Croce, which was perhaps the greatest single work of art ruined. Two of the bronze doors by Ghiberti at the Baptistery were damaged. More than a thousand panel paintings were partly or completely inundated, as were the National Library and State Archives with their many rare books and documents. The losses were tragic, but an international rescue operation made it possible to restore at least some of the ravaged buildings and artworks.

Forecasting Floods

In forecasting floods, scientists calculate both the probability of flooding in any one year and the frequency of flooding over a period of years. For the purpose of the planning and design of flood control measures, forecasting is usually done for moderately long intervals in the range of from fifty to one hundred years. To design measures that would control frequent floods represents too high a risk. Provisions against unusual floods that recur less than once a century may involve impossible expense. Complete flood protection is only possible in special circumstances. The artificial Lake Kariba on the Zambezi River in southern Africa, for example, has a large enough capacity to retain a year's runoff.

Although the relationship between weather and floods is far from simple, changes in atmospheric circulation may disrupt the normal incidence of floods and may affect the flood magnitudes as well. Shifts in atmospheric circulation patterns in low latitudes disrupt monsoonal and other weather systems and commonly increase the risk of droughts in some years and of floods in others. During the last decade, the Sahel area of Africa and the semiarid-to-arid regions of inland eastern Australia have experienced prolonged droughts that were ended by extensive flooding. It may eventually be possible to refine the forecasting of floods to make allowance for shifts in weather patterns.

In areas where agriculture depends on flooding, a shift in the weather and flood patterns can also have disastrous effects. There is archaeological evidence that the First Dark

Mid-August monsoon rains and river flooding in Bangladesh not only killed more than 800 residents in 1974 but led to a cholera epidemic, which caused the deaths of at least 15,000 others, and to a famine, which left untold animals and an estimated 15 million persons suffering from hunger and malnutrition.

Age of ancient Egypt, which saw the destruction of the Old Kingdom, resulted primarily from a succession of famines, which caused widespread starvation and a breakdown of the social order. It seems likely that the famines resulted from failures of the monsoon rains that feed the Blue Nile and promoted the annual irrigation floods.

River Differences

The hazard of extensive river flooding is obviously greatest where extensive areas adjacent to a major river channel lie below the level reached by flood crests. Except for its delta, the Mississippi in its lower six hundred miles occupies an alluvial trough cut principally by glacial meltwater at a time of low sea level. The later rise of the sea level as much as five hundred or more feet and the outgrowth of the delta have caused the river to elevate its bed. In many places, the surrounding land slopes down and away from the river. The lowest lying areas are undrained backswamps.

Although natural levees along the Mississippi's banks have been raised and strengthened and have been supplemented by artificial levees constructed on the floodplain, the flood risk over large areas continues to be severe. Considerable success has been achieved with control measures in some areas. A floodwall built in 1955 was estimated to have saved the city of St. Louis, Mo., a potential $340 million of damage in the 1973 flood.

The lower Huang Ho enters its alluvial plain at Meng-chin, nearly five hundred miles from the sea and only four hundred feet above sea level. The very gentle gradient is insufficient to allow the river to transport its sediment load, more than forty percent of which is deposited upstream from the mouth. Some of the large sediment deposits are distributed by floodwater. But the deposits upstream have also raised the level of the river one to two yards above the level of the surrounding countryside. At ordinary low flows the water is as much as three yards higher than the surrounding area. During floods the difference may reach more than eight yards.

The building of the Mississippi Delta upward and outward as well as settling near the delta margins has caused the Mississippi to switch its main outlet from time to time. The process usually results in the rapid reestablishment of a new main channel, but the point of diversion lies one hundred and fifty miles or less from the river's mouth. In addition, the area

Differences in the structure of the surrounding land help determine susceptibility to river flooding. The low-lying areas along the Amazon River in Peru (above) are much more likely to be flooded than are the highlands along the tributary Urubamba River (right).

of the Mississippi Valley upstream from the delta proper is somewhat protected from flooding by bluffs.

By contrast, the lower reaches of the Huang Ho traverse a vast area that slopes gradually away from the main channel. Switching of the river's outlet occurs as far as 280 miles upstream from the coast. Switching may displace the mouth through an area more than two hundred miles long and may cause extensive flooding. A deliberate breaching of the Huang Ho levees during the high water of 1938 resulted not only in a change of course but also in the displacement of an estimated six million refugees, of whom possibly half a million died.

In the plains of semiarid regions, the lack of continuous vegetation permits rapid surface runoff. In addition the stream channels in such areas are very shallow, and heavy rainstorms cause extensive flooding. Wide flooding may also occur in basins that have interior drainage if the streams that flow into them rise. Such is the case in the Lake Eyre basin of central Australia, which has been widely inundated twice in the last generation.

On the large Siberian rivers (the Ob, Yenisei, and Lena) that flow north the annual thaw occurs earlier in the southern upstream areas than in the northern downstream areas. The downstream areas may remain frozen and ice-jammed

long after the spring meltwater reaches them. These areas are also bordered by extensive waterlogged marshes, which contribute to flooding. Disastrous fish kills occur if the spring meltwater contains large amounts of humus.

Many characteristics influence the form of the flood peak. One of the most important is the size of the basin. Small basins, which roughly correspond to the areas of individual storms, are subject to rapid increases in discharge and inundation. In small basins the floodwater quickly drains off when the peak has passed. By contrast, the large downstream basins of rivers are typically affected by a slow rise and fall of the flood crest. The peak discharge in such areas may be maintained for some days.

These contrasting characteristics have given rise to what is known as the upstream-downstream controversy. Small-to-moderate floods in small basins can be controlled by simple conservation measures and by the construction of small dams. Protection in downstream areas requires extensive and expensive engineering works.

The Effects of Floods

Most rivers tend to scour their channels as their discharges rise to peak values. Then rivers fill the channels in again as the floods subside. It is unusual for even very large floods to produce significant changes in channel size. When such changes do occur, they are normally corrected within a few years. Although flooding may erode channel banks, erosion of the floodplain is uncommon. Whereas the flow velocity within the channel may be between six and ten feet per second, the sheet of floodwater moves at less than two feet per second. The average depth of deposits on floodplains during inundation is usually measured in fractions of an inch.

Some rivers, however, are raising their floodplains significantly. The River Severn, upstream of Shrewsbury, England, for example, has reduced its channel capacity to three-quarters of what is required to contain the most probable annual flood. Consequently, inundation of the floodplain has become more frequent. Areas cultivated in medieval times are now frequently under water.

Flood risk and flood damage have increased as flood-prone areas have come under use. For generations the floodplain of India's Ganges River was used mainly for seasonal farming. The pressures of India's population growth have produced permanent agricultural settlement on the plain. Flood dam-

The damage from river flooding depends largely on the use of the surrounding land. A flood on this section of the Connecticut River (above) is a hazard to trees and vegetation. Flooding along many rivers, as on this section of the Missouri River (below), also endangers man-made structures that are expensive to replace.

age in the plain, mainly to crops, is now assessed at an average of $1 million a year. The 1973 floods on the Indus in Pakistan alone extended over nearly two thousand square miles and ruined crops worth $250 million.

Statistics for flood damage are most readily available in the United States. Damage due solely to river floods, as opposed to hurricane and tidal flooding, can be separated into two categories. The damage from smaller, merely "disastrous," river floods, as measured in 1975 dollars, has been increasing during the twentieth century at a rate that will reach about $1.2 billion by the year 2000. The damage from larger, or "catastrophic," floods has been increasing more steadily and will reach $6.25 billion by the year 2000.

Flood risk is greatly increased by urbanization. The swift runoff from construction sites and the sediment it carries reduce the size of stream channels. The spread of masonry and paved surfaces, combined with the extension of storm drains, may increase the frequency of overbank flows in affected streams five or six times.

Responses to Floods

People's responses to the hazards of floods depend on their perception of the risks involved. Responses can be divided

Heavy rainfall is a common cause of local flooding. After a night of thunderstorms, parts of Damascus, Va., lay under floodwater.

into three general categories: passive, precautionary, or alleviatory measures. Taking out flood insurance, taking emergency actions during actual floods, and accepting public relief are among the most common responses. Long-term precautionary actions include structural adjustments such as the erection of levees and the flood-proofing of individual structures, the regulation of land use in catchment basins and on floodplains, and measures designed to reduce the probability that a river will overflow.

The probability of overflow can be reduced by installing flood-storage reservoirs where practicable, by embanking, and by enlarging the natural channel. Unfortunately, these solutions are to some extent all self-defeating. Reservoirs may prove unable to contain the waters of unusually high floods. Bypass channels and artificially enlarged channels may also prove inadequate and may increase the flood risk in downstream areas. It may be impracticable or uneconomical to excavate and maintain a channel capable of accommodating large but infrequent floods. Moreover, artificial channel enlargement in some agricultural areas of the Midwest has caused gullying in the basins of tributary streams. Artificial embanking increases the flood risk if the banks are breached.

It seems likely that flood warning systems will be improved in the future. On some rivers, flood control structures will be progressively improved. It does not seem likely that people will stop using land along rivers that are subject to flooding. It seems that accepting the risk of flooding will remain the principal human response to this disaster.

The loss of life from most flooding can, however, be substantially reduced by basic precautionary measures. At any danger of flooding, low-lying areas should be evacuated. Those who must remain in a flood-prone area should have bottled water, canned food, and other necessary supplies. One flood-related hazard is electrocution from current traveling through water that has come into contact with electric appliances or with a power source. In homes and buildings this hazard can be eliminated by turning off the electricity at its main source before flooding occurs. People should not enter a flooded basement, or a structure of any type, in which water is in contact with a source of electricity.

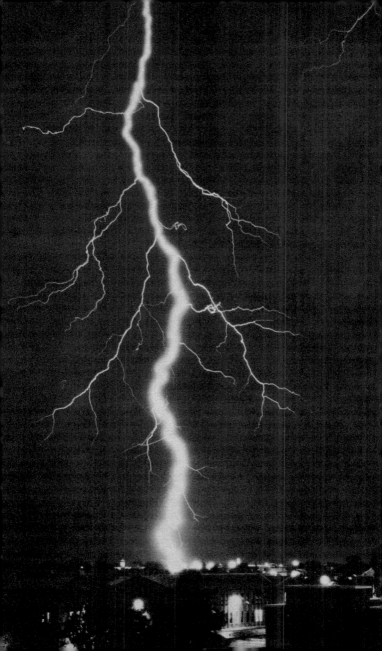

5.
Thunderbolts

Lightning strikes the Earth about a hundred times every second. Each year in the United States alone, 90 million gigantic bolts of electrical energy kill more people than do tornadoes, destroy about 18,000 houses, and cause property damage in excess of $100 million. Strikes by lightning to the world's forests and grasslands typically occur upwards of two hundred million times a year. These strikes produce thousands of wilderness fires each year in the United States alone that cost approximately $100 million to control, about one-third of the country's total annual fire control expense.

Not all lightning damage occurs on the ground. Ships, in days when they were not properly grounded, were often damaged by lightning. Commercial airplanes are involved in lightning strikes about once in every five thousand flying hours. The damage is usually slight, however, and only rarely is a plane lost. The extent of the damage to an airplane depends on the characteristics of the particular lightning flash.

Lightning and Man

Thunder rumbled overhead as professional golfers Lee Trevino and Jerry Heard sat under an umbrella at the thirteenth green on the Butler National Golf Club course in Oak Brook, Ill. It was the afternoon of June 27, 1975, and the course was crowded with players and spectators for the second round of the Western Open Golf Tournament. Suddenly Trevino fell to the ground and rolled over twice. "I thought he was kidding at first," one bystander recalled, but then Trevino yelled, "I've been hit!" The people around him realized that Trevino had been struck by lightning. His injuries were not serious, but he and Heard were both treated for minor burns at a nearby hospital.

Elsewhere on the course, Bobby Nichols was also struck by lightning. At about the same time Arnold Palmer, Jim Ahern, and Tony Jacklin had their clubs knocked out of their hands by lightning, but they were not hurt. This widely reported event was an almost playful demonstration of the power of lightning.

Human beings have been aware of the power of lightning

—for both evil and good—from the beginning of time. It was from lightning that people first got fire, which was so important in the development of human culture. Lightning was often considered one of the principal manifestations of divine power. When a man was killed by a bolt from heaven, it seemed natural to assume that God had stricken him down as punishment for some misdeed. The Book of Psalms says that to destroy his enemies, God "sent out arrows and scattered them; lightning and discomfited them."

Even after Benjamin Franklin and others had determined the true nature of lightning by scientific experiments in the eighteenth century, people still remained fascinated by it and fearful of its unpredictability. Writers of popular melodrama continued to use thunderstorms to create a mood of foreboding. In his *Autobiography*, Mark Twain tells of the effect a storm had on him as a boy:

> *A prodigious storm of thunder and lightning, accompanied by a deluging rain that turned the streets and lanes into rivers caused me to repent and resolve to lead a better life. I can remember those awful thunderbursts and the white glare of the lightning yet and the wild lashing of the rain against the windowpanes. . . . With every glare of lightning I shriveled and shrank together in mortal terror.*

In the United States, an average of more than one hundred people are killed by lightning each year. Its victims are usually killed instantly. Many more people, like Trevino and his fellow golfers, are only stunned or receive superficial injuries.

There are accounts of what it is like to be struck by lightning. One description was given by a farmer who was packing fruit in his barn with some helpers during a storm in the summer of 1959. He and another worker, a woman, went to the door to look out at the rain. The man wore rubber boots; the woman wore sandals. As they watched, lightning hit a willow tree some distance away and traveled along power lines to the barn, which was not equipped with lightning rods to deflect it. The lightning entered the barn, and both the man and the woman collapsed. One of the other workers ran to get help. When she returned, the farmer was beginning to regain consciousness, but the woman was dead. Questioned about his experience, the farmer said that he had felt as though he had been hit by a giant hammer. When he regained consciousness, he felt no more than a slight pain in his shoulder and a tingling feeling in his fingers.

Most victims of lightning are not struck directly. People hit while standing under a tree, for example, usually get only a small part of the current that passes through the tree and onto the surface of the ground. But the human body cannot tolerate more than a very small amount of electricity. A fraction of an ampere for one or two seconds can easily cause death. It is unusual for anyone to be killed by lightning while indoors. By far the greater number of fatalities occur outside, where the victims are unprotected by buildings or vehicles.

People at sporting events like the Western Open Golf Tournament seem to be especially frequent targets. Another instance occurred at England's fashionable Ascot racetrack in 1955. A week-long heat wave was broken by a sudden violent thunderstorm on the afternoon of July 14th. The spectators in the uncovered enclosures at Ascot were huddling around tents to shelter themselves from the rain when lightning flashed through the crowd. According to a newspaper report, it seemed to flicker down the final stretch of the track opposite the stands. People were "bowled over like ninepins"; some were lifted into the air and flung down again. While many people wandered around in a daze, others began to panic. The police were able to prevent a stampede, but two people were killed and forty-four were injured.

In February 1959, lightning killed two soccer players and injured seventeen during a match near Paulo de Farias, Brazil. In 1949, lightning struck a baseball field in Baker, Fla.; it dug up twenty feet of the infield, killed three players, and injured fifty spectators.

An automobile or railroad car is particularly effective in protecting its occupants from harm during a thunderstorm, principally because it is made of metal. Ships or boats, on the other hand, no matter what they are made of, are quite vulnerable to lightning. Floating high on a flat body of water, they naturally attract an electrical charge descending out of the air. Today it is rare for an oceangoing vessel to be seriously damaged by lightning, but it does happen. A Greek tanker, the *Kriti Sun*, exploded, broke into three sections, and sank when it was struck by lightning off Singapore in October 1975. Although this was considered a freak accident, lightning has taken a heavy toll of ships and seamen over the centuries.

Among sailors lightning is associated with Saint Elmo's fire, the glow that appears at the top of a ship's masts when the air is charged with electricity, and which was traditionally believed to be the sign of a supernatural protecting presence. But the lightning that often followed the appearance of this "protecting" fire could shatter the masts, or even damage the hull, causing the ship to sink.

In the eighteenth century the British navy tried to protect its ships by using "electrical chains," which were hung from the masthead down into the water during a storm, but their effectiveness was limited. In 1847 Sir William Snow Harris published a study of two hundred and twenty naval vessels hit by lightning. In nearly fifty cases the ships were set on fire, and many were damaged or disabled. In the incidents reported, ninety seamen were killed and nearly two hundred were injured. The navy adopted Harris's recommendation that the mast itself be made a conductor by having a copper band nailed along its whole length and by connecting the band to copper plates on the keel and hull. This helped to solve the problem, and the introduction of metal ships later in the century sharply reduced the number of losses due to lightning.

Aircraft. The French airship *Dixmude* had been built in Germany during World War I as Zeppelin L-72. After Germany's defeat in 1918 it was handed over to the French navy. The craft established an endurance record in September 1923, traveling 4,500 miles in 118 hours. But its commander, Lieut. du Plessis de Grenedan, expressed doubts about the dirigible's ability to repeat the performance since it had not been designed for such long flights.

On December 18, 1923, the *Dixmude* left its hangar near Marseilles with fifty people aboard for a flight to North Africa. On the 21st, when it was over Biskra, Algeria, on its way back to Marseilles, it was warned by radio about a storm over the Mediterranean Sea. On the 23rd, an Italian vessel received a wireless signal from an airship that seemed to be in trouble. Two days later some fishermen recovered Grenedan's body off the coast of Sicily. The *Dixmude* had gone down with everyone aboard. Subsequent examination of pieces of the wreckage indicated that its storage tanks had exploded after being struck by lightning.

Dirigibles were especially vulnerable to lightning because they were filled with highly combustible hydrogen gas. The cause of the *Hindenburg* disaster in 1937 is still a subject of controversy, but an investigation by the U.S. Department of Commerce found that the most probable explanation was that a hydrogen leak had been ignited by an electrical discharge.

Other aspects of thunderstorms were also dangerous to such lighter-than-air craft. In 1925 the U.S. naval airship *Shenandoah* ran into electrical storm activity over Ohio on a flight from Lakehurst, N.J., to St. Louis, Mo. An updraft suddenly raised its altitude by more than three thousand feet; immediately afterward, it plummeted toward the earth at twenty-five feet per second. Under the pressure of these violent movements, the ship broke into three parts. They floated gently to the ground, and only fourteen out of the forty-three people on board were killed. Passengers on the British airship R-101, which crashed under similar circumstances in 1930, were less fortunate: forty-eight out of fifty-four were killed in the tragedy.

Today's airplanes are not as likely to be damaged by thunderstorms, but at times the effects of storms can still be devastating. On December 8, 1963, a Puerto Rico-to-Philadelphia jetliner was struck by lightning and exploded during a thunderstorm, only moments after taking off from the Baltimore, Md., airport where seventy-one passengers had been discharged. All eighty-one of the persons remaining aboard were killed. On September 26, 1964, an aircraft successfully sustained five separate lightning hits in twenty minutes while in a holding pattern over Chicago. During a storm on July 23, 1973, an Ozark Air Lines twin-engine turbojet was on its way into Lambert Airport at St. Louis. The airport control tower lost radar contact with the flight when it was about a mile from the runway. According to the pilot, his plane was hit by lightning "at least once" before it crashed into a ravine in the midst of a wooded area in the St. Louis suburb of Normandy. Debbie Schwab, whose home was about a hundred yards from where the plane crashed, said that she heard "a boom like lightning, followed by more booms." Her husband ran out of the house and saw a ball of flame light up the sky. Thirty-six of the forty-four people on board were killed.

Forest Fires. Trees, like ships, are natural targets for lightning. Because they are full of moisture, they are good conductors of electricity, which is why it is so dangerous to stand under a tree during a thunderstorm. When a tree in the middle of a forest is hit, the result is frequently a forest fire.

Lightning flashes within a cloud produce what is called "sheet lightning," but flashes between clouds produce a forked channel (above). Cloud-to-ground lightning (left) discharges often strike isolated tall objects such as trees. Triggered lightning (below) has the appearance of a cloud-to-ground discharge but actually begins from a tall object, which "triggers" the discharge.

On the average, cloud-to-ground discharges in the United States start ten thousand forest fires each year, of almost all are extinguished while small. It is the remaining three to five percent that burn out of control and cause virtually all of the damage. These relatively few fires can be extremely destructive. In 1970 alone, fires burned such large parts of southern California that the region was declared a disaster area. Fourteen people were killed. Eight hundred homes and buildings were destroyed, and 600,000 acres of timber and watershed cover were burned.

In Canada between 1969 and 1973, there was a yearly average of 2,500 such fires, and well over two million acres of forest were burned as a result. In 1974 alone, nearly two million acres, or ninety-four percent of the total area burned in Canada, were destroyed by lightning-related fires.

Marvin Dodge of the California Department of Conservation has warned that more and more disastrous fires can be expected because of the accumulation of dead fuels in the wildland areas of the western United States. It is in areas protected by the federal government that the accumulation and the hazard of such conflagrations are greatest. Dodge has argued that prescribed burning may be the solution and that critics of the practice fail to recognize the difference between high-intensity wildfires that destroy everything and low-intensity fires that may cause little or no damage.

A similar view has been expressed by Alan Taylor of the U.S. Forest Service. Although recognizing that there must be research into ways of controlling the few lightning fires that become holocausts, Taylor has emphasized that the greatest challenge is to learn about the roles of lightning and fire in plant and animal communities. This knowledge, Taylor believes, should be coupled with man's technological capabilities and used to prevent disasters associated with lightning. At the same time, Taylor argues, man should allow fire as a natural agent of change to pursue its course. It appears that in the 1970s the principle of total fire prevention taught by Smokey the Bear is giving way to the evidence that lightning and the fires it causes may play a natural role in the ecological balance of forests.

Anatomy of a Lightning Discharge

A lightning flash is a transient, high-current electrical discharge in the atmosphere. It usually occurs within a cloud (intracloud discharge) or between the cloud and the ground

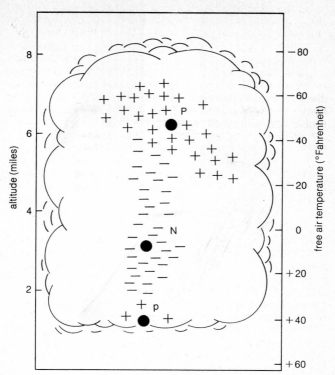

Some scientists believe that the electrical charges within a cloud that produce lightning have a distribution related to altitude and temperature (P = net positive charge; p = smaller positive charge; and N = net negative charge).

(cloud-to-ground discharge). Only infrequently does a flash occur between clouds (intercloud discharge) or from a cloud to the surrounding air (air discharge). Intracloud discharges are the most frequent, but those from clouds to the ground cause the most damage and deaths. A less well known type of lightning is the discharge that originates at the ground from a tall conducting object, such as a tower or skyscraper, and travels to a cloud above. This type is caused by the presence of the man-made conductor and would not occur in its absence. Because the flash is "triggered" or initiated by the conductor, it is called triggered lightning.

To understand the danger of lightning and the damage it can cause, it is helpful to examine the physical events that occur in a lightning discharge to the ground. The source of a lightning discharge is the accumulation of electrical charges in regions of a cumulonimbus cloud (commonly known as a thundercloud). Just how these charges build up is a mystery. Apparently, natural processes generate an area of net positive charge in the top of a cumulonimbus cloud and a net negative charge in the bottom. Both charges have magnitudes of perhaps forty or fifty coulombs (a charge equal to the electricity transferred by a current of one ampere in one second).

Frequently, a small positively charged region with a magnitude of a few coulombs is detected near the cloud base. The charge resides on ice crystals and water drops. If the electrical field in the cloud exceeds a few hundred thousand volts per yard, the charge drains from the droplets and ice crystals to initiate a lightning flash. If this occurs in the base of the cloud between the large negatively charged region and the small positively charged region, a cloud-to-ground discharge begins in the form of a stepped leader, which is visible as a downward branching pattern.

The visible process begins when a channel of light emerges from the cloud base. It is very faint and is composed of an electrically charged column with a luminous core only an inch or so in diameter. The leader moves in a steplike pattern toward the ground. Each step is typically a little more than fifty yards long and is traversed in less than a microsecond (a millionth of a second). Each step is followed by a pause before another fifty yard step. Several channels may develop toward the ground and give the appearance of downward branching.

The stepped leader is characterized by a velocity of about 125 miles a second (only a tiny fraction of the speed of light). The leader typically has a current of a hundred amperes that deposits five coulombs on the channel in the twenty milliseconds (thousandths of seconds) that it takes to reach the ground. When one of the leader branches comes to within about fifty yards of the ground, one or more discharges originate from the ground. The upward discharge that connects with the leader short-circuits the cloud to the ground, and the return stroke then begins.

The return stroke can be thought of as a high-current flow that drains the negative charge from the channel. As the

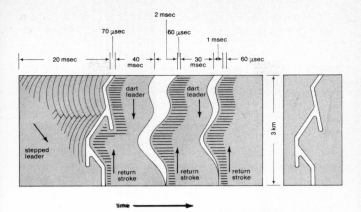

A diagram of the phases of a lightning stroke (left) shows that the process takes only a small fraction of a second. If photographed on stationary film (right), the steps of the process are not visible (msec=milliseconds and μsec=microseconds).

electrons in the lightning channel flow toward the ground, the luminosity moves up the channel at a speed approximately one-third that of light.

This is the instant at which damage occurs to objects that are struck by lightning. Peak currents typically reach 20,000 amperes and occasionally exceed 200,000 amperes. The channel expands at supersonic speed to a luminous diameter of perhaps two or more inches, and the acoustic wave resulting from this expansion is heard as thunder. The pressure in the channel may be many times that of the atmosphere, and the temperature may exceed 45,000° F. These peak currents, pressures, and temperatures in the channel are generally attained in a few microseconds. They diminish as the current decreases to one-half its maximum value in forty or fifty microseconds. The luminous return stroke takes only seventy microseconds to reach the cloud base from the ground. Current continues to flow in the channel for a few hundreds of microseconds. In less than a millisecond, the return stroke is over.

The completion of the return stroke sometimes ends the lightning event. But usually another phase begins in about forty milliseconds with the emergence of a dart of light from the cloud base. It typically follows the old channel and moves at a speed one-hundredth that of light. There is no stepping, just a downward progression of a luminous dart about fifty yards in length. The dart carries a few hundred to a thousand amperes and deposits a few coulombs of charge on the channel. No branching occurs, and the dart usually contacts the same point as did the stepped leader. Consequently, the cloud is again short-circuited to the ground, and another return stroke occurs. Typically, three or four leader and return phases occur to produce a lightning flash with an average duration of two-tenths of a second. As many as twenty-six leaders with return strokes have been reported, however, in a lightning flash that lasted two seconds.

About one-fifth of the cloud-to-ground discharges have more than one contact point with the ground. This occurs when the dart leader encounters a section of the channel "older" than a hundred milliseconds and forges a new stepped leader to the ground. When more than one contact point with the ground is made, the damage that can be caused by the flash is increased.

The cloud-to-ground discharge is not the only kind of lightning flash that involves the ground. Studies at New York City's Empire State Building in the late 1930s showed that lightning sometimes begins at the ground and moves to the clouds. A detailed study of these triggered discharges was recently made by Karl Berger at the Mt. San Salvatore Lightning Observatory near Lugano, Switzerland. There, two instrumented towers, each more than two hundred feet high, are involved in more than a hundred lightning flashes each year. More than four-fifths of these are triggered lightning, and the remainder are "normal" cloud-to-ground discharges.

A detailed study of photographs and of the characteristics of the electric currents revealed that the triggered lightning begins with a stepped leader originating from the tower top. It may carry either a positive or negative charge. The upward leaders have many of the same characteristics as the downward leaders. The principal difference becomes apparent, however, when the upward leader contacts the cloud. No return stroke occurs. The channel luminosity increases along the entire channel, and there is an increase in the current. If a subsequent stroke occurs, it is initiated by a dart leader that begins in the cloud and moves toward the tower.

Not all triggered lightning involves thunderstorms or objects on or near the ground. H. T. Harrison of United Air Lines reported in a one-year survey of airline flights that thunderstorms were conspicuously absent in many of the incidences of lightning discharges involving the planes. Pilots usually separate their reports into lightning strikes and static discharges, the latter occurring primarily in the absence of thunderstorms. Visible damage is reported in one-third of the incidents, and there is no apparent difference between the damage that occurs during thunderstorm conditions and that which occurs without thunderstorms. It appears, therefore, that "static discharges" involving aircraft are, in fact, lightning that is initiated or triggered by the presence of the airplane.

By far the most common type of lightning is an intracloud flash that occurs within a cloud. The ratio of intracloud to cloud-to-ground lightning is estimated to be ten to one in tropical latitudes, but the ratio decreases at higher latitudes. In Norway, at latitude 50° N, the intracloud and cloud-to-ground frequencies are approximately the same.

In an intracloud flash a leader process develops within the cloud at average velocities of more than 28 miles a second. During this time the cloud has a low luminosity punctuated by random periods of brightness that occur when the leader reaches pockets of charge within the cloud. No return stroke occurs. The electrical charge is estimated to be twenty coulombs, similar to that in a cloud-to-ground flash, but measurements indicate that it can range from less than one to as much as a hundred coulombs. The vertical range of the intracloud discharge averages about one-third mile, whereas the horizontal extent is from nearly two-thirds of a mile to more than six miles, with a mean of nearly two miles. The flash appears to be predominantly a horizontal flash within a cloud.

Aural and Visual Effects

By far the most dramatic evidence of lightning is the flash of light that is seen and the thunder that is heard. Scientists have developed extensive instruments and techniques to record these emissions. From such recordings the physical characteristics of the flash can be deduced.

Arthur Few of Rice University in Houston, Texas, has made a detailed study of the "acoustical signature," or thunder, of the lightning flash and has mapped its path in space. He has discovered in several cases that the normal cloud-to-ground flash has a long horizontal section in the cloud that may be ten times longer than the short vertical section that can be observed below the cloud base. Furthermore, this horizontal section is largely within a horizontal slice of the atmosphere that is defined by the isotherms, or areas of constant temperature of between 32° F and 50° F. It seems, therefore, that lightning originates in a region of the cloud known to contain both ice crystals and water drops.

Rough estimates of the distance to a flash and of its channel length are made using a simple formula that is based on the great difference between the speed of light and that of sound. First, the time interval between light emissions and the thunder is recorded in seconds, and then the duration of the thunder is measured. Dividing the time interval by five yields the approximate distance to the channel in miles. The lightning channel, furthermore, is an instantaneous but geometrically spread-out source of sound. The thunder from the various parts of the channel arrives with a time delay determined by the distance to the channel segment. Consequently, dividing the duration of the thunder by five gives the approximate minimum length of the lightning channel in miles.

It is difficult to specify the exact distance over which thunder can be heard. Characteristics of the atmosphere such as wind and temperature as well as the height of the lightning source are all factors that determine how far the sound travels. The distance, however, is typically no more than fifteen miles and may be considerably less.

The visual effects of the lightning flash are always impressive and have led to reports of many different types of lightning. These differences, however, can mostly be explained by the fundamental properties of a flash. "Forked lightning," for example, is actually a cloud-to-ground flash with many branches. "Bead lightning" refers to lightning in which sections of the channel that remain luminous for a longer time give the appearance of luminous beads. "Heat lightning" refers to the distant red flashes of a thunderstorm from which no thunder is heard. The flashes are red for the same reason that the setting sun is red; the blue light is scattered more than is the red. No thunder is heard because the sound waves are refracted up into the atmosphere and pass overhead. "Sheet lightning" refers to the luminous appearance of a cloud in an intracloud flash. The channel is not visible and the cloud, illuminated from within, resembles a white sheet.

Occurrence and Distribution

Thunderstorms can occur whenever moist air is cooled and condensed by moving through large vertical distances. The

Lightning can be a damaging phenomenon, but it can also be a beautiful sight.

greatest frequency of lightning is on the island of Java, where thunderstorms occur on the average of 223 days of the year. Within the United States, lightning occurs most frequently in Florida. There is an ample supply of moisture in Florida from the surrounding water, and the solar heating of the land lifts the moist air. The resulting cumulonimbus clouds extend to several miles in height and produce regions in Florida that have approximately ninety days of thunderstorm a year.

An area of low thunderstorm frequency is found along the West Coast of the United States. Although the Pacific Ocean provides the region with a sufficient source of moisture for thunderstorms, the area is dominated by an anticyclone, or high-pressure, area, which suppresses movement. Consequently, the West Coast is favored with fair weather. In his investigations of triggered lightning, Harrison noted a disproportionately high frequency of lightning strikes involving airplanes in the vicinity of airports on the West Coast. He has suggested that the few thunderstorm days that are reported from airport meteorological offices in the region may in part be the result of aircraft triggering discharges.

Destructiveness

By far the greatest damage is done when lightning strikes the Earth's surface. The average of more than one hundred persons killed in the United States each year, however, is down from an average of more than four hundred a year in the early decades of this century. Recent research indicates that the loss of life can be even further reduced.

When lightning strikes the human body, it sometimes only causes burns and tissue destruction, injuries that do not necessarily cause death. Far more serious effects are the loss of respiration and interference with the rhythmic beat of the heart (ventricular fibrillation). If either occurs, the body suffers irreversible damage unless first aid is given within five minutes. In the absence of breathing, artificial respiration should be given. In the absence of a heartbeat, heart action can be simulated by placing the victim on his back and pressing firmly on his chest with the heel of the hand once every second or slightly faster. In this way prompt first aid may "reverse" death by lightning.

Precautionary measures, however, remain the surest way to avoid becoming a lightning death statistic. People should stay inside during a thunderstorm and keep away from metal objects such as electrical appliances, plumbing, the sink, the phone, and the television set and avoid doorways, porches, and fireplaces. The safest place is inside a metal structure; therefore people traveling by automobiles in a thunderstorm should remain inside them. If caught swimming or boating in an open craft they should go ashore and leave the beach area. If caught in the open, they should avoid hilltops and high places and not seek shelter under isolated trees but should find the lowest spot possible and crouch so as to cover only a small area of ground. They should get off the golf course before the rain starts and should avoid wire fences. Everyone should remember that getting wet is preferable to participating in a lightning flash.

Each year lightning strikes to property cause dangerous, extensive, and expensive damage. People with a home in an area with twenty to thirty thunderstorm days a year can expect a strike on the average of once every hundred years. People cannot prevent lightning from striking their home, but they can provide a safe path to the ground by installing a lightning rod with a conductor to the earth for safe grounding. Benjamin Franklin's invention of the lightning rod more than two hundred years ago has in principle remained unchanged; it is still the most reliable way to protect a home against lightning. Boats with grounded masts and metal objects are also safe if the occupants avoid contact with metal.

A Look Ahead

Basic research is being conducted in predicting and controlling lightning. There have been, however, only a few experiments in modifying thunderstorms and reducing the harmful effects of lightning, and they have been inconclusive. Individual research institutes have traditionally worked alone to determine the physical properties of the lightning discharge. Yet, prediction and control can only be achieved when scientists understand the complicated meteorological patterns of airflow and precipitation that are associated with the buildup of charged regions in the thundercloud. This degree of knowledge will require a comprehensive and coordinated scientific effort that uses the latest technological advances to study all aspects of the thunderstorm simultaneously. Such an effort will make prediction, and perhaps limited control, of lightning a technological possibility.

6.
Blizzards, Avalanches, and Glaciers

Like so many of the small things in nature, a snow crystal has an interesting, even beautiful, structure. Considered as a single particle, it is ineffectual as an element of force or destruction. Only when snow crystals occur in huge quantities of countless numbers does their presence cause concern or terror.

Floating in the rare air of the high atmosphere, the tiny pointed or flat-ended hexagonal columns and thickened hexagonal plates of snow crystals form colored halos, pillars, arcs, and circles in the light of the sun. Snow is formed in the upper parts of turbulent clouds. The reactions between snow crystals and undercooled water cause the development of electrical charges that are often manifested as cloud-to-cloud or cloud-to-ground lightning, radio static, or less noticeable kinds of atmospheric electricity. Sweeping over and smashing onto an airplane's wings and fuselage, snow crystals cause electrification that may appear as Saint Elmo's fire and may illuminate the trailing edges of the wing tips.

Accompanied by intensively strong, cold winds, snow creates blizzards. At times snow may become so deep and unstable on a mountain slope that it forms a terrifying avalanche, or it may become consolidated in massive layers of blue-green glacial ice that flow down a mountain like a slow-moving river.

Blizzards

Long, severe snowstorms combined with buffeting winds result in blinding, freezing conditions in which unsheltered people and animals have little recourse. One such blizzard in the United States resulted in the notorious Donner Party incident. The Great Blizzard of 1888 in the Northeast and a record-breaking month of snowstorms in Europe in 1956 are among other historic blizzards. Large cities can be particularly vulnerable to severe snowstorms. A total of more than 23 inches of snow fell on Chicago in a 24-hour period in 1967. Enormous drifts had been shaped by winds that reached 53 miles per hour, and the city was immobilized.

California, 1846–47. At its maximum the Donner Party emigrating to California included twenty-nine men, fifteen women, and forty-three children, with twenty-three ox-drawn wagons. Under the leadership of George Donner, they separated from the main body of the westward migration on July 20, 1845, leaving the established trail to follow the so-called Hastings Cutoff south of Great Salt Lake in Utah. In an ill-advised move, they broke a new trail through the Wasatch Mountains and lost about two weeks' time. The party suffered great hardships and lost many oxen while crossing the Great Salt Lake Desert. The group was further plagued by internal dissensions (resulting in a homicide and a banish-

Trying to cross the Sierra Nevada en route to California, the Donner Party was caught in a severe blizzard in 1846–47. Exhaustion, injuries, malnutrition, and starvation killed forty-two persons.

The members of the Donner Party experienced the worst effects of a blizzard—the isolation and immobility that prevent people from finding food or shelter.

ment), by depletion of food supplies, and by Indian attacks on their oxen.

On October 31, weary and short of food, they approached the pass across the Sierra Nevada and found their progress completely blocked by heavy snow. Most of them built crude cabins near what is now known as Donner Lake; others made a similar camp a few miles farther east on the trail. Eight days of almost continuous blizzard followed, during which time many of the oxen, the chief reserve of food, wandered off and were lost. Other snowstorms followed. On December 15 the first death occurred, due to exhaustion and malnutrition rather than to actual starvation.

On December 16, ten men and five women set out on

snowshoes to cross the mountains. They struggled on during a month of harrowing, often overwhelming, hardships from cold, blizzards, deep snow, and inadequate food. Eight of the men died, and the bodies of some were eaten by the others. Two men and all of the women reached the Sacramento Valley.

Settlers in California then organized a relief party that left Fort Sutter (now on the site of Sacramento) on January 31, 1847. Struggling heroically through the deep snow, seven men reached the lake camp on February 18. They took twenty-three of the starving people, including seventeen children, back to the California settlements, but several deaths occurred on the way. Other relief parties followed, but because of illness and injuries it was impossible to remove everyone. When one group was reached by rescuers they not only ate all the food given to them but the laces from the snowshoes that the relief party had brought for them to wear.

Once during the ordeal some members of the party built a fire, erected a shelter, and retired for the night. By morning their fire had melted through the snow to ground level—a distance of thirty feet.

On March 6 one of the survivors, J. F. Reed, described the prevailing blizzard conditions in his diary:

> With the snow there is a perfect hurricane. In the night there is a great crying among the children, and even with the parents there is praying, crying, and lamentation on account of the cold and the dread of death from hunger and the howling storm. The men up nearly all night making fires. Some of the men began praying. Several of them became blind. I could not see the light of the fire blazing before me, nor tell when it was burning. The light of heaven is, as it were, shut out from us. The snow blows so thick and fast that we can not see twenty feet looking against the wind. I dread the coming night. Three of my men only, able to get wood. The rest have given out for the present. It is still snowing, and very cold. So cold that the few men employed in cutting the dry trees down, have to come and warm about every ten minutes. 'Hungry!' 'Hungry!' is the cry with the children, and nothing to give them. 'Freezing!' is the cry of the mothers who have nothing for their little, starving, freezing children.

After the dogs and cowhides had been devoured, more deaths occurred, and the survivors were forced to resort to cannibalism. The last survivor did not leave the camp until April 21. Five died before reaching the mountain camps; thirty-four died at the camps or on the mountains while attempting to cross, and one died just after reaching the settlements in California. Two men who had joined the party at the lake also died. There was a total of forty-two deaths, the worst disaster of the overland migration to California.

Northeastern Seaboard, 1888. Between the 11th and 14th of March nearly thirty inches of snow fell over an area extending from Maine to Maryland. The high winds, offshore waves, and freezing temperature produced a horrifying blizzard that killed more than four hundred people. Dozens of fishing boats, schooners, and barks—in cargoes, ports, and the open ocean—were battered, driven ashore, or capsized. As communication wires were blown down, cities and towns were isolated.

Parts of the area had never experienced such a storm before and were totally unprepared for it. With its vast and concentrated population, metropolitan New York City took a severe beating. Winds of up to one hundred miles per hour blew off the roofs of homes and blew the heavy snowfall into vast drifts that covered fences and public monuments, filled up driveways and building entrances, and made transportation, even on the elevated trains, impossible. One man who tried to walk the one block from his place of business to his home froze to death. Another man actually managed to make it from Wall Street to his club on 25th Street; it took him four exhausting hours, however, and he later reported having seen "bodies sticking from the snow." The city's electrical and fire alarm system failed. The hotels were so glutted that people slept in corridors; and most stores, theaters, and restaurants closed. It was so cold that the East River froze over and then cracked into hazardous ice floes.

Europe, 1956. During the month of February an onslaught of blizzards, accompanied by intense cold, wreaked havoc throughout England and Western Europe. (The cold penetrated as far south as the Mediterranean Sea. On February 9 the low temperature on the island of Sicily was 5° F.) The accumulation of heavy snow and later thawing caused many destructive avalanches in mountainous areas, particularly in Austria and Yugoslavia. Rivers froze for long distances, and explosives had to be used to break up ice jams.

The 1956 blizzard in Europe was very destructive both of human life and of agriculture. More than nine hundred deaths were attributed to the blizzard or to its aftereffects. The snow and the accompanying cold, particularly because they reached so far south, had disastrous effects on plant life. Olive trees along the Mediterranean, for example, were destroyed. It was estimated that the crop damage alone was more than $2 billion.

Avalanches

An avalanche is a large mass of snow and other materials, frequently including a considerable amount of rock debris, that moves rapidly down a mountain slope. An avalanche begins when the mass overcomes the frictional resistance of the sloping surface, often after its foundation has been loosened by spring rains or rapidly melted by a warm, dry wind or other factors. Thunder and artillery fire or other man-made noises can start the snow in motion.

Avalanches, often referred to as "white death," can be extremely destructive. In periods of exceptionally heavy snow, for example, whole villages have been destroyed, in some cases with considerable loss of human life. Several incidents have been well documented.

Leukerbad, Switzerland, 1718. The small spa town of Leukerbad had barely survived a devastating avalanche in 1518, when most of the town was destroyed and sixty-one persons were killed, and would again suffer avalanches in 1720 and 1758. Leukerbad's avalanche on January 17, 1718, however, was the worst of the four. With no warning, tons of snow rolled over the town at about 8:00 P.M. knocking down every building — Saint Laurentius church, the famous baths that had made Leukerbad a tourist center, the hotels, every residence, and even those avalanche-proof structures that had been specifically built to withstand such force. The avalanche was so sudden that the residents were trapped kneeling at altar rails, sleeping in their beds, and in one case, selecting a bottle from a wine cellar. Fifty-five persons were killed.

Saint Gervais and LaFayet, Switzerland, 1892. The two small resort villages of St. Gervais and LaFayet were both wiped out on July 12, 1892. One hundred and forty persons were killed, and all of the buildings were destroyed. Saint Gervais was located below an overhanging glacier on the west slope of Mont Blanc. At 2:00 A.M., when most of the residents were in bed, the overhang suddenly broke off and showered tons of snow, ice, water, and glacial debris over the village. The avalanche continued rolling downhill and obliterated the neighboring village of LaFayet.

Wellington, Washington, 1910. The most disastrous avalanche in U.S. history took place in the Cascade Mountains of Washington on March 1, 1910, following heavy snows in an area where forest fires had decimated trees and ground cover the previous autumn. For nine days in late February heavy snow trapped a crowded passenger train at the mountainous Wellington station. When the snowfall finally stopped on February 28, it was followed by warm winds and rain. At 1:20 the next morning from the slopes above Wellington a great twenty-foot-thick slab of snow loosened. About a half-mile long by a quarter-mile wide, the slab slid directly toward the small station town. It hit the stalled train, a snow plow, the water tower, several locomotives and boxcars, and dozens of persons and pushed everything into a deep gorge. The avalanche miraculously missed a small hotel, whose residents grabbed shovels and ran to remove the buried. Twenty-two persons were saved, but ninety-six others had been killed.

Ranrahirca, Peru, 1962. At 6:13 P.M. on January 10, 1962, a great ice cap suddenly cracked off a glacier atop Mount Huascarán, an extinct volcano in the Andes Mountains of South America. It fell onto a lower glacier, starting an avalanche of incredible size—about thirteen million cubic yards of rock and ice weighing an estimated twenty million tons. Described as a "hellish roar," it rushed ten miles down a funnellike canyon in just seven minutes. On its way it smashed the village of Ranrahirca, where all but 98 of the 2,456 residents were killed, completely obliterated the next five smaller villages and all of their residents, and hit ten other settlements, taking dozens of other lives. In all, more than four thousand persons and ten thousand animals were killed and more than $1 million worth of crops was destroyed. One survivor said that the avalanche "came rushing at us like the end of the world," and another stated that "everything went—vanished, like a nightmare."

Stewart, Canada, 1965. On a foothill of the three thousand-foot-high Granduc Mountain in British Columbia, a copper mine known as the Le Duc Camp was buried at 9:57 A.M. on February 18, 1965, by an icy avalanche that swept down from a nearby glacier. The twenty workmen who were trapped in a newly opened eleven-mile tunnel were lucky. The frozen tunnel did not collapse, and they were able to dig their way out of the partially open entrance within a few hours. The workmen who were manning the power plant, the carpenter and machine shops, the cookhouse and the coffee shack, and outside equipment, however, were carried away and buried alive. Nothing remained of the campsite but a rubble of snow and debris. A few of the buried men eventually dug through the snow to freedom, and rescue work went on at a frenzied pace until the others were saved or their bodies found. Of the 154 men involved, only 27 were killed, causing one avalanche expert to remark that "the avalanche was merciful, if such a word can be applied to a blind force."

Avalanche Formation and Control. In mountainous terrain an avalanche is a fearful natural phenomenon that can sweep and grind everything in its path. With the tremendous increase in the popularity of skiing in the snowy mountains of the world, considerable attention is now being paid to avalanche danger in such regions. Despite the construction of avalanche protection works in most parts of Switzerland, avalanches still occur there following periods of intense snowfall and cause death and destruction. In some of the older towns of Switzerland buildings constructed in open areas likely to be swept by avalanches are built like the prows of ships in order to divert the flowing snow.

Because most of the ski areas in mountainous regions in the United States are located within national forests, avalanche danger is monitored by the Forest Service of the Department of Agriculture. Rangers of the Forest Service, specially trained for avalanche forecasting and control, monitor the resort areas and other mountainous slopes where avalanches might endanger highways or other structures. At present much of the control consists of lobbing explosives into the upper reaches of the avalanche zones, intentionally causing snow to slide before it would do so from natural forces.

It is believed that one of the causes of avalanches is the slow formation of depth hoar under the snow pack. Depth hoar is a hexagonal cup-type of ice crystal that first begins to form at ground level. The zone of depth hoar slowly spreads upward within the snow pack. Depth hoar crystals develop from the evaporation of the original snow particles and from the simultaneous formation of larger, denser ice crystals near the ground. In this transformation of the snow the depth hoar crystals grow by vapor deposits. The crystals develop in a loose array so that, although the actual density of the snow remains the same, the "strength" of this area of the snow pack is so low that it can flow like sugar. There is, therefore, a zone of weakness within the snow pack near the ground, the particles of which act as a lubricant when the upper layers of the snow start sliding down a mountain.

Other mechanisms caused by the instability and flow characteristics of snow also play a role in producing avalanches. The extremely heavy "wet" avalanche is perhaps the most dangerous because of its great weight, heavy texture, and tendency to solidify as soon as it stops moving. The dry type is dangerous because it contains great amounts of air, making it act like a fluid. It is this kind of avalanche that may run part way up the opposite side of a narrow valley.

All forms of avalanches may be triggered by the formation of depth hoar. Although avalanches may develop during a heavy snowstorm and slide while the snow is still falling, more often they occur after the snow has "seasoned." In many instances the avalanche is triggered by a large slab of snow breaking from a projecting shelf, called a cornice, which forms on the lee side of a mountain ridge from wind-blown crystals. Such massive snow cornices may extend outward as far as fifty feet or more. Although they tend to be controlled by plastic flow, at times they break from the sheer weight of the accumulated snow.

Glaciers

A glacier is a body of ice originating on land by compaction and recrystallization of snow and showing evidence of present or past movement. Glaciers occur where the snowfall in winter exceeds the melting in summer, conditions that now prevail only in high mountain areas and polar regions. Because they are restricted to cold, remote places and because their destructive processes move so slowly, glaciers are less familiar to most people than are other, more immediate phenomena that cause natural disasters. Nonetheless, the presence of extensive ice-covered areas is an extremely important feature because of their direct and indirect effects on the Earth and its inhabitants.

Glaciers occupy a total of nearly six million square miles, or about ten percent of the Earth's land surface, an area almost as large as South America. About ninety-five percent of all present glaciers are concentrated in Antarctica and

Greenland; the remainder are widely scattered on all continents, except Australia, and on many islands in high latitudes. The exact volume of glaciers is not known, but conservative estimates suggest that there is enough ice in them to encase the entire Earth in a mantle between one hundred and two hundred feet thick. Because appreciable changes, either increases or decreases, in the volume of glaciers would adversely affect the distribution of people and their economic relationships, variations in the existing amount of glacier ice are highly critical to man. If all existing glacier ice were to melt, for example, the resulting rise in the sea level of about two hundred feet would submerge every major coastal city in the world.

There are three major types of glaciers. The largest, which are called ice sheets or ice caps, cover huge areas and in many cases are thick enough to bury entire mountain ranges except for their highest peaks. Practically all of Antarctica, an area of more than five million square miles, is covered by an ice sheet eight thousand feet or more thick in places. The Greenland ice sheet covers about 650,000 square miles and has a maximum measured thickness of nearly eleven thousand feet. Smaller ice sheets occur on Iceland, Spitsbergen, and several other Arctic islands; still smaller ones are located in the highlands of Norway.

Valley glaciers, the second type, are ice streams that flow down mountain valleys. The Alps, Rockies, Himalayas, and other high ranges of the world contain many valley glaciers. The smallest valley glaciers are thin patches of ice covering only a fraction of a square mile. At the other extreme is Beardmore Glacier in the Antarctic, which is about one hundred and twenty miles long and twenty-five miles wide. Hubbard Glacier in Alaska is about seventy-five miles long. Many large valley glaciers are up to three thousand feet thick.

A third and more rare type are piedmont glaciers, which are intermediate between ice sheets and valley glaciers. They are valley glaciers that spread laterally over the lowland at the foot of a mountain range. The Malaspina and Bering glaciers in Alaska, each of which covers about fifteen thousand square miles, are examples of piedmont glaciers.

Differences in size between these three types of glaciers depend on climatic factors that determine the amount of snow that accumulates. The differences in the form result from the fact that glacier ice flows and therefore molds its form according to the topography.

Takhin Glacier in Alaska is a valley glacier, an ice stream flowing down a mountain valley. Other types are ice sheets and piedmont glaciers.

Formation of Glaciers. Glaciers originate in snowfields. The lower limit of a perennial snowfield is called the snow line. The snow line is at sea level in polar regions but rises gradually as one moves toward the equator. The maximum altitude of the snow line (about twenty thousand feet) occurs not at the equator but in the horse latitudes, a dry region about 30° north and south of the equator. Climatic conditions, which are determined by geographic position and altitude, affect both the winter snowfall and the summer melting. They are the major factors affecting the locations of snowfields and glaciers. It is for this reason that some very

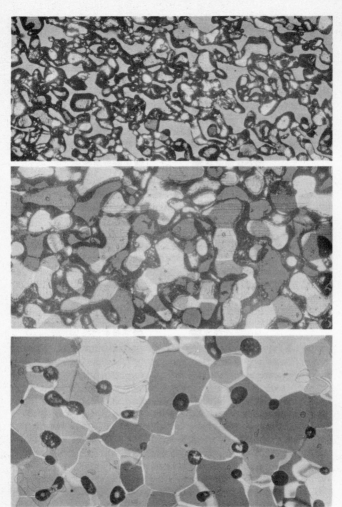

These thin-section photographs show the transformation of snow to ice in a glacier. At depths of about one yard (top) and twenty yards (center), the uniformly gray areas between the grains of snow represent pore spaces. At about one hundred yards (bottom), the snow has become ice, and the pore spaces have become rounded because of the compression of the trapped gases.

cold but dry areas have no glaciers, whereas other warmer areas with abundant snowfall support large glaciers.

As snowfields grow in thickness, solid ice is formed through gradual recrystallization of the accumulated snow. In the first step, which takes place near the surface, melting, evaporation, and compaction transform fluffy flakes of new-fallen snow into a porous mass of small, rounded granules called firn, or neve. This stage in the change of snow to solid ice can be seen in any melting snowdrift. The weight of snow that accumulates year after year buries the firn of previous years to greater and greater depths. The increasing pressure causes melting and recrystallization at the edges of the grains until all of the air space is gone and solid crystalline ice is formed.

The thickness of the snow firn and ice can increase only until the strength of the ice is exceeded by the pressure exerted by the weight of the accumulation. At this point movement begins. As a result of the pressure from above, the ice at the bottom moves in much the same way that cold molasses or tar will flow. Although ice in small pieces is a brittle substance incapable of flowing, ice under sufficient pressure behaves like a plastic material. It flows readily, though quite slowly. The thickness required to initiate movement depends somewhat on the slope of the land surface, the temperature of the ice, and other factors, but some flow occurs in ice masses as little as fifty feet thick.

Flow causes a glacier to move downward or laterally into a zone where its losses exceed the annual accumulation of snow. If the glacier descends below the snow line, the losses are due mostly to melting and evaporation. If a glacier extends into the sea, much of the loss, or wastage, may result from the breaking off of icebergs that float away. Thus, the changes in the size of a glacier depend on the degree of balance between its accumulation and wastage rates. A glacier that is in equilibrium (a rare condition) does not fluctuate in size because the flow from the zone of accumulation exactly compensates for losses sustained in the zone of wastage.

Glaciers move so slowly that the motion cannot be seen, but the speed of movement can be estimated in various ways. There are records, for example, of the bodies of mountaineers buried by avalanches in the Alps having been carried several miles to a glacier's terminus, or head, within a few decades. Likewise, the movement of large rocks or other objects on a glacier's surface can be determined by successive observations or measurements from some fixed point off the ice. Somewhat more precise ways of measuring a glacier's speeds include drilling deep holes in the ice and inserting pipes that are progressively deformed or setting up rows of stakes and measuring their movement by surveying techniques. Maximum velocities of up to one hundred and fifty feet per day have been recorded, but a few inches or a few feet a day are more typical.

The various parts of a glacier move at different rates. The movement of a valley glacier is similar to the flow of a river in that the velocities are greater in the center than near the edges, as is shown by the fact that a straight row of stakes soon becomes curved. Ordinarily the flow is more rapid in the middle part of a glacier than near its terminus. The upper one hundred to two hundred feet of a glacier is composed of rigid, brittle ice that does not flow but is carried along by the mobile ice underneath. This brittle zone fractures easily and is characterized by long cracks called crevasses, which are caused by forces that result from different rates of flow in various parts of the underlying ice. Especially at places where the gradient of the bedrock floor changes abruptly, the upper surface of the glacier may be broken into a jumbled maze of ice pinnacles called seracs.

Catastrophic Effects of Glaciation. Glaciers are the most powerful of all the forces that erode the Earth, and their effects on land features usually are both distinctive and spectacular. Glaciated mountains are much more rugged than nonglaciated mountains. Sharp-pointed peaks like the Matterhorn in Switzerland and deep, U-shaped valleys like Yosemite in the Sierra Nevada of California owe their form mainly to glaciation. The fjords of Norway, Patagonia, and Alaska are glaciated valleys now partially submerged by the sea.

A glacier abrades and polishes the bedrock floor over which it passes; rocks and sand pushed along by the ice have the effect of a giant rasp or piece of sandpaper. Frost action, landslides, and avalanches carry rock debris onto a glacier surface from the land protruding above it. The material carried by a glacier ranges from house-sized boulders to clay particles. When the glacier melts, all of this material is laid down as an unsorted deposit called till, or boulder clay. At the terminus of a glacier the melting ice drops its load in the form of mounds and ridges referred to as a terminal moraine.

Valley glaciers also commonly have lateral moraines between the edge of the ice and the valley walls as well as medial moraines formed by the confluence of tributary glaciers that have lateral moraines.

Drumlins are clusters of elongated hills that are oriented parallel to the direction of ice movement. They are composed of till laid down near the margins of large ice sheets. Much of the material laid down by glaciers is reworked by meltwater streams, which build outwash plains and outwash terraces composed of stratified sand and gravel. Kettles are depressions on outwash plains that are formed by the melting of ice blocks buried in the outwash deposits. Eskers are winding ridges of stratified gravel and sand believed to have been deposited by subglacial streams.

Ice Ages: the Ultimate Disasters. Present-day glaciers are in part remnants from the last great Ice Age, or Pleistocene epoch, when the ice-covered area of Earth was three times its present size. The Antarctic and Greenland glaciers were not much larger than they are now, but large areas in North America and Europe were covered by ice sheets. Exactly when the period of Pleistocene glaciation began is not known, but it was probably between two and three million years ago. Available evidence indicates that during that epoch there were at least four or five major glacial periods, and some climatologists believe that there were as many as twenty, separated by intervals when the climate was even warmer than it is now.

So far as can be determined by the use of the radiocarbon method for dating wood and other organic matter found in glacial deposits, the last major ice advance in North America and Europe reached its peak between seventeen and eighteen thousand years ago. At this time the snow line was twelve thousand to fourteen thousand feet lower than it is now, and the mean annual temperature may have been about 14° F cooler. The final shrinkage of the North American and European ice sheets began about eleven thousand years ago, and by about 3000 B.C. glaciers were less extensive than they are now. After about 2000 B.C. glaciers again expanded slightly and in most parts of the world attained sizes slightly greater than they were even during the "Little Ice Age" from about 1550 to 1850. A warmer climate during the last half of the nineteenth century, and especially the first half of the twentieth century, has caused extensive shrinkage of glaciers throughout the world. Although recession has been the general rule during the last century, a few glaciers have either advanced or remained stable, and in 1971 alone the ice cover in the northern hemisphere increased twelve percent.

Both the remnants of Pleistocene glaciers and the landscape over wide areas of the Earth bear the direct or indirect imprint of glaciation. Areas that were formerly covered by ice are strewn with till and characterized by typical land forms, including moraines, drumlins, and eskers. Drainage features reflect the influences of glaciation. The courses of some rivers like the Missouri were determined by the position of the glacier's margin. Furthermore, the thousands of lakes and swamps in Canada, the northern United States, and northern Europe occupy basins formed by glacial erosion and deposition. The close of the Pleistocene era caused a wave of extinction of animal life, severely depleting the variety and numbers of large mammals. The indirect effects of the Pleistocene glacial period extend far from the areas actually covered by ice. Belts of sand dunes and blankets of windblown silt, called loess, occupy large areas south of the boundaries of the former North American and European ice sheets.

Terraces caused by variations in the stream load accompanying glaciations and deglaciations are prominent features in many valleys. Terraces were also formed along the coasts as a result of sea level fluctuations during glaciations and interglacial periods. As a result of greater precipitation and less evaporation during glacial times, large lakes developed in regions now arid. Great Salt Lake is a remnant of a formerly much larger glacial lake referred to as Lake Bonneville.

Before the Pleistocene Ice Age, there were two earlier major ice ages, both of which occupied large areas in belts that are now tropical. One glaciation occurred during the Intra-Cambrian period (about five hundred and seventy million years ago), and the other occurred during the Early Permian period (about two hundred and eighty million years ago). All three of the known major glacial episodes were apparently rather brief, and during the long intervals between them glaciers were not present even in high mountain and polar regions. Each, however, affected terrestrial and marine plant life. We are living during an unusual period. During most of geological time the climate was considerably warmer than it is now, and subtropical types of trees grew even in polar areas that are now covered by ice. It has been theorized that we may now be entering another "little ice age" or even a "great" one.

Glaciological Research. Although an impressive amount is known about glaciers, many important problems are unanswered. Much remains to be learned about the physical properties and behavior of glaciers, especially the large ice sheets. The flow speeds of many glaciers have been determined, but there is no satisfactory explanation of the mechanism by which the flow of ice occurs. The relationships between glacier fluctuations and climatic variations are highly complicated and not well understood. The cause of worldwide climatic changes that resulted in the three major glaciations is still a mystery. Variations in astronomic, atmospheric, oceanic, and continental tectonic factors have been considered as causes; and migration of the poles has recently been suggested.

All of these and many other related problems are the subjects of intensive study by glaciologists throughout the world. Apart from purely scientific interest, there is a practical aspect to such investigations because of the potential effects on man that would accompany changes in the present amount of glacier ice. Studies of the past behavior of glaciers have as yet been too limited in scope to be of significant value in forecasting future trends.

7.
Landslides, Droughts, and Dust Storms

Although the seas have been credited with being the source of life, it is on the land itself that civilizations have sprung up and flourished. Mankind has resided on the soil for almost half a million years. The Earth's valleys, plains, mountains, coastlines, deserts, and marshes have all served as man's dwelling places.

Yet it is these same terrains that under certain conditions have withheld their gifts or have seemed hostile to both man and beast. Land masses move down unstable slopes; rocks erode, soil particles break apart, and dust is transported by winds; vegetation fails to get the water essential to sustain life. The resulting landslides, droughts, and dust storms have been responsible for untold calamitous events and human misery. There are few positive attributes about such phenomena, yet each is a natural part of the Earth's drama that man has documented through scientific and historical records.

In another way, the Earth's debris has preserved history. Archaeologists unearthed the fabled Greek city of Troy and other ancient settlements around the Mediterranean, uncovered and cleared dozens of great pre-Columbian centers throughout Latin America, and salvaged King Tutankhamen's treasure in Egypt by sifting and removing more than 200,000 tons of grit. They are currently digging out such diverse finds as Caesarea, the city built by Herod the Great in what is now northern Israel, from beneath 8,000 acres of drifted sand many feet deep, and an American Indian site from beneath the black dirt of southern Illinois that in successive layers contains twelve different settlements from different periods. All of these civilizations had been covered for centuries, and therefore preserved, by the Earth's restless soil.

Landslides

The transport of rock debris is not confined to the channels of streams, rivers, avalanches, and glaciers. On every slope gravity exerts a pull that sometimes results in large-scale movement of soil, broken rock, and even large masses of bedrock.

Abrupt landslides are the most spectacular example of such movement. Every year large numbers of slides occur in mountainous country—the Alps, Himalayas, Rocky Mountains, and other areas of steep topography. The sliding masses range in volume from a few cubic yards to a cubic mile or more. Some large slides, starting without warning and moving at high speeds, have overwhelmed entire towns and caused other catastrophes. (The worst landslide in French history obliterated an Alpine resort chalet in 1970, killing 43 persons.) A sliding mass sometimes blocks a stream to form a lake, thus complicating the process of erosion. In regions subject to strong earthquakes, sharp shocks often start landslides involving masses that were nearing the point of release.

Chronic landslides, which move slowly and intermittently on steep slopes, are more common than are catastrophic slides. Masses of soil and broken rock may move by slow flowage and by slipping over the firmer base. In cold seasons such masses may be frozen and practically stationary; thawing in spring causes saturation with water and renewed flowage or sliding on the slippery base. Different rates of movement often create an uneven surface. Trees growing on a slope are often tilted at various angles and even uprooted.

Chronic slides include all gradations between abrupt landsliding and the imperceptibly slow downslope movement known as creep, which operates on every slope covered with loose, weathered material. Even soil covered with close-knit sod creeps downslope, as indicated by the slow but persistent tilting of poles, gravestones, and other objects set into the ground on hillsides. There are so many different kinds of landslides because of the many factors involved—differences in rock structure, coherence of material, degree of slope, amount of water, extent of undercutting at the base of the slope, rate of movement, and quantity of material.

The wearing down of land masses is natural and usually inconspicuous. Yet occasionally, when this process is accelerated, a landslide may start without warning, gather momentum as it moves downward, and overwhelm whatever is in its path. Such devastation has taken place in many places throughout the world.

Chiavenna, Italy, 1618. More than twenty-four hundred persons were killed during a sudden landslide in the Chiavenna Valley on September 4, 1618, considered one of the worst landslide disasters in history. Only three persons managed to survive by digging their way out of the debris by hand.

Elm, Switzerland, 1881. On the evening of September 11, 1881, the residents of Elm, located in the Sernf Valley, in the shadow of a mountain called Plattenbergkopf, were quietly going about their evening business. For more than twenty years the Plattenbergkopf had been mined and quarried for its valuable slate. Little concern was shown for buttressing the weakened sections of the mountain, which resulted in small rockfalls, quarry cave-ins, and eventually a five-yard-wide crack near the mountain's pinnacle.

At about 5:30 P.M. the villagers heard a rumbling near the mountain's peak. Trees and boulders began moving and falling together. The slide stopped, and all was quiet for seventeen minutes. Then another rumble was heard, but this time trees, boulders, soil, and rocks descended in a rolling mass that enveloped everything in its path. After another pause a third slide leveled the upper portion of the mountain. When the dust had cleared, more than ten million cubic yards of rock from the upper part of the Plattenbergkopf had fallen, filling a portion of the valley four hundred and fifty yards deep and a million square yards in area. One hundred and fifty persons were killed and another two hundred were injured.

Aberfan, Wales, 1966. Perhaps the worst disaster in Welsh history resulted when an 800-foot-high slag heap collapsed on October 21, 1966, and released two million tons of debris onto the town below. The moving mass buried a school and twenty homes and killed 144 persons, including many children who were attending the school that was located at the base of the heap.

For more than one hundred years slag heaps have been accumulating around mining towns like Aberfan as by-products of mining operations. Because of their diverse composition, such heaps are highly plastic and fluid. The Aberfan slag heap was also weakened by a natural stream that ran beneath it. For days before the disaster, residents of the town had complained to local authorities that the heap seemed to be moving.

On the morning of October 21 mining officials sent a maintenance man to the top of the heap to check the validity of the complaints. While he was surveying the mound, a section of two million tons of rock and stone fell away, crashed down the side of the man-made mountain, and fell onto Aberfan. The sound of the cascading debris was heard a mile away. Rescue efforts began immediately. The town's miners rushed to the surface and toward the devastated area, and the townspeople carefully dug at the site of the school to try to unearth the trapped children.

Los Angeles, California, 1969. A torrential rainstorm that dropped ten inches of rain on Southern California produced a series of landslides that killed at least 100 persons and caused damage estimated at more than $60 million in January 1969. The rains washed away topsoil and undermined the supports used to hold up homes built on the hillside. More than 9,000 homes were destroyed or damaged, the residences in Mandeville Canyon suffering the most extensive damage. To aid in recovery, President Richard M. Nixon declared the affected site a disaster area and made it eligible for $3 million in federal relief funds.

Canyonville, Oregon, 1974. On January 16 heavy rains and freezing temperatures caused 26,000 cubic yards of land to fall and slide down the slope of a mountain. The moving flow smashed a telephone company relay station at the base of the mountain and killed nine men. The station's eight-inch-concrete walls were smashed by the moving mud.

Peru, 1974. Unusually heavy rains caused a mudslide on April 25 that blocked the Mantaro River and created a lake nearly eight miles long and about six hundred feet above the surface of the normal riverbed. Further heavy rains in June caused the mudslide dam to overflow, destroying homes in the valleys downstream. The flooding caused $5 million in damage to roads, $3 million in damage to property, and $4.5 million in damage to agriculture. In all more than 1,000 persons were killed.

Colombia, 1974. A landslide in the Quebradablanca Canyon, located about fifty miles east of the capital city of Bogotá, killed more than 200 persons and injured about another 100 on June 28. Much of the nearly 400,000 cubic yards of rock and mud loosened by the slide fell onto the main highway linking Bogotá and Villavicencio. Six crowded buses and 20 other vehicles carrying passengers along the road were buried in the slide. Then on September 29 a landslide fell onto a slum settlement on the outskirts of the city of Medellín 150 miles northwest of Bogotá, killing an estimated 90 persons.

Droughts

From 250 miles in space, U.S. astronaut Neil Armstrong called the Earth the blue planet and "a beautiful jewel in space." The Earth's blue color is testimony to its abundance of water just as Mars, the red planet, derives its color from its arid, stony deserts.

The Earth carries with it through space a fixed amount of water that man can neither increase nor diminish. On a per capita basis there are more than 450 million cubic yards of water per person. Yet there have been times in recorded history when no rain has fallen in certain areas for extended periods. In such cases famine has often accompanied drought, and natural catastrophe has produced human tragedy. Throughout recorded history famines resulting from droughts have killed hundreds of millions of people.

Drought cannot be defined simply as a shortage in rainfall. The amount of water that is needed must be taken into account. Further, the effect of a shortage of rainfall depends on the amount of moisture in the soil at the beginning of the dry period. Drought begins only when the vegetation can no longer absorb water from the soil rapidly enough to replace that lost to the air. A drought does not necessarily begin on the day that rain ceases; it begins when the moisture in the soil is exhausted.

There are three basic types of drought. The first, called permanent drought, is characteristic of the driest climates. The sparse vegetation in such areas is adapted to drought, and agriculture is impossible except by irrigating throughout the entire crop season. In regions of permanent drought, there is no stream flow and no runoff except when a rare rain occurs.

The second type, seasonal drought, is found in climates that have well-defined rainy and dry seasons. The natural vegetation is made up of plants that produce seeds during the rainy season and then die and of plants that remain alive but become dormant in the dry season. For successful agriculture, the planting dates in such areas must be adjusted so that the crops develop during the rainy season; otherwise, irrigation is necessary. Stream flow is periodic, and all but the largest streams may become completely dry during the dry season.

The third kind of drought results from the fact that rainfall everywhere is irregular and variable. These droughts are

The jagged mountains, the plateaus cut by extinct rivers, the boulder-strewn plains, and the shrinking lakes are remnants of the Sahara's past, when its climate was quite different. Today, the region is one of the driest on Earth, an area of permanent drought. Even a short-term change in weather patterns can produce drought and famine that upset the delicate balance between life and death.

contingent and they are due to the accidental failure of rainfall. Although they may occur in any season, they are most probable in summer when the water needs of plants are greatest. Contingent droughts may occur almost everywhere, even in areas of seasonal drought, but they are most characteristic of subhumid and humid climates. They are usually brief and irregular and often affect a relatively small area. Contingent droughts vary in intensity and cannot be anticipated.

Scientists sometimes distinguish a fourth type of water shortage, an invisible drought. Even when summer showers are frequent, they may not supply enough water to restore what is lost by evaporation. The result is a borderline water deficiency that cuts crop yields. When water is supplied to the crops by irrigation to compensate for the deficiency, the crop yields may increase two- or threefold.

Today, scientists believe that natural fluctuations are still the dominant element in the Earth's climatic changes. The current climatic trend has produced a colder Arctic and increased ice since about 1950. The trend seems to have caused on the average a slight shift of the main zones of global wind circulation and of the climatic belts that accompany them. This shift, in turn, has produced continued droughts over many years just south of the Sahara Desert and fewer Indian monsoons. In middle and higher latitudes the shift has altered the character of the prevailing wind circulation patterns, with more frequent anticyclones that persist for weeks or months and give rise to more frequent droughts.

Although meteorologists and climatologists have made advances in predicting scarce water periods, they have not altered the most lethal characteristic of these catastrophic conditions. Droughts are still the most serious hazard to agriculture in nearly every part of the world. Since both precipitation and the demands for water vary from one year to another, there is a great variation in the magnitude of droughts. To be able to forecast the incidence and intensity of droughts a season, or even a few weeks, in advance would be of inestimable value to agricultural, commercial, and industrial interests.

But even more useful than the forecasting of droughts would be the ability to control them through the artificial production of rainfall. There were sensational reports of experiments in cloud seeding with dry ice and silver iodide in the late 1940s that led to the formation of many rainmaker firms throughout the world. Before the end of the 1950s, however, it became clear that the potentialities of rainmaking were limited and that there was no reason to expect that droughts could be controlled or reduced to any real extent.

Despite such limitations, droughts and accompanying famine are claiming fewer fatalities than in past years. This is partly due to greater relief efforts, improved medical attention, better communication, and closer international cooperation.

Still, the historical record regarding famine is highly selective and generally poorly documented. Most famines have occurred in areas lacking adequate communication with the rest of the world. Many famines have occurred without the knowledge of those outside the affected area and have been lost to history. Others have become known only after it was too late to help. Still other reported famines may never have occurred. In some cases sympathetic local officials may have claimed that a famine existed in order to obtain tax or rent relief or to induce other measures to prevent distress. Whatever the inadequacies of the historical record, the documented record does reveal the unimaginable suffering of tens of millions of human beings.

Egypt, A.D. 1064–72. During one period in Egypt's history the Nile River failed to flood for seven years. The resulting famine was so bad that cannibalism among the people was reported.

India, 1630 . . . 1972. India has been severely affected by droughts and famines throughout its history. A famine occurred in 1630 during the reign of Shah Jahan, the builder of the Taj Mahal, who undertook relief efforts. To obtain money for food, parents sold their children. In the city of Surat 30,000 persons were reported to have died. The drought was followed by floods.

In the province of Bengal in 1769–70 there was a severe famine caused by drought. The estimates of the number of deaths ranged from 3 million to 10 million (a third of the entire population).

A famine caused by drought, war, and locusts occurred in western India in 1803–04. There was a migration of starving people, and thousands were reported to have died. In northwest India in 1837–38 a famine caused by drought killed 800,000 persons.

In Bengal and the neighboring province of Orissa in 1866 a famine was caused by poor distribution of rainfall. One and a half million persons died. In 1868–70 a famine caused by drought affected the northwestern and central provinces of Punjab, Bombay, and Rajputana. The deaths in Rajputana were estimated at one-fourth to one-third of its population.

In 1876–78 India, along with China, suffered one of the worst famines in history. The basic cause in both countries was drought. The monsoon failed in the south in 1876 and in the north in 1877; in the south in 1877 the monsoon was irregular and caused additional damage to crops. The greatest distress was in the province of Madras where, of a population of about 20 million, it was officially estimated that 3.5 million persons died from starvation and disease.

Although major relief efforts were attempted (at one time more than 2 million received relief in Madras), the famine came so soon after the famine of 1868–70 that it put a great strain on the government. Local officials feared that further relief efforts would destroy the government.

Then in May 1972, on the eve of its 25th anniversary of independence, India again suffered drought. The failure of the erratic monsoons and prolonged temperatures as high as 110° F claimed more than 800 lives and caused an estimated crop loss of $400 million. In August, prolonged starvation conditions in the state of Bihar cost the lives of at least another 250 persons.

China, 1876–79. Measured by the number of deaths, the Chinese famine of the 1870s may well have been the worst famine in human history. The immediate cause was drought; almost no rain fell for three years. Poor communications prevented the outside world from learning of the famine for a year. In one area the only way to dispose of the dead bodies was to dig huge holes, which today are still called "ten-thousand-men holes." National and international relief efforts were attempted but to little avail because of the difficulties of transportation. It was estimated that between 9 million and 13 million persons died from hunger, disease, or violence.

Sahel, 1972–74. The great West African drought was a disaster that took the world by surprise. Yet it was no sudden development but was the result of a long process of climatic change, ecological rape, and political mismanagement that could have been predicted some years before the news first broke in 1973.

It is easier to understand these failings if one remembers the remoteness of the Sahel lands where the tragedy began.

The people of the Sahel, an area that lies at the southern boundary of the Sahara Desert in West Africa, search the barren ground for anything that might be edible. Caused by overpopulation and drought, the famine in the Sahel in the early 1970s caused an estimated 50,000 to 200,000 deaths.

The Sahel (the name comes from an Arabic word meaning "shore" or "boundary") is the area between the true desert of the vast Sahara and the beginning of the fertile lands and forests that stretch to the West African coast. The Sahel, therefore, is essentially an area of marginal land, supporting Tuareg and Fulani nomads with their camels and cattle in the north and thousands of villages, dependent on subsistence crops of millet, maize, and sorghum, in the south.

The Sahel region stretches from the Atlantic Ocean on the west through Mauritania, Mali, Upper Volta, Niger, and Chad to the center of the African continent. Much of Senegal, Ghana, Cameroon, Nigeria, and the Central African Empire is also Sahelian in ecology, and it can be argued that the Ethiopian drought that had begun in 1972 formed the eastern flank of the great dry belt that extended across Africa by 1974. Kurt Waldheim, Secretary-General of the United Nations (UN), estimated in March 1974 that as many as 25 million Africans were directly affected—even though this is one of the least densely populated parts of the Earth.

The human roots of the problem go back to 1960 when France began to give independence to its West African colonies. A handful of tiny countries, none economically viable and all more or less dependent on French monetary and administrative aid, were left with a highly centralized, French-style civil service in a region where slow communications impeded administration. Without a census, tax rolls, or statistics, the embryonic countries began the task of development.

The first decade of independence began well, with eight years of good rains. International aid provided new wells and vaccination programs for the cattle and the nomads. The growing economies of coastal countries like Nigeria and the Ivory Coast provided ready markets for the expanding herds. In short, the 1960s saw a population explosion among the Sahel's human and animal inhabitants.

In 1968 bad rains served the first warning that the fragile ecological balance of the desert could not support so much life. Few cattle died in that year, but around most of the new wells there were great patches of dead land where the cattle and goats had overgrazed until not a tree or bush or blade of grass remained. The governments of the Sahel, meanwhile, were wondering what to do about the "nomad problem." Culturally different from the settled blacks of the south who dominated politics, the nomads had little time for tax collectors and less for the man-made national frontiers that cut across their traditional trading routes. Sporadic guerrilla warfare plagued the Sahel throughout the 1960s.

Equally shortsighted were the relatively rich neighbors of the Sahel nations. The fast-developing coastal countries of the Ivory Coast, Ghana, and Nigeria took up to forty percent of the young adult males of the Sahel countries and the bulk of their livestock exports, without ever attempting to integrate their economies. Nomads from Niger still have to drive their cattle down the long trail to the slaughterhouses of northern Nigeria, where they are paid in Nigerian money. Because this money cannot be spent in Niger, the nomads buy Nigerian goods at inflated prices and smuggle them home. In 1973, according to an estimate of the European Development Fund, two-thirds of Niger's peanut exports had been "imported" by nomads from Nigeria.

The greatest tragedy of the Sahel came after the disastrous year of 1972, when almost no rain fell. By December the vast cattle herds had devoured what little desert pasture there

As do all severe droughts, the drought in the Sahel killed plants and animals as well as humans. It was estimated that more than half of the cattle in the area died within two years.

was. The herds moved south to the Niger and Senegal rivers, where they were met by angry peasants whose own crops had failed. By May 1974 the flow of the mighty Senegal had become so feeble that the river was salt 155 miles from the sea. The dry riverbeds were choked with dead cattle. The losses ranged between fifty and eighty percent of the herds. With the dwindling herds came a swelling mass of refugees. The town of Rosso on the Senegal grew from 8,000 to 40,000 within six weeks.

The first warnings of the disaster had reached the UN Food and Agriculture Organization (FAO) in Rome in October 1972, but there was no effective means of evaluating the scale of the emergency until the herds and refugees began to reach the major centers in early 1973. Nor were the local governments eager to undermine their precarious authority by admitting to the world that their people were starving. By June 1973 the nature of the crisis was beginning to emerge. Between one-half and two-thirds of the cattle herds were dead, and the bulk of the survivors had trekked far to the south. The nomads who had driven their cattle south had left families and dependents in the north, where at least two million scattered people were in desperate need of food. Another million peasants from the marginal villages had fled to the cities and were living in makeshift, disease-prone encampments. Behind them a vast tract of land was bereft of trees, of desert scrub, of pasture, and of the hardy Sahel vegetation that normally held back the desert.

The nomads and peasants of the Sahel are a hardy people, accustomed to deprivation and disease. Even in the good years of the 1960s, infant mortality among the Tuareg rarely fell below fifty percent. But some of the new diseases that came with the refugees led to disaster. In the remote villages of the Air Massif Mountains in northern Niger about half the school-age children perished in a measles outbreak. In Mauritania in 1974 influenza and chicken pox became killers; in Chad diphtheria was widespread. When the FAO's regional administrator visited northern Chad in mid-1973, he was asked by local chiefs not to send any vaccine because diphtheria would bring a faster and more merciful death than starvation.

There will never be wholly reliable statistics on how many people died in 1973 because of the drought. Estimates run as high as 200,000. *Disaster in the Desert*, a Carnegie Endowment report made by two researchers with no firsthand experience of the disaster, estimated the death toll at 100,000. The Sahel countries' own coordinating office placed the death toll at not less than 50,000. The truth probably lies between the figures, and the toll for 1974 was probably similar. Of greater long-term importance is the effect of malnutrition, which will blight the children who did survive for the rest of their lives. One British journalist reported that the only children he had seen alive in a series of nomad encampments were deformed or suffering from speech and motor impediments.

The immediate result for the Sahel countries was economic disruption, further weakening their already frail economies. Before the drought, Upper Volta had an annual per capita gross national product of $55, and the inhabitants of Niger had an average annual income of $85. In Niger the decimation of the cattle herds removed the thirty-five percent of the tax base that came from the head tax on the nomads' animals. By late 1973 the international oil crisis was adding its own savage financial effects on the Sahel countries.

When the cattle died in 1973 they were eaten—a major contributory factor in the mixture of luck and muddle that staved off mass starvation. Beginning in May, an international airlift of essential supplies was organized. President Hamani Diori of Niger later pointed out that the cost of the

During droughts in the 1970s, forest fires burned in western France (above), an area that is normally free of such fires, and many reservoirs that supply water to California cities dried up (below).

airlift in his own country would have paid for the irrigation of 27,000 acres of land near the Niger River that could have produced the 110,000 tons of food that Niger needed. In Mali a team of three U.S. Hercules transport aircraft used one ton of aviation fuel for every ton of food they flew to the worst-hit area. In Chad it took nineteen tons of aviation fuel to fly in one ton of medical supplies. And the aviation fuel had to compete with the food for the country's rail transport facilities.

The distribution of the 550,000 tons of food donated in 1973 fell into three stages. First, it was transported to the overloaded ports of West Africa. In Dakar, Senegal, grain that had arrived in July was still stored on the docks as late as November, soaked and partially ruined by the rainy season. The second stage involved moving the food from the ports to regional centers. The Dakar–Mali railroad was the vital link, moving up to 10,000 tons a month. But both road and rail transport ceased to be reliable after the rains began to wash out the dirt tracks and undermine the railway lines. The third stage of distribution, from regional centers to the famine area and refugee camps, depended on trucks. In the Sahel, UN officials reported that the life of a modern truck was about a thousand hours because of the desert conditions and lack of maintenance facilities.

In September 1973 an FAO investigating committee estimated that 650,000 tons of food would be needed for 1974, which meant that distribution from the ports had to begin in January if the food was to reach the affected areas before the rains began. The Sahel governments themselves put their food needs at 1.2 million tons. Bureaucratic and budgetary delays at the FAO in Rome and at the U.S. Agency for International Development headquarters in Washington, D.C., meant that 1974 food shipments did not begin to arrive in great quantity until late March. The situation was saved, ironically, by the spread of the drought into Nigeria, where it cut the peanut crop by sixty percent. This crop failure freed the vast Nigerian truck fleet. More than four hundred Nigerian trucks were hired by the FAO in early June and used as a nonstop shuttle to the Sahel, moving up to 50,000 tons of food each month.

It was in 1974 that the political consequences were felt. In Niger the social strains of the drought, combined with a political crisis, led to a military coup that overthrew the civilian government of President Diori in April. In Ethiopia the drought brought social unrest and dissatisfaction that led to Emperor Haile Selassie's downfall in September.

Research into the climatic changes that had brought on the drought pointed to a long-term, fundamental shift that would render much of the Sahel uninhabitable within two decades. The study, compiled at the Massachusetts Institute of Technology, was cited by the U.S. delegate to a July conference of the UN Economic and Social Council. He argued that emergency food aid must continue but that long-term attempts to irrigate or rehabilitate the Sahel would be doomed to failure.

Four years later, in 1978, Ethiopia reported that it was again in the grip of a drought, worsened by climatic changes and deforestation. As many as a million of its residents were said to be starving from the renewed famine.

The evidence for a long-term climatic change is not yet conclusive, but it is strong enough to make impractical the expensive option urged by the Sahel governments of a billion-dollar investment in irrigation and restocking of the region. An entire way of life, based on nomadism and cattle raising, appears destined for extinction throughout the affected region. Much of the nomads' economic role in camel-borne trade, particularly of salt, has been taken over by trucks, and the expansion of the desert has significantly reduced the amount of grazing land left to the nomads. If the expansion continues, the way of the Tuareg could be doomed, and the proud but impoverished nomads could be forced to become resettled cultivators.

Dust Storms

Although the word *dust* suggests finer particles than does the word *sand* the distinction between a dust storm and a sandstorm is somewhat arbitrary. *Dust storm* is the more popular term in the United States, and *sandstorm* is used more often in North Africa and the Middle East. The terms cover a class of phenomena that result from large amounts of dust or sand being raised from the ground into the air. Such storms are common to most semiarid and desert regions of the continents. Those of Africa's vast Sahara are perhaps the most legendary.

Embracing about 3.5 million square miles of northern Africa between the Atlantic coast and the Red Sea, the Sahara is the world's largest desert. It is also one of the most hostile environments on Earth, one in which air temperatures exceeding 130° F have been recorded and an area in which ground temperatures commonly rise to 170° F or more. It is therefore most appropriate that the name of the region was derived from the Arabic word *sahra*, meaning "wilderness" or "desert." Ever harsh and unforgiving toward the careless or unwary traveler who would trespass on its interior vastness, the Sahara has been the burial place for thousands of men since ancient times. Even group efforts have met with disaster upon occasion. Before trade routes became well established, whole caravans devoted to trade in slaves, ivory, gold, or salt vanished into the blowing desert sands without a trace.

Periodic sandstorm conditions and droughts have produced tragedies of far greater scope. The latest of these is resulting in unprecedented devastation, affecting millions of people in more than a dozen countries where desert winds blow and famine stalks. Events have yet to run their course, and predictions of the ultimate magnitude of the disaster vary. It is clear, however, that *catastrophe* is the only truly suitable word for describing what is happening.

Meteorologists have long studied the occurrence of dust storms—their appearance, severity, distribution by region, season, and hour, and associated meteorological conditions. Observations in the Sahara on the physics of blowing sand have been made and checked with theory and laboratory experiments. It has been found that when the wind at the ground exceeds a certain speed, its stress on the exposed sand causes the lighter grains to bump into the larger ones, rolling and bouncing them along the ground. Drifting reaches greater heights as the wind speed increases, but under thermally stable air conditions it does not exceed several hundred feet. In unstable air, however, fine sand and dust may be carried upward as high as the rising currents go, an altitude that sometimes surpasses 15,000 feet.

The critical wind speed for starting a sand drift depends on the distribution of the different sizes of exposed grains and on their stability. Long exposure to a wind pattern may sort the grains into an arrangement that resists erosion. Livestock and motor traffic can disturb this balance and promote wind erosion. It has been determined that rising particles heated by the sun may warm the air as much as 5° F a day in summer, increasing the thermal instability and thereby increasing the lifting of dust.

It is generally agreed that there are only two essential requirements for a dust storm to begin. The wind speed at the ground must exceed a certain critical speed, generally between fifteen and thirty miles per hour, depending on the shape, size, specific gravity, dampness, and temperature of the ground particles. In addition, the ground cover must contain loose, dry particles light enough that they can be lifted.

Most dust storms fall into one of two broad types. The khamsin of Egypt is perhaps the best example of the first type. In the khamsin blowing dust occurs over an extensive area in which one or more large moving air masses are produced by a barometric depression. The haboob of the Sudan is a common example of the second type, which is associated with a local cumulonimbus or thunderstorm cloud.

The Khamsin. Primarily a phenomenon of the colder season, the khamsin tends to occur in the late winter and spring. It is probably the most common weather situation producing dust storms over coastal North Africa. A low-pressure area passing eastward along the Mediterranean coast often produces a strong flow of warm desert air from the south, followed by a burst of cold air from the north. As a result of its desert origin and its force, the southern wind is always dusty or hazy, and in the spring and fall it is likely to produce severe sandstorms. Made unstable by its movement over the warm Mediterranean and desert, the cold air itself may pick up sand and contribute to the storm.

The frequency, thickness, and extent of the dusty air produced by a khamsin are usually greater during the daytime. The sandstorm may begin and end at any hour, and it often continues all night or for several consecutive days. The khamsin dust that follows a cold front may approach as a wall, but the dust in the warm-air current generally begins gradually as the wind increases. The extent of the dust is variable, from scattered areas of a few hundred yards to solid belts of more than one hundred miles. Extensive dust storms similar to the khamsin occur in Asia Minor, Iran, the Soviet Union, India, China, Australia, and the United States. The many severe dust storms over the Great Plains of the United States are mostly formed by dried-out unstable polar air that originates in the Pacific Ocean.

The Haboob. This kind of dust storm, which occurs frequently in the Sudan, usually forms at the edge of a thundercloud. Dust is blown upward from the ground and often resembles smoke from a fire on a windy day. A billowing wall of dust develops, rises to the bottom of the cloud, and later rises even higher. Some haboobs are red in color, but they may be yellow or black, depending on the type of dust or sand involved.

From a distance, a haboob may appear as a light-colored haze below the cloud, a phenomenon due to the reflection of sunlight. The storm arrives with a sudden increase of the wind. The squall is often severe, and the visibility decreases almost instantaneously. The wind gradually decreases, and visibility improves. Most storms are over in less than an hour or so, but occasionally they may last several hours. Many short haboobs end with rain, which washes the dust out of the air and wets the ground, preventing further dust storms. If a haboob moves away from the storm cloud, it usually lasts longer.

Most haboobs begin between noon and dusk. They occur in warm seasons, especially the late spring and early summer, and in dusty regions, particularly in areas of India, the Middle East, Australia, and West Africa.

In addition to khamsins and haboobs, local sandstorms or areas of blowing sand and dust may occur. All that is required is unstable air, wind speeds of more than fifteen to twenty miles per hour, and loose material on the ground.

Effects of Dust Storms. Once raised into the atmosphere, dust takes on a variety of appearances. The typical dust wall in the haboob forms when a sudden and marked increase in wind speed raises dust along a broad and continuously advancing front. One characteristic of some khamsin-type dust storms is a dust ceiling or overcast. This forms when a warm, dust-laden air mass overruns a shallow, cooler air mass; a heavy fall of dust follows. Dust falls around the Canary and Cape Verde islands are sometimes so thick that navigation is endangered; birds roost out such storms on ships' riggings. Dusty air drawn into a cyclonic wind system and forced to rise over a colder air mass may precipitate muddy rain or snow. Mud rains are most common in Europe but are recorded occasionally in the United States, Australia, and China.

As the wind and instability associated with a dust storm subside, the larger particles soon fall to the ground. The upper air currents, usually moving more rapidly than the surface air layers, may carry the finer particles for several thousands of miles. This fact explains the widespread dust hazes often observed in regions far removed from the areas of dust storms. A sufficient amount finally settles out or the dust becomes so diffused that the visibility and color of the sky are no longer noticeably affected.

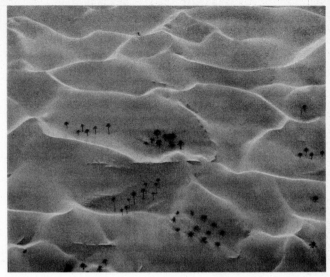

These advancing dunes in the Sahara are overcoming a desert oasis, and only the tops of palm trees remain visible.

Dust from haboob-type squalls in the Sudan is spread by the prevailing easterly winds so that for much of the year all of western and central Africa from latitude 5° to 30° N has a persistent dust haze. The haze changes in density from day to day and season to season, sometimes becoming troublesome to aviation.

Wind Erosion. The movement of sand and dust by wind is an important geologic process, particularly in desert regions. It produces highly distinctive landscape features and widespread sedimentary deposits. The process involves three stages: erosion, transportation, and deposition. Erosion involves the picking up and blowing away of loose, fine-grained material. This occurs wherever dry, sandy, or dusty surfaces unprotected by vegetation are exposed to strong winds. Coarser material the size of sand is usually carried along close to the ground. As the sand is driven by the wind, it exerts an abrasive effect on rocks and other objects in its path, thus continuing the work of erosion and carving out uniquely sculptured surfaces. The movement of the material continues until the velocity of the wind slackens or until it encounters an obstacle. Blowing sand often accumulates to form heaps, mounds, or ridges that are known as dunes.

Finer powdery dust, classified technically as silt, can also be set in motion by the wind. It is quickly carried upward by turbulent air currents, sometimes to great heights, and is transported in suspension. Under suitable conditions blowing silt may result in dust storms, and the material may be carried long distances. The silt eventually settles; if the process is continued long enough, a deposit known as loess is formed. Ash, the fine-grained material from volcanic eruptions, is transported in similar fashion and forms deposits known as tuff.

Around deserts such as the Sahara, dust storms have been known for centuries. They lead to falls of reddish dust over much of Africa and southern Europe and occasionally as far as England. A single storm in 1901 was reported to have deposited from three to thirty tons of dust per square mile over an area of at least 300,000 square miles—a total of about two million tons of dust in Europe alone.

The dust that settles to the ground may be held in place by vegetation and become a part of the soil. Ordinarily individual dust layers are too thin to retain their identity. If dust storms recur frequently over a long enough period of time, however, the accumulated dust may gradually build up a loess deposit, blanketing broad areas to depths of from a few inches to many feet. Such deposits are currently building up near the glaciers of Greenland and Alaska. Loess is distinguished from other types of sedimentary deposits by its lack of distinct layering or bedding, by its occurrence on hills and valleys alike, and by its homogeneity and excellent sorting.

Loess deposits dating back to the Pleistocene epoch are widespread in many countries and form some of the world's best agricultural soil. Examples are found in central and western Europe, southern South America, China, and the central and northwestern United States. In the Missouri-Mississippi drainage basin, the thickness of the loess is up to more than one hundred feet, and in China it is reported to reach several hundred feet. Where thick loess is exposed along valley sides, it commonly forms steep bluffs with conspicuous vertical cracks.

The ash blasted into the air by volcanic explosions reaches much greater heights than ordinary dust and is carried farther and deposited in greater thicknesses. After the eruption of Mount Katmai in Alaska in 1912, an area of about 2,000 square miles was covered by ash deposits a foot or more in thickness, and a much larger area received at least a quarter of an inch of ash. Ash from some volcanic explosions is carried halfway around the world. In many areas deposited ash is an important natural fertilizer. When concentrated in sufficient quantity and thickness, ash is an important source of material for scouring powder, ceramic processes, and other uses.

Wind erosion takes place partly by deflation, the simple blowing away of loose, fine-grained material, and partly by abrasion, the gradual wearing away of hard material through the continued impact of wind-driven sand. In general, the effects of deflation are important only on soil and on unconsolidated materials. The marks of abrasion are visible on rock and other resistant materials.

Deflation occurs mainly in desert basins and along streambeds that are dry during a part of the year. It works primarily on material already loosened by weathering and running water. Frequently the erosive effects of the wind are canceled out by the washing in of new material. In many situations the layer removed is so thin and the area from which it is removed is so broad that the erosion is imperceptible. In certain locations where rainfall is nearly zero, however, erosive effects are more concentrated. They may result in a gradual lowering of the land surface, producing topographic forms ranging from small shallow depressions to broad basins hundreds of feet in depth.

Small depressions and basins are found in the plains and deserts of the western United States. They are found on a larger scale in the deserts of Peru, Mongolia, and northern Africa. The Qattara depression of the Libyan desert has a length of roughly 175 miles, a width of up to nearly 80 miles, and a maximum depth of more than 400 feet below sea level.

Another effect of deflation in some places is the formation of desert pavement, a thin layer of pebbles that occurs where the material originally exposed to the wind consisted of a mixture of pebbles and finer material. The gradual removal of the fine material by the wind leads to an accumulation of the pebbles.

Blowing sand acts as a powerful abrasive agent. Under artificial conditions it is used to clean the masonry surfaces on buildings and to etch designs on monumental stone. Under natural conditions, the effects of blowing sand quickly become evident on glass, metal, and wood. Bits of glass lying in windy, sandy areas, for example, soon lose their luster and take on a dull, frosted appearance. Automobiles caught in severe sandstorms have had their paint removed and their windshields frosted to translucency in a short time. Individual pebbles and rock fragments are etched, faceted, smoothed, or eroded in irregular patterns and commonly assume forms known as ventifacts. Larger masses of rock and bedrock surfaces are eroded on a larger scale and take on a distinctive appearance.

Ventifacts and wind-eroded rocks occur in some places where sandstorms no longer occur and where vegetation is now well established. In such circumstances, the rocks serve as indications of past climatic conditions much different from those of the present.

The Great Plains "Dust Bowl." In the 1930s, the name "Dust Bowl" was applied to an area in the Great Plains section of the United States, including portions of Kansas, Oklahoma, Texas, New Mexico, and Colorado. Known in the early nineteenth century as the Great American Desert, it has always been subject to periodic droughts; even in good years the rainfall does not exceed fifteen inches.

The first white settlers in the area were mostly ranchers, but farming was introduced in the 1880s, and by 1930 one-third of the land was given over to corn, winter wheat, cotton, and a variety of other crops. During the thirties, and especially in 1933, 1934, and 1936, the Great Plains suffered from disastrous drought conditions and repeated crop failures. The Dust Bowl was hardest hit. Sparse rainfall dried out the soil and led to the dust storms that gave the area its name. One of the worst, in November 1933, sent the topsoil swirling five miles into the air, darkening the sun, covering houses with sand, and bringing all activity to a halt. The dust clouds from that storm drifted as far east as New England, where they deposited twenty-five tons of dust per square mile and caused "black blizzards" of discolored snow.

The Dust Bowl disaster was aggravated by the fact that it came in the midst of the Depression, when general economic distress was widespread throughout the country. As rivers and water holes dried up and livestock perished in droves, thousands of families like the Joads in John Steinbeck's novel *The Grapes of Wrath* left their homes and migrated to California to seek work as landless laborers. Some counties lost as much as sixty percent of their populations. Those who stayed behind became increasingly dependent on govern-

In 1936 a father and his sons cross barren land in Cimarron County, Oklahoma, a part of the Great Plains "Dust Bowl." Dust storms during the 1930s were caused by several factors, including drought and poor conservation.

ment aid for their survival. In 1936 more than one out of every five households was on relief. In some localities the figure was as high as eighty-five percent.

The United States Soil Conservation Service blamed the disaster on the fact that too much of the land was being used for agriculture and recommended that, to prevent future soil erosion, half of the Dust Bowl's farmland be returned to pasturage. The Federal Government instituted programs to show farmers how to rehabilitate their land, encouraging them to let part of it lie fallow each year, to allow time for moisture to build up in the subsoil. Trees were planted to impede blowing soil, and contour farming—following the contour of the land when plowing—was recommended to conserve water and further reduce erosion.

The drought was over by the early forties, but during

World War II farmers in western Kansas and Oklahoma began to overuse the land for wheat crops again, and a new dry period in the early 1950s threatened to bring another crisis. This time disaster was averted by the federal Soil Bank Program, which gave subsidies to farmers in return for retiring acreage from wheat production.

Sand Dunes. Perhaps the best known and most striking result of wind action is sand dunes. They cover great areas in the deserts of Africa, Asia, and Arabia and lesser areas in the deserts of North and South America. Sand dunes are also prominent features along many seacoasts and some lakeshores and, in inactive form, are found in various interior areas of the United States, Germany, Poland, Hungary, and other countries.

Dunes, in general, may be classified as being either active or stabilized. Active dunes—those still being built up, shaped, or moved by the wind—may be subdivided into those with and those without vegetation, the forms of the two being distinctively different. In the absence of vegetation, blowing sand moves freely, much like drifting snow, until some obstacle or resistance causes accumulation. In many places, dunes develop on relatively flat surfaces in the absence of any distinguishable obstacles. Such dunes commonly are shaped either like crescents or ridges and display remarkable regularity in their characteristics.

From the human standpoint the development of dunes may be a destructive process. Fields, forests, buildings, roads, and even villages have been overwhelmed and obliterated. Various means have been devised to stabilize dunes and control the movement of sand. In some places the planting of grasses, shrubs, or trees is effective. In other places various types of mechanical barriers or protective coatings have been used.

Active dunes sometimes become stabilized by the growth of a continuous cover of vegetation, due primarily to a change in climatic conditions. Extensive areas of such "dead" dunes occur in the central United States and in various European countries. If the vegetation on stabilized dunes is destroyed, wind action may begin again.

Many sandstone formations, some dating back to early periods of geologic time, have been identified as ancient dunes that became consolidated. Some of these formations are of considerable extent and thickness and serve as evidence of former deserts. Windblown sand is characterized by physical properties different from those of other types of sand deposits and is helpful in the identification of ancient dune sands that have lost their distinctive shapes.

Prediction. Dust storms have serious consequences. They obstruct vision, damage machines and material, cause electrostatic discharges and radio static, erode soil and deposit dust, impair human health, and bring death to animals and man.

In order to predict dust storms, the weather forecaster must have experience with the local vulnerability to blowing dust, a knowledge of the usual behavior of storms, and an ability to forecast the winds and the thunderstorms or low-pressure systems with which dust storms are associated. Continuing research will doubtlessly lead to even greater accuracy.

II. Observations

"Ultimately, great destruction can only spell out reconstruction. Loss of life leads to a need for new births."
—William E. Maloney

"Two of the newest and most important of American
institutions concerning themselves with the Earth and
its natural occurrences are the Center for Short-Lived
Phenomena and the National Center for Atmospheric
Research."
—Lord Ritchie-Calder

"Nature cannot be commanded except by being obeyed"
—Sir Francis Bacon

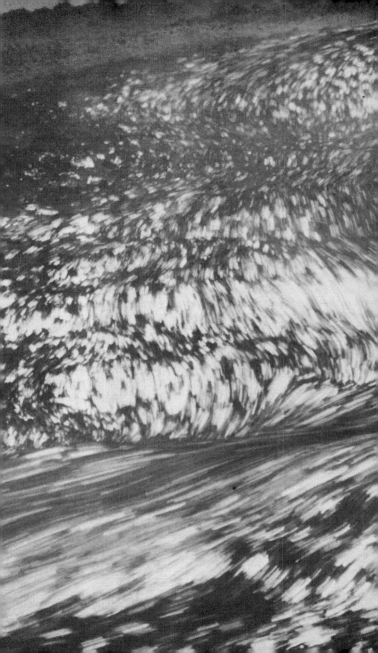

8.
The Turbulent Earth

Modern man has lived in indifferent harmony with nature. Despite the overwhelming evidence of the power of nature—periodic earthquakes, volcanic eruptions, destructive winds, droughts, and avalanches—man has considered the planet Earth to be his world. The land he has used to construct his cities and highways belongs to him, he has thought. The wastes and oil that he spills into water and the choking effluents that his factories feed into the air will forever be absorbed, man has believed, for the supply of water and air has been thought to be inexhaustible.

With the development of the atomic bomb these assumptions have begun to change. When man first learned to harness the enormous energy of nuclear fission, the immensity of his achievement made him begin to question his responsibilities. Man began to recognize his own potential for destruction and for initiating or aggravating the "natural" disasters threatening the ecology of the planet. For the first time, those who sounded the alarm were not just a handful of environmentalists, conservationists, biologists, or politicians. For the first time, mankind as a whole began to be aroused. Consequently, there has been in the nuclear age a quickened interest in the state of the Earth, an enlightened self-interest in man's activities that affect the planet that both supports all life and causes catastrophes. The need to understand the Earth more fully has become a top priority.

Recognizing the urgency of the need to know more about the Earth, the Smithsonian Institution in January 1968 established the Center for Short-Lived Phenomena. Five years earlier, scientists from throughout the world had flocked to witness the birth of Surtsey, a new volcanic island off the southwestern coast of Iceland. Impressed by the amount of information that the scientists were able to collect, the scientific community began to consider setting up a permanent center to gather and dispense information on the sudden, unpredictable, and transient activities of the Earth. One of the scientists involved in this movement was Sidney Galler, who subsequently became assistant secretary for science of the Smithsonian Institution in Washington, D.C. Galler's plans for the center began to be implemented in 1967.

Established in an office at the Smithsonian Astrophysical Observatory in Cambridge, Mass., under the directorship of Robert Citron, the center had hardly begun to function when it encountered its first major challenge. On Dec. 6, 1967, a new island erupted in Telefon Bay near Deception Island in Antarctica. The action had begun, according to the center's reports, at 2000 hours Greenwich Mean Time on December

A 100-foot-deep rift on Deception Island in Antarctica was formed by volcanic action in 1970. The first event reported by the Center for Short-Lived Phenomena—the creation of a volcanic island in Telefon Bay near Deception Island—occurred three years earlier.

4 when "there occurred an undulatory movement of the surface followed by three major explosions." The volcanic events formed an island 984 yards long, 273 yards wide, and 131 yards high, with three craters and a zone of vents.

The center had been located in Cambridge in order to take advantage of the international communications network that the Astrophysical Observatory had set up for its worldwide optical satellite tracking stations. The network was used by the center to contact people in or near the area of the Antarctic volcanic eruption, including members of expeditions from the Argentine Antarctic Institute and members of scientific teams from Chile and the United Kingdom. Information was requested from the United States embassies at Santiago, Chile, and Buenos Aires, Argentina, and from the Smithsonian observing station at Comodoro Rivadavia, Argentina.

Photographs of the eruption and a description of the event were obtained from the Argentine Antarctic Institute and from the naval attaché of the U.S. embassy at Santiago. Geological samples of the new island and samples of the gases and sediments from the craters and vents were collected by the Argentine Antarctic Institute. Samples of volcanic ash were collected aboard the Argentine vessel *Bahia Aguirre*.

Samples of eruption material from a total of seven different locations were gathered. The commentary provided by the center to geologists was later supplemented by published reports that were prepared by the men who had conducted the on-site investigations. Thus, coincidentally, the first event that the center investigated was the birth of a volcanic island like the birth of Surtsey, the very event that had provided the stimulus for the establishment of the center itself.

Mission of the Center

From the beginning, the mission of the center has been "to obtain and disseminate information on short-lived natural events such as volcanic eruptions, major earthquakes, the birth of new islands, the fall of meteorites and large fireballs, and sudden changes in biological and ecological systems." Its purpose is to encourage the mobilization and dispatch of research teams to take advantage of the opportunities to study important short-lived events. Receiving news of such an event quickly permits such teams to travel with instruments and equipment to the scene in as short a time as possible to collect important data that otherwise might be irretrievably lost.

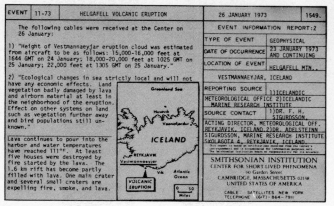

Event information reports prepared by the Center for Short-Lived Phenomena furnish scientists with up-to-date information on recorded events.

In the introduction to their book about the center, *The Pulse of the Planet,* James Cornell and John Surowiecki note: "One of the greatest scientific problems of the twentieth century has been finding a means to observe large-scale changes in the earthly ecosystem while they are actually occurring. Many important natural events ... occur suddenly and unexpectedly in remote corners of the world. Often, too, they end as abruptly as they began. . . . Yet, while the events may be transitory and short-lived, their effects are sometimes long-lasting. Volcanic islands may erupt, subside, and disappear in a matter of days, but volcanic pollutants may linger in the atmosphere for years, the disruption of local biology may persist for centuries, and the alteration in geological substrates may remain forever." The center's job is to create a continuing record of the Earth's transient natural phenomena.

Scientists and institutions that have become "correspondents" of the center have accepted a concomitant responsibilty to provide information to the center about short-lived natural events occurring in their areas and, when called upon, to verify reports made by other sources. By the end of its first year the center had documented 70 geological, astrophysical, and biological events, including 20 major earthquakes, 12 volcanic eruptions, 11 fireballs, 5 major oil spills, 5 fish kills, 2 rare animal migrations, 2 meteorite falls, 1 red tide, 1 seiche (the sudden oscillation of the water in a lake or bay that causes fluctuations in the water level), 1 sea surge, 1 locust swarm, and 1 major drought.

Geophysical Events

Between January 1968 and mid-1978 the center received reports of more than 400 geophysical events. This by no means included all such events that occurred during that time. The nearly 200 reported earthquakes, for example, met the selective criteria of being greater than magnitude 7 on the Richter scale, of occurring in unusual areas, or of being of exceptional interest because of crustal movements, faulting and fissuring, major land movements, or landslides. Among the nearly 200 volcanic eruptions reported were those involving underwater eruptions, the birth of new islands, island eruptions and disappearances, caldera collapses, fissure extrusions, *nuées ardentes* (swiftly expanding clouds of hot gases, ashes, and lava fragments), and major mudflows. (It is interesting to note that, before systematic documentation was begun by the center, most scientists believed that volcanic eruptions occurred at a rate· of only ten to twelve a year.)

Geophysical events reported on also include earthquakes under the seafloor greater than magnitude 7 on the Richter scale or those that considerably affect the marine geophysical environment, tsunamis (sea waves produced by undersea eruptions), and sea surges. Polar and subpolar events included are the formation of ice islands, unusual breakups of sea ice, and surging glaciers. A listing of any year's geophysical events covers a wide range of phenomena, some bearing such exotic names as the Izu-Oshima earthquake swarm (a total of 399 earthquakes recorded between Jan. 14 and 25, 1972, around the Izu-Oshima Volcano in Japan); the Piton de la Fournaise volcanic eruption at Réunion Island in the Indian Ocean, and the tongue-twisting Grimsvotn Jokulhlaup, a glacial outburst flood in Iceland.

One of the most serious events monitored by the center was the violent earthquake in Managua, Nicaragua, in December 1972, a shock of magnitude 6.25 that produced losses estimated at 6,000 to 7,000 dead, 20,000 injured, and 300,000 homeless. The loss of property was about $1 billion. While the city's electrical power was out of service during the period immediately after the earthquake, the center kept in contact with an amateur radio operator. Broadcasting

The disastrous earthquake that occurred in Nicaragua in 1972 was one of the most serious events monitored by the center.

from a portable rig located in his automobile, the man provided information that was relayed throughout the world.

Astrophysical Phenomena

From 1968 through mid-1978 the center recorded more than 100 major fireballs and about 60 meteorite falls. The Smithsonian Astrophysical Observatory operates a worldwide network for astronomers that includes the Central Bureau for Astronomical Telegrams of the International Astronomical Union. The center does not duplicate the observatory's efforts, and it does not deal with predictable astronomical events such as eclipses. What the center does deal with, and with maximum speed, are fireballs. With luck, these blazing chunks of rock fall to the Earth in places where they can be recovered quickly enough to provide scientists with important data about the universe beyond our own planet.

In August 1972 an exceptionally bright fireball was observed over a large area of the United States and southern Canada. The object was observed from Las Vegas, Nev., to Edmonton, Alta., a distance of more than a thousand miles. There were reports from towns in Montana of sonic phenomena occurring from one to three minutes after the sighting, followed by an earthquakelike rumble. Observers reported that the fireball was visible for periods ranging from

A meteor moving through the Earth's atmosphere becomes a spectacularly luminous object, called a fireball. Meteor showers are one of the concerns of the Center for Short-Lived Phenomena.

several seconds to nearly a minute, with a smoke trail persisting for up to two minutes afterwards. There were human eyewitness accounts of the event, and the fireball was also observed by a satellite for more than a minute and a half. According to the satellite's sensor, the maximum brightness of the object exceeded that of the moon.

Assuming that the surface temperature of the meteor was that of the melting point of an iron-nickel-chromium alloy, astronomers speculated that it had a diameter in excess of fifty miles. The brightness of the object indicated a very large body, and the long duration suggested a trajectory nearly tangent to the Earth. Astronomers consider it conceivable that the meteor skipped through the atmosphere, approaching to within twenty-five miles of the Earth's surface, and then skipped out again at about longitude 114° west in a northerly heading. If the meteor had struck the Earth, the impact would have been similar to that of the explosion of a nuclear bomb.

Another remarkable astronomical event recorded by the center was the fantastic meteorite shower that fell on Pueblito de Allende, Mexico, in February 1969. Early in the morning of February 8, a blinding blue-white fireball turned night into day over a thousand-mile path from southern Mexico to El Paso, Tex. Hundreds of observers throughout Mexico reported seeing the brilliant flash of light and hearing a tremendous explosion. U.S. Air Force meteorologists calculated the wind direction and velocities at the time of the event by guiding a B-57 airplane through the dust train. Special filter traps aboard the plane collected samples of atmospheric dust.

Meanwhile, thousands of individual meteoritic stones rained down over a large area of rural Mexico. They were recovered and identified almost immediately. Not only was this the largest strewn field on record but it was also the most productive. According to some estimates, at least four tons of material actually reached the ground, and an estimated two tons of meteoritic material were removed from the area. The meteorites were carbonaceous chondrites, but among the component minerals were two (grossularite and sodalite) not previously recorded in meteorites.

Other Activities

In addition to geophysical and astrophysical events the center also deals with important archaeological and anthropological events and with biological and ecological phenomena. By mid-1978 more than 3,000 event reports had been issued and distributed on well over 1,000 short-lived events to more than 2,000 scientists and institutions in 144 countries throughout the world.

The center is also concerned about the impact of natural disasters on humans. In 1971 the center conducted an international survey to determine the number, distribution, and characteristics of facilities for warning against and monitoring such catastrophes. The survey also documented current research in natural disasters. The published directory of the center's findings is being used as a guide to plan a global warning system for natural disasters. The center was also instrumental in compiling and publishing in 1974 the *Directory of National and International Pollution Monitoring Programs*, a first step toward the goal of enabling man to understand and protect his environment.

In October 1975 the center was reorganized, becoming an independent, nonprofit organization, no longer affiliated with the Smithsonian Institution. Under the directorship of Richard Golub since April 1976 the Center for Short-Lived Phenomena, Inc., has continued to pursue its original goals and by mid-1978 was seeking ways to expand the spectrum of events covered.

9.
The Restless Atmosphere

Twice a day at more than five hundred locations throughout the world, balloons carrying radiosondes and rawinsondes (radio transmitting devices) and other instruments are sent into the upper atmosphere. Before bursting in the thin, cold air of the stratosphere, well above the highest-flying aircraft, the balloons radio back to Earth information about the temperature, pressure, humidity, and winds at different altitudes.

Every day—especially important during the hurricane and typhoon seasons—long-range aircraft measure the weather conditions over remote parts of the oceans and over the polar regions. At the same time weather satellites passing overhead in their orbits send back pictures of the clouds and measurements of the Earth's air and surface temperatures.

It is data from these various sources that the World Weather Centers in Washington, D.C., Moscow, and Melbourne, Australia, use to make the daily weather forecasts that are familiar to everyone within the reach of radio, television, or newspapers.

Other more specialized probes are also being carried out. Gigantic balloons launched from Palestine, Tex., carry thousands of pounds of instruments to altitudes far above those reached by the radio balloons. Some of these balloons stand more than 800 feet high before being released and, when fully inflated in the stratosphere, have volumes of up to one and one-third million cubic yards. A Lockheed Electra airplane is used to carry a long-nosed boom that supports sensitive motion and temperature sensors. Lodged in the boom's base is the most accurate inertial navigation system available. U.S. Air Weather Service RB-57F jet aircraft with oversized engines and wings fly at altitudes unattainable by ordinary aircraft. These planes sample the rare upper atmosphere, where they can detect traces of volcanic particles, trace gases like the fluorocarbons, and debris from man-made nuclear explosions.

Occasionally, experiments directed toward a particular problem are carried out. In 1974, for example, crews of meteorologists and their assistants from all over the world set up headquarters at Dakar, Senegal, to make the first

NCAR's outfitting of a war-surplus de Havilland Buffalo airplane with a long boom carrying a highly accurate inertial navigation system and placing sensitive wind and temperature sensors well ahead of the aircraft was so successful that a Lockheed Electra was later similarly equipped.

long-term comprehensive measurements of the tropical atmosphere. These measurements have provided new insights about how hurricanes begin and how in other ways that crucial part of the globe affects the world's weather.

All of these adventures into the unknown have been motivated by man's desire to probe and understand the Earth's atmosphere, weather, climate, and natural disasters. The programs are largely the creation of the National Center for Atmospheric Research (NCAR), an organization whose sole mission is to make such studies.

The History of NCAR

The weather that so greatly influences the affairs of mankind is determined by the complex atmosphere that covers the Earth. As adventurous sailors began to travel about the Earth during the Age of Discovery, the general patterns of the atmosphere began to be understood. These early explorers learned to use the steady winds of the tropical belts to push their square-riggers across the oceans. They also learned about the movement of hurricanes, and they developed simple ways of predicting the weather from the directions of the wind and the patterns of clouds. But the real key to understanding the complex atmosphere, each part of which interacts with every other part, came only when there were ways to observe it as a whole.

Recognizing the difficulties of studying the atmosphere in its entirety, meteorologists have for many years sought a cooperative approach. Under the leadership of Matthew F. Maury of the U.S. Navy, sea captains of several countries began to exchange observations from all parts of the globe on a regular basis as early as the 1850s. This informal activity eventually resulted in formation of the World Meteorological Organization, through which the weather services of most of the countries of the world now cooperate in exchanging information on a twice-daily basis. This exchange allows meteorologists to draw complete weather maps twice a day, to trace changing patterns as they develop, and to predict weather conditions.

But exchanging observations is not enough. More than fifty years ago Cleveland Abbe, an American meteorologist, wrote:

> What I most long to see, and what I believe is of fundamental importance in atmospherics—the want of which is a real obstacle—is the existence of a laboratory building specifically adapted to atmospheric experiments and the association therewith of able students trained in mathematics, physics, and mechanics. When all this is realized, the intellectual work that will be done there will gradually remove all obstacles to the perfection of our knowledge of the atmosphere. Does this seem like a long look ahead? Not so. The time is ripe for the institute.

It was not until recently, however, that—on the recommendation of the U.S. National Academy of Sciences—the U.S. National Science Foundation (NSF) appropriated funds for the creation of an institution along the lines envisioned by Abbe. A group of universities, each with its own teaching and research program in atmospheric science, worked out the details of the organization.

These universities saw the institution as an important extension of their own capabilities as well as a valuable center

The headquarters of NCAR is located on the slopes of the Rocky Mountains in Boulder, Colo.

for studying the atmosphere. As the tasks and activities were planned for the center, the highest hopes of the founders were distilled into a single sentence that appeared in a planning document: "The institution . . . is to be thought of as a center at which high scientific competence and consummate technological skill can be combined in a free and natural alliance to master our atmospheric environment."

Under the leadership of Walter Orr Roberts, its first director, the new organization was formally established as the National Center for Atmospheric Research in Boulder, Colo., in 1960. With support from NSF, Roberts assembled the expert staff and specialized facilities needed to create a comprehensive approach to atmospheric problems by scientists from various disciplines, institutions, and countries.

NCAR is situated on a magnificent site on the eastern slopes of the Rocky Mountains. Most of the NCAR staff of approximately six hundred people work in Boulder, but there are several contingents elsewhere. In Palestine, Tex., a group launches large weather balloons; a smaller group in Christchurch, New Zealand, flies globe-circling constant-density balloons. Scientists and technicians at Mauna Loa, Hawaii, observe the corona and activity of the sun.

Models of the Atmosphere

Man always has been subject to the vagaries of the weather. In 1816, for example, there was no summer in New England; snow fell during June, July, and August. Not only did the rains that fell in southern California in 1978 cause flooding but they were totally unexpected, coming after a year of drought. Man's dream has been to be able to predict what the weather will be a few hours or days ahead, to control it if possible, and, more recently, to preserve the quality of the air in which he lives.

The basic force behind the weather is easy to understand. The atmosphere is a restless fluid covering the entire planet. Near the equator the air receives much more heat from the sun than it can radiate back into space, but near the poles the opposite occurs—the air loses more heat to space than it receives from the sun. Heat is transported from the equator to the poles, and it is in this process that the motions of the atmosphere are generated.

Even a casual look at a weather map indicates that the motions of the atmosphere are very complicated. Movements such as the trade winds in the tropics and the higher-latitude westerlies are large-scale, relatively stable motions. But there are also motions of lesser size—sea and land breezes, cyclones and anticyclones, hurricanes and squall lines—that range in intensity from gentle to ferocious and in size from a few miles to many hundreds of miles.

Although it is true that scientists must observe the atmosphere as a whole before they can understand its variety and complexity, observation alone is not sufficient. To refine the understanding of atmospheric processes, ways must be developed to digest the vast amount of information collected. One of the more difficult tasks confronting meteorologists is to perform calculations on these data within a theoretical framework.

The main tool being used to relate theory and data is a "model" of the atmosphere. This is not a laboratory model that meteorologists can see or feel but rather a mathematical model stored in the memory of a computer and manipulated by its computational ability. Theoreticians continue to isolate problems that can be studied analytically, and field studies measure processes such as motion energy, water, and momentum in limited portions of the atmosphere. Only when the numerical model in the computer brings this data

Using a model of circulation patterns, NCAR produces computer-created weather maps that indicate cloud covers and low-pressure systems (H = high and L = low).

together can scientists determine the impacts of isolated processes on the system as a whole or predict accurately measured atmospheric quantities to check their theories.

The working of a mathematical model, like the real atmosphere it tries to simulate, is rather simple in concept but immensely complex in execution. The model obeys well-established laws of physics that are written in the form of fewer than a dozen equations. These equations relate factors such as pressure forces and the rate of change of momentum of air masses, the addition of heat to the air and the rate of temperature change, and the water evaporated from the oceans and the heat released when this water falls as rain or snow. The application of these general laws must be made while taking into account factors such as the actual areas of the oceans and continents, the temperature of the ocean surface, and the effects of mountain chains. The computer, therefore, must be supplied with a great deal of information.

To complicate matters further, all applicable laws must be applied simultaneously. In addition, any changes produced by applying them must be taken into account by the model as it runs through time. If the model (or the real atmosphere), for example, produces snowfall at a particular location, the color of the ground at that point changes from brown or green to white. This, in turn, changes the amount of heat absorbed by the ground from the sun, which then affects the heat radiated into the air by the ground, and so on through a lengthy chain of interactions. The computer must keep up with the results of its calculations and adjust its subsequent calculations accordingly.

Because no computer yet built can deal with each individual particle of air, each section of the model must be used to represent a fairly large volume of air. For purposes of calculation, the most sophisticated global model in use at NCAR divides the air into separate volumes, each about one hundred and fifty miles square and almost two miles deep. Each volume is considered to have constant factors—temperature, clouds, and so on—throughout. In models of weather changes for a more limited area, each volume carries less of a burden, representing averages over smaller distances.

Weather and Climate Predictions

Assuming that a model is sufficiently realistic, that its calculations are based on accurate observations of the real weather, and that the computer can calculate faster than the weather changes, a model of the atmosphere can be used to make forecasts. Numerical models are being used by the National Weather Service to make predictions of the weather from one to four days in advance. Because research must constantly test new approaches, the NCAR model and those used by other research institutes are somewhat more elaborate than the models used by the National Weather Service. Eventually, the research models will serve as the basis for greatly improved operational forecasting.

Forecasting long-term changes in climate involves very different considerations. The time scale for such predictions must be tens or hundreds of years instead of days. Although scientists believe that many factors influence the climate, there is as yet no suitable way of showing how these factors operate over very long periods of time. Now that some of man's activities influence an entire region of the Earth, and conceivably the planet as a whole, the ability to predict climate has become particularly urgent. The accumulation of particulate matter and of carbon dioxide that are injected into the atmosphere by the burning of vast amounts of fuel and the large amount of heat that is released from power sources such as generators, automobiles, and buildings in cities are likely to affect climate.

In order to understand long-term changes in climate, it is first necessary to understand the relationship between the major source—the sun—and the major reservoir—the oceans—of the Earth's energy. Astronomers have not been able to establish the changes in the amount of heat the sun sends to the Earth to an accuracy of better than about 0.3 percent, but even a change of only this amount probably causes an appreciable change in global weather. It is known that the sun's output of X-ray and ultraviolet radiation does change, but the amount of energy in these variations is small compared to the total amount radiated by the sun. Furthermore, the variations are clearly noticeable only in the upper atmosphere. Such changes occur in an eleven-year cycle, which is sometimes called "the sunspot cycle." This subtle eleven-year change in the sun may affect the climate in a small way. Climatologists are now looking for evidence of solar change over longer periods of time. Evidence is coming not only from measurements of the sun but also from the Earth's climatic history as registered in tree rings and in the geological record in cores drilled from the ocean bottoms and the polar ice packs.

Severe Storm Research

Among the most obvious features of the weather are the local storms that pass across the face of the Earth, bringing with them abrupt changes of temperature along with winds and rain or snow. The more intense storms can also produce damaging hail. Because northeastern Colorado has one of the highest frequencies of hail in the United States, NCAR is well located for the study of such severe storms. Since 1967 the study of thunderstorms in northeastern Colorado has been a cooperative project among NCAR, the National Oceanic and Atmospheric Administration (NOAA), and a dozen universities. This work has involved the use of radar to detect storms and to observe their characteristics; aircraft to measure conditions around them; balloons carrying instruments to measure conditions aloft; and ground networks to observe conditions under the storms.

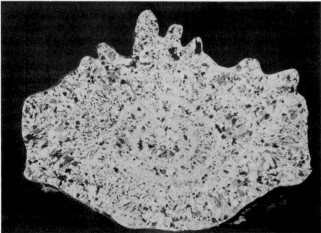

The study of hail is one of the concerns of NCAR. A radar antenna in Colorado searches clouds for signs of hail. Taken with polarized light, a photograph of a cross section of a huge hailstone, about seventeen inches in diameter, shows the pattern of ice crystals.

As NCAR scientists and their colleagues study actual thunderstorms in nature, a companion effort is under way to learn how to make mathematical models of thunderstorms. Just as a group of equations describing various physical processes can be combined in a computer to simulate the global atmosphere, in the same general way it is possible to simulate a cumulus cloud as it grows into a giant thunderstorm. Such a model must take into account the way the air is drawn into the cloud at the bottom, the growth of small cloud droplets into raindrops in the air updraft, and the freezing of the raindrops to snow and ice and their continued growth as they reach the colder upper levels.

Investigating the Boundary Layer

The first 3,200 feet of the atmosphere are called the boundary layer. This is the region below the clouds in which most of the atmospheric processes of interest to our daily lives take place. Dust and smoke enter the atmosphere in this layer. It is relatively calm and stable at night, but begins to mix during the day because of the convection started by the sun. Patterns of pollution are seen in the boundary layer.

Boundary-layer research at NCAR includes experiments using computer models; experiments done in the laboratory; and experiments carried out in the field. NCAR scientists and their colleagues combine aircraft, radar, and networks of ground-based instruments in their study of the ways in which mass, energy, and movement change in the boundary layer.

One site for boundary-layer experiments is a tower 900 feet high near NCAR in Erie, Colo. This facility, administered jointly by NOAA and NCAR, is called the Boulder Atmospheric Observatory (BAO). The tower uses an elevator to carry instruments to any of its ten levels. Measurements made by aircraft at various heights can be calibrated against measurements made by the tower instrumentation. The BAO is one of the few facilities in the United States available for this kind of research.

Global Chemical Reconnaissance and Air Pollution

NCAR has for many years studied the mysteries of the natural sources and sinks of trace gases and particles in the atmosphere. Trace gases such as carbon dioxide and ozone have a very important effect on the global heat balance because they can absorb both solar and infrared radiation and thereby influence the temperature of the air. It is becoming increasingly obvious that dust and smoke particles also affect air temperature.

Since the beginning of the Industrial Revolution, enough fossil fuel has been burned to produce an appreciable increase in carbon dioxide in the atmosphere, and it is predicted that by the year 2000 there will be about a twenty-five percent (or even greater) increase from the present level of more than three hundred parts per million by mass. This increase will raise the surface temperature slightly, having a small but possibly significant effect on the climate of the Earth unless there is some counteracting influence.

To understand trends in the atmosphere as a whole, scientists must make observations in remote parts of the world, far from the direct influence of mankind, although there is now virtually no part of the globe where it can be said that man has no influence at all. NCAR scientists have made measurements of trace gases and dust particles in Antarctica, the Arctic, and the jungles of Panama and Brazil, on long flights over the Arctic and the Pacific Ocean, and on the peaks of volcanoes in the Hawaiian Islands. Their purpose is to determine the natural background of such materials against which man's activities can be measured, thereby determining whether man influences the atmosphere as a whole.

The question of preserving the atmospheric environment is increasingly urgent. (Although the air in our large cities has become dangerously polluted, there are many mechanisms, particularly precipitation of rain and snow, that continually cleanse the air in and around cities.) Along with their colleagues in universities and government laboratories, scientists at NCAR are attempting to define the chemical processes that produce smog and haze particles as well as the more irritating by-products of air pollution. Perhaps they also will discover ways either to alter the chemistry of the atmosphere or to reduce the sources of pollutants.

The Sun and Upper Atmosphere

The weather cannot be considered without taking into account the sun—the ultimate source of energy for the Earth as well as the determinant of conditions in the Earth's upper atmosphere. The sun has a fascinating and complex atmosphere of its own, and scientists at NCAR are trying to unravel the secret of solar activity. Indications have been

initial

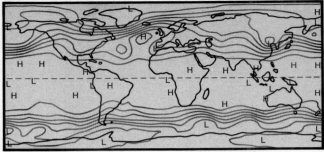

96-hour forecast

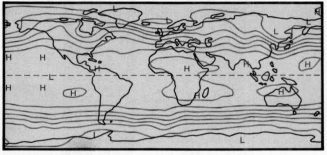

96-hour verification

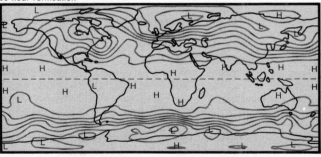

To test an experiment in forecasting the weather, the NCAR computer records patterns of air pressure on microfilm. Real weather conditions (top) serve as the starting point of the experiment. The computer produces a forecast (middle) based on these conditions. The forecast is then compared with weather conditions as they actually develop (bottom). (H = high and L = low.)

uncovered in the past few years that the sun may be less fixed and constant than has been thought. Historical sunspot studies, observations of the sun's magnetic field, and the unsuccessful search for solar neutrines have all led to speculations that the sun may change its output over decades or centuries. The search for such changes now forms an exciting focus for solar research.

For many years scientists studying the upper atmosphere have been aware that this region responds to changes in solar activity. For example, from time to time there are major emissions of energetic particles, X rays, and ultraviolet radiation from the sun. The emissions cause storms at levels above fifty miles to about one hundred and ninety miles, the region called the ionosphere, and still farther up in the region called the magnetosphere. During such events the magnetic fields of the Earth may change rapidly. Moreover, such magnetic storms often are accompanied by intense displays of aurorae in high latitudes and by difficulties in transmitting high-frequency radio waves over long distances.

Tools of the Atmospheric Scientist

To understand and predict the larger phenomena, the atmosphere must be studied in depth on a global basis. For small-scale investigations of events such as boundary-layer experiments and thunderstorm studies, the phenomena must be investigated in three dimensions and in more detail. To conduct such a wide range of investigations, scientists have had to develop an array of vehicles and instruments with which they can probe and measure the atmosphere.

The most obvious way to probe this complex medium is to carry an instrument directly into it. Because aircraft have proved extremely useful in this respect, NCAR owns and operates two twin-engine Beech aircraft, a twin-jet Sabreliner, and a Lockheed Electra. It also has access to a Schweizer sailplane (glider) owned by NOAA. All of these craft have instruments to perform special kinds of research such as measuring winds and temperatures with great accuracy, sampling the air for trace gases, particles, and cloud droplet samplings, and measuring the radiation from the sun and Earth.

Long before aircraft were employed, balloons were used to probe the atmosphere. In about 1904 the first successful observations of the stratosphere by balloons were made by Leon Teisserenc de Bort, a French scientist. Balloons, of course, have developed greatly in the twentieth century. They now have volumes of more than thirty million cubic feet and can carry loads of more than eleven hundred pounds far into the stratosphere, where they can float for many hours or even days. NCAR usually launches balloons from its National Scientific Balloon Facility site at Palestine, Tex.

NCAR has also developed smaller constant-density balloons that can circle the Earth at a constant level for more than a year. In addition, balloons of various sizes are used to carry instruments for special purposes such as measuring the distribution of ozone or the vertical flux of radiation that determines the air temperature.

The dream of the meteorologist always has been to be able to sit on the ground and to observe the behavior of the air above him. He still cannot do this in every respect, but NCAR's radar can probe the heart of a thunderstorm and see the distribution of rain and hail inside it. The pulsed laser (infrared radar) or "lidar" can measure the distribution of airborne particles. A new portable automated network of weather stations can report what is happening simultaneously over a large area to scientists seated in front of a computer console. New telescopes can probe the solar atmosphere. Many of these efforts are experimental, but the potential of being able to observe events from a remote location spurs NCAR's scientists to improve such techniques.

The computer, of course, is one of the most important tools of the atmospheric scientist. NCAR operates the world's largest computer facility devoted exclusively to atmospheric research. The computers are used to construct comprehensive numerical models of the general circulation of the atmosphere and are also used for many other studies, including those of convection clouds, interactions between the atmosphere and the surface of the land and oceans, and circulations in the oceans themselves. The computers are used to coordinate the masses of data gathered in field experiments and to speed the analysis of experimental information. The NCAR computer complex is also used by many outside scientists.

Global Atmospheric Research Program

Because atmospheric research deals with a global system, it lends itself to important international undertakings. One such undertaking that first emerged in the 1960s is the Global Atmospheric Research Program (GARP), which utilizes the most capable research scientists from all member countries of the United Nations. As a key U.S. participant in GARP, NCAR has joined with scientists in NOAA, the National Aeronautics and Space Administration, and many universities to undertake global observations of the circulation in the lower atmosphere. Balloon and satellite systems aid in measuring wind velocities and in obtaining pressure and temperature data to supplement observations from satellites and from the ground-based global meteorological network. At the same time, NCAR has also undertaken experiments with models to simulate and compare various combinations of observing systems.

A large and important part of the atmosphere that has been neglected until recently is the tropical belt. Tropical meteorology has now become an important part of NCAR's work with GARP. In 1974, NCAR participated in the GARP Atlantic Tropical Experiment, an ambitious, multinational field experiment headquartered in Senegal in western Africa. This experiment consisted of intensive observations of the tropical atmosphere using ships, aircraft, radar, surface weather stations, and pictures from weather satellites directly overhead. This combination permitted a new view of tropical weather systems.

The peak of GARP will be an intensive observation program that will end in the early 1980s to obtain data that can, for the first time, adequately define the conditions in the atmosphere on a global basis. This program, known as the Global Weather Experiment, will involve the combined use of all the tools available to the meteorologist, including meteorological satellites, constant-density balloons, radio-equipped balloons, aircraft, and other devices such as drifting buoys.

In a sense, the activity of GARP symbolizes the kind of enterprise for which NCAR was created. There are problems too large and too complex for individual atmospheric scientists to undertake. NCAR provides a means by which scientists in the United States can cooperate with those from other countries to study the atmosphere of the planet as a single system in order to piece together the riddle of the gaseous envelope that covers the Earth.

10
The Evolving Planet

If the "doomsday" thesis is correct, human society and the Earth's systems that support it will suffer a catastrophic collapse within the next century. Although it is true that industrial societies have disrupted the natural cycles of minerals, carbons, and water, there is some evidence that ways may be found to avert such a disastrous collapse. As man tries to deal more effectively with the problems that he has created and to live in better harmony with the Earth that supports him, the Earth sciences will develop in new directions, to become even more important than they are today.

The Framework

The Earth may be thought of as a series of approximately concentric shells of various materials. The core, mantle, and crust of the Earth are surrounded by two fluid envelopes—the hydrosphere (the Earth's oceans, rivers, lakes, and polar ice) and the atmosphere. All living matter is concentrated in the biosphere near the boundaries between the solid Earth and its fluid envelopes.

All geological study of the Earth is dominated by the broad cycles of motion within the Earth's layers and by the cycles of the materials that cut across the concentric layers. The water cycle, for example, extends from the water layer on the Earth into the atmosphere and into the solid Earth. These cycles operate on different time scales, ranging from months to millions of years.

In another sense geologists are Earth scientists who study rocks. They may be primarily concerned with history, with utility, or with theory. Historians try to decipher the history of the Earth and of its life during the past four or five billion years, the time since the Earth first took form as a planetary body. Practitioners, or prospectors, search for Earth materials that can be of use to man. Theoreticians are concerned with causes—why mountains rise; how the oceans originated; why oil forms and accumulates in the pores of sedimentary rocks; and what causes earthquakes and volcanic eruptions.

In the Earth sciences predictions of developments and events are generally based on the theory of plate tectonics.

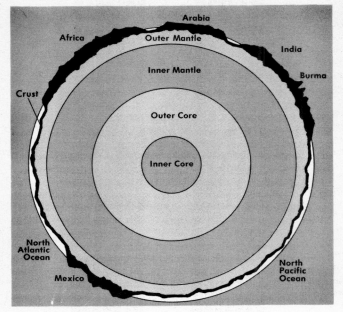

The Earth may be thought of as a series of concentric shells. This cross section shows the core, mantle, and crust of the Northern Hemisphere.

Essentially, the theory holds that slow motions within the Earth's solid interior cause lateral motions in the rigid and shell-like outer layer of the Earth. The continents drift with the shells or plates at rates of a few inches per year. Until recently, the geological creed for more than a hundred years had been that "the present is the key to the past." Using the past and present as a guide to the future, plate tectonics theory can be used to make predictions of what is to come. Unfortunately, the time scale involved is so great that there is some question as to whether or not there will be any humans surviving to test such predictions. In addition, there are many factors, some of them outside of human control, that may influence the future of the Earth and its suitability for human habitation. There is some evidence that the Earth may be entering a new ice age. Other evidence indicates that the increase of carbon dioxide in the Earth's atmosphere — largely a result of the modern industrial age — is warming the

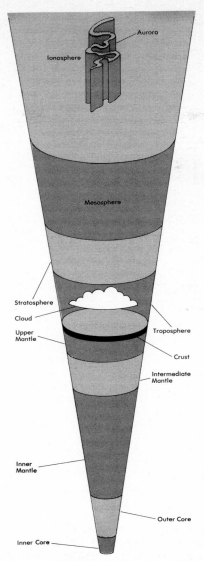

The Earth and its atmosphere contain layers in gaseous, liquid, and solid form. Geology studies the cycles of change within these layers.

Earth. Recent shifts in wind patterns, if they become permanent, might also have serious effects. Desert areas in Africa, for example, seem to be expanding. Whether the Earth becomes a frozen globe, a Venus-like hothouse, or a giant desert, such changes would have catastrophic effects on man.

The Outlook

The following predictions are not imaginative or inspired guesses but are based on known scientific facts and reasonable extrapolations of them:

1. The Earth sciences, once predominantly an outdoors study, will become increasingly theoretical as more chemists, physicists, and mathematicians join in the study of the problems of the Earth.

2. Global mathematical models will be formulated for the circulations of the atmosphere, the oceans, and the Earth's interior.

3. The knowledge of the physical properties of the Earth, which is required for mathematical models, will be determined from laboratory experiments at high pressures and temperatures and from refined geophysical probes of the Earth.

4. The distributions of chemical elements within the Earth's layers and their migrations between layers will be determined in detail.

5. The new theoretical models will guide investigators to critical historical evidence and to potential mineral deposits. Thus, theoretical advances will be accompanied by advances in the historical and practical aspects of geology.

6. Improved instruments for remote sensing of the Earth's interior from satellites, planes, ships, and the ground will facilitate the discovery of concentrated deposits of minerals and fossil fuels.

7. Climatic changes on a global scale will become predictable, but not controllable.

8. Within a hundred years—at least one densely populated city in the western United States will be devastated by a major earthquake; like other faults, the San Andreas Fault will be controlled by scientific means, and California will suffer no more major earthquakes; the world's supply of oil and natural gas, produced within the Earth during the past three hundred million years, will be completely used up; continued shifting of global climatic belts will cause drought and famine, and deserts will extend their boundaries.

The European Space Agency's Meteosat is one of many weather satellites being used to survey the Earth's weather patterns. Accurate surveillance of the weather will help scientists develop better predictions of important shifts in the global climate.

9. Within thousands of years—the sea level will rise tens of feet as the ice sheets melt, flooding world ports and many square miles of arable land; later, the ice sheets will spread from the polar regions toward the equator, causing the sea level to fall, stranding world ports inland, and decreasing the amount of land suitable for habitation; a large meteorite will strike the Earth's surface with sufficient force to generate a crater with a diameter measured in miles.

10. Within millions of years—the drift of Africa toward Europe will once again seal the Straits of Gibraltar, and the Mediterranean Sea will evaporate completely, leaving an enormous basin floor of salt flats as deep as ten thousand feet below sea level; movements in California will bring the present site of Los Angeles adjacent to the present site of San Francisco in ten million years and adjacent to the coast of southern Alaska in sixty million years.

11. Within hundreds of millions of years—the Pacific Ocean will have closed up, and the Atlantic Ocean will be as large as the Pacific is today; the Japanese islands will have been compressed and uplifted into a mighty mountain range between Asia and North America; Australia will have moved northward to form a supercontinent with Asia and North America; oil that is today in the early stages of formation in sediments on the coast of eastern North America and other continental margins will have migrated into reservoirs suitable for drilling and exploitation.

The Cycles of the Earth

The prediction of events thousands or millions of years in the future appears rather futile against prophecies of the catastrophic collapse of human society in one hundred years or so—the consummate "natural" disaster. The explosive growth of world population and the accompanying growth of technology and industry have already placed severe strains on natural resources. Estimates of demand and supply during the next century make it clear that no easy solution is in sight.

It is true that unanticipated discoveries or inventions can nullify scientific predictions, but man is faced with the fact that natural resources are finite, whereas the demand for them is theoretically infinite. Concentrated deposits of minerals, metals, and fossil fuels are generated by the Earth in cycles with durations of millions of years. Most existing deposits will have been used within the foreseeable future.

Additional requirements can be met only by expensive extraction from rocks with low concentrations, by substitutions of one material for another, or by the recycling and reuse of extracted materials.

We have lived through a brief period of abundance when humans could exploit the environment. We must readjust our social and economic systems in the realization that the human species and its activities constitute an integral part of the cycles of the Earth. Our future activities must become integrated into the cycles in such a way that what we take from the Earth is used efficiently and then replaced with minimum disruption and contamination.

Within a hundred years we will have developed efficient water management systems using rivers, lakes, and oceans. The salts extracted from the oceans will supplement chemical elements extracted from the ground. Water used in cities will be purified and returned to the water cycle, and sewage will be processed for its many metals.

The part of the carbon cycle involving photosynthesis of organic materials and the slow generation and accumulation of oil and natural gas in rocks will be artificially reproduced within a relatively short time. Waste vegetable matter and manure from farms, sewage from cities, and a harvest of plankton from the oceans will be treated with bacteria to produce fertilizer and methane. The fertilizer will, of course, replenish the soil for food production, and methane—a natural gas—potentially at least will provide a significant proportion of the energy requirements for mechanized farming. According to some estimates, if the problems of harvesting plankton can be solved, we may have an energy supply equivalent to the present consumption of oil and natural gas.

The prediction and modification of earthquakes, volcanic eruptions, and weather phenomena will save countless lives. Medical advances and the control of epidemics and plagues will also prevent needless deaths. The human life span will doubtless be lengthened.

Despite the facts that some natural resources will be exhausted within the next century—in addition to local pollution at intolerable levels and widespread food shortages and famines—many scientists remain confident that a succession of world crises will not lead to a doomsday catastrophe. Many scientists believe that the progressive adjustments that these crises will force on society will lead man to find a more harmonious relationship with the Earth's cycles.

III. Myths of Natural Catastrophe

"I personified the earthquake as a permanent individual entity. . . . It stole in behind my back, and once inside the room had me all to itself, and could manifest itself convincingly. . . . It expressed intention, it was vicious, it was bent on destruction, it wanted to show its power. . . . I realize now, better than ever, how inevitable were men's earlier mythological versions of such catastrophes, and how artificial and against the grain of our spontaneous perceiving are the later habits into which science educates us. It was simply impossible for untutored man to take earthquakes into their minds as anything but supernatural warnings or retribution."
— William James
(after experiencing the
San Francisco earthquake, 1906)

"As long as there is the rhythm of day and night, winter and summer, man will continue to dream, to believe in being saved."
— Mircea Eliade

11.
Flood and Fire: Themes of Disaster

Man has always been awed by such natural catastrophes as floods, volcanic eruptions, forest fires, and tidal waves. He has feared them, studied them, and today, through modern science, partially understands and controls them. In terms of human history, however, scientific explanations are quite recent. Only within the last few years, for example, have scientists reached a consensus about the origin of earthquakes, and new developments in the earth sciences are being reported daily.

For the greater part of history man has tried to explain the natural catastrophes that he endured, or feared he would endure, through folklore, mythology, and religion. In folklore, for example, earthquakes are characteristically attributed to the movements of a subterranean creature, often a god or supernatural being who holds the Earth on his shoulders and tries periodically to shift the weight. In Greek mythology the role is performed by the rebellious Atlas, a Titan undergoing punishment for opposing the rule of the superior deity, Zeus. In some areas of the Far East the function is carried out not by a human figure but by a great fish—asleep with its tail in his mouth—that periodically awakens, bites its tail, and moves in pain.

Such stories contain considerable psychological symbolism. They often belong to complicated cosmologies that not only help explain the myths but also describe an overall relationship between man and nature. In many myths the accounts of natural catastrophes, particularly such world catastrophes as the biblical flood, help explain certain qualities of human society—its origins, its relationship to the divine world, its members' relationships among themselves and with outside groups, and, in some cases, its destiny.

Oral and written stories of natural catastrophe occur throughout the world. As legends and folktales these stories follow predictable patterns. In fact, there are only four general themes:

1. Catastrophes are caused or abated by magic powers, usually in the control of a supernatural figure—a ghost, druid, saint, demon, Satan, or the like—but sometimes influenced by magic objects or rituals.

2. Catastrophes occur in order to mark great events—a royal birth, the death of a holy man, or the loss or return of a hero.

3. Human beings help to bring about or stop catastrophes by breaking or observing taboos or by insolence or arrogance toward nature, gods, or other men.

4. The natural forces or objects that cause or are affected by catastrophes are given human characteristics and motives: earthquakes are "caused" by the weariness and pain of an Atlas; an erupting volcano is imagined as the breath of a confined monster; and a solar eclipse is explained as the "anger" of the sun over some human misdeed.

Since it is the local context of a story that determines its precise form, the number of variations within these common themes is almost incalculable, but the four ideas remain basic. What are the psychological or intellectual impulses that account for these underlying themes? Do the four simple motifs say something more than what is immediately obvious—that prescientific people imagine nature in terms of themselves and as possessing magical and moral qualities? How can we discover the "meaning" of such themes?

An astonishing number of catastrophe myths are concerned not with local events—such as landslides, tornadoes, and hurricanes—but with world catastrophes. This can be explained in part by the fact that it is only since the advent of modern news media that people have been exposed to world events. For those living in earlier times, especially preliterate societies, the scope of local events was doubtless exaggerated by sheer ignorance of everything beyond the immediate environment. Nevertheless, the existence of so many world catastrophe myths suggests that they appeal to the imagination because of their capacity to illuminate something fundamental about human life.

Stories of the inundation of the world, for example, occur in virtually every mythology on Earth: North American Indian, Irish, Greek, Egyptian, Hindu, Indonesian, Eskimo, African, and so forth. The notion of a battle of gods with each other or with monsters at the end of the world, accompanied by vast natural upheavals, occurs in the traditions of India and Ireland, in the book of revelation, and in Norse, Jewish, and Lithuanian mythology. That there will one day be a continuous world eclipse is told in Indian, South American, and Norse mythology. A world fire occurs in Norse, Greek, Lithuanian, Jewish, Babylonian, Chinese, Maori, North American

Indian, and other myths. Because the stories occur world-wide, examining several world catastrophe myths and their interpretations may help provide a better understanding of their appeal.

Genesis, Utnapishtim, and Ragnarök

The notion of a great deluge or flood is by far the most common catastrophe story in world mythology. The biblical flood is directly paralleled by a Babylonian myth, the story of Utnapishtim that is preserved in the oldest narrative poem in the Akkadian language, the Epic of Gilgamesh. The differences between the flood in the Bible and in Gilgamesh are striking. In the story of Utnapishtim the gods are simply angry with men for overpopulating the Earth (a motif that appears in other disaster stories) and for making noises that interfere with the gods' sleep. One of the gods, Ea, takes pity on men, however, and in a dream warns Utnapishtim of what is to happen. Within seven days Utnapishtim builds an ark and loads it with his family, craftsmen, animals, and possessions. The rains come with such violence that the gods themselves are frightened and, regretting their scheme, take refuge. The rains last for six days and nights; on the seventh, Utnapishtim sees a mountain in the distance and brings the ark to rest on it. After another seven days Utnapishtim releases a dove, then a swallow, and finally a raven—which fail to return. He makes sacrifices to the gods, and except for Enlil, who is angry that any man has escaped, they are pleased with his salvation. Ea approaches Enlil for his hatred of men and pleads for more moderate punishments in the future. Enlil relents, and Utnapishtim is granted eternal life, the only human being to enjoy this blessing.

Unlike the account of the biblical flood—to which the myth is related historically—there is no clear sense in the Utnapishtim story of a purpose for the events. As is the case in other Babylonian flood stories, the gods have little or no reason for what they do, and they behave like spoiled adolescents when the trouble they have caused begins to get out of hand. Utnapishtim is scarcely a distinguished figure like Noah, and there is no sense of the anguish he ought to suffer as he sees the world around him destroyed. Some of the indifference of the myth to the gods' motives or to human emotions may be explained by the imperfect form in which the text survived. It is apparent, nevertheless—particularly in light of the lack of certainty in the epic over the fate of the rest of humanity—that the story is presenting ideas that are not fully integrated into a meaningful pattern.

The tendency to include poorly justified events in a myth is not necessarily a sign of incompetence in the intelligence that created the story, however. The events that a myth describes have a cultural meaning that is independent of the attempt to dramatize them. A myth presents certain "facts," like a universal flood, because such facts have an implicitly recognized meaning within the community. The story does not have to explain causes and effects, motives, or emotions. It is in this way that myths can explain the social milieu of a people. In reading a myth for its social meanings, therefore, one asks what a mythological event or series of events seems to explain about the values of the mythmakers' own social group.

Social meaning is only one type of meaning, but it is clearly something very early and important in the history of a myth's meaning and should not be ignored. Flood myths lend themselves to such interpretation. Writing about Genesis, the noted British anthropologist E. R. Leach suggested that the main sequence of stories in the opening chapters shows, in part, an attempt to work out patterns of ancestral descent and of permissible sexual relationships among the Israelites. According to Leach, the story of the flood, whatever else it may say about morality and God's grace, is a vital part of this pattern. His theory is a concrete way to begin understanding the significance of the world disaster story.

Genesis shows that sexual relationships among the Israelites are linked to the expulsion from Eden. The relationship of Adam and Eve is, until the eating of the fruit, nonsexual. Since Adam and Eve have a single origin, their discovery of sexuality can be seen as brother-sister incest. In the same way, Cain and Abel represent the possibility of homosexual incest between two brothers. (Indeed, given the absence of females on Earth, Cain and Abel are unmarriageable, a problem that Genesis solves by sending Cain to the land of Nod where, inexplicably, he finds a wife.) Father-daughter incest occurs in the story of Lot and his daughters. The story of Ham and Noah confirms the taboo against a sexual relationship between father and son. Finally, in marrying Sarah, Abraham forms a union with his half-sister, a relationship that, in time, God blesses above all others.

As it explores these relationships Genesis also consistently portrays sexual relationships outside the close-knit society of

The book of Genesis, including the story of Adam and Eve, has been interpreted as an attempt to sanction certain human relationships and to forbid others.

the tribal group as undesirable. Cain is punished for the slaying of Abel by exile and marriage into the land of Nod. The angels who visit Lot are at all costs to be spared homosexual relations with the Sodomites. Abraham is punished for offering Sarah to the Pharaoh. Reduced to its simplest form, Genesis can be interpreted as a sequence of repetitive stories that approve of sexual unions within the close kinship ties of the Israelite community but disapprove of relationships that involve homosexuality or close family incest. The best relationship is like that of Sarah and Abraham, neither clearly incestuous nor clearly exogamous.

Each stage in the Genesis story attempts not only to give man a history but also to repeat in different contexts an essential message from God to man. The loss of Eden introduces man not just to sin, death, and woe but also to sexuality and sexual reproduction, to animal and plant husbandry, to kinship groups and family hierarchies, to economics and language diversity—to the world of culture and contradiction that is opposed to the unified, self-sufficient, presexual world of Eden. Though oversimplified, the essence of this interpretation is that Genesis links sexuality in ancestral and present-day marital practices with man's place and prosperity in the world. Man can never return to the precultural innocence of Eden, where Adam and Eve could live without knowledge of incest and where nature provided for all human needs without effort. Man's prosperity in the world depends on maintaining social and sexual relationships that are pleasing to God.

Apart from other dramatic themes and moral issues, Genesis repeatedly ties man's welfare and nature's benevolence to the observance of essential kinship and incest regulations. The story of the great flood becomes a crucial part of this scheme. The flood is the most sweeping solution possible to the problem of ancestral incest created by the union of Adam and Eve. Unlike the flood of the Utnapishtim story, the flood in Genesis annihilates every living creature except those in the ark. The chain leading back to the original incestuous pair is broken or significantly modified. After the flood no one's immediate ancestors can be more closely related than the sons of Noah and their wives, who, thanks to their anonymity, may be descendants of Cain, or of Seth (the third son of Adam and Eve), or, like Cain's wife, entirely unaccounted for. The covenant of the rainbow sets God's seal on the permanence of this solution. The suggestion of a sexual relationship between Ham and Noah after leaving the ark and the later accursed union between Lot and his daughters are ways of testing the validity of the resolution reached by the great flood.

One function of a world catastrophe story is to allow a way of solving a common dilemma—a paradox such as taboos against incest and the logical necessity of tracing all descent

Like the story of Adam and Eve, the account of the biblical flood helps explain human relationships, but it also explains man's relation to nature as well as his relation to God.

back to some incestuous pair. A myth presents the dilemma on a fictional level at which a resolution is possible because of the unique ability of a world catastrophe to test or alter the social order. The biblical flood and the Utnapishtim story attempt to codify social mores and explain questions men have about their origins. Of course, they also explain feelings and answer questions that human beings have about their environment.

One compelling catastrophe myth from the ancient world is the story of Ragnarök, a Norse myth that continues to have an audience through its recreation in the German composer Richard Wagner's opera *Götterdämmerung*. The details of the myth, which can be combined into a composite version of the story, appear in several of the Icelandic poems known as the *Eddas*:

> The world is created from an original void, Ginnun-gayap, in which ice meets with sparks and fire from the region of the south, Muspell, to form life. A giant creature, Ymir, is created and becomes the ancestor of the race of the giants.
> When he is killed by the earliest gods—one of whom is Odin, chief of the Norse pantheon—the parts of his

body are used for the construction of the cosmos. Before his death Ymir is nursed by an enormous primordial cow, and this same creature is responsible for creating the original ancestor of the gods by licking blocks of ice with its tongue. A cosmos is thus created, consisting of men, gods, and giants. Each race lives in a different part of the cosmos, but these different areas are connected with one another like parts of a great tree, Yggdrasil. The peacefulness of the world is shattered by constant quarreling between a great serpent gnawing

According to the Norse myth of Ragnarök, Loki was punished by being chained beneath a poisonous snake. When his wife could not protect him from the dripping poison, Loki's agonized movements produced earthquakes.

*at the roots of Yggdrasil and an eagle sitting in its
branches.*

Among the gods are Odin's son, Balder, the most
handsome and loved of the gods, and Loki, a trickster
figure descended from the giants and therefore of uncertain loyalties in the competition between gods and
giants. In addition to other moral lapses the gods cheat
the giants of the payment agreed upon for help in
building their palace, and then, through the schemes of
Loki, Balder is killed. In punishment Loki himself is
tied to a rock beneath the dripping jaws of a poisonous
snake. Loki's faithful wife catches most of the poison in
a bowl, but when she empties the bowl the poison
reaches Loki and his tortured movements at these times
are felt by men as earthquakes.

This state of affairs ends with Ragnarök, the "fate"
or "destiny" of the gods. It is a time of human corruption when brother fights brother and children turn
against parents. The orderly cycles of nature begin to
decay. The sun is eaten by a wolf that pursues it every
day and gradually overtakes it. Endless winter begins.
The mountains move and massive earthquakes occur.
Yggdrasil is shaken from top to bottom. Fenrir, an
enormous wolf previously imprisoned by the gods, and
the great Midgard serpent, which has been lying
beneath the waters that encircle the Earth, both mon-
strous offspring of Loki, attack toward the center of
the world. The giants, led by the escaped Loki, attack
the gods, traveling in a ship made of dead men's finger-
nails. Surt, a fire giant from Muspell, joins the assault.
In the great battle that ensues Odin is killed and eaten
by Fenrir. Fenrir in turn is killed by Odin's son Vidar.
Thor and the Midgard serpent die a mutual death, and
all the gods, giants, and monsters fight and die until
only Surt is left. The fire giant then casts fire over the
Earth, destroying mankind as well as the gods. All
creation is engulfed in these flames and by the sea that
simultaneously floods the Earth.

In time, however, Earth again rises from the sea,
renewed and purified. A new generation of gods takes
charge. Balder returns from the dead to be with them,
and two human creatures who have been hidden in the
trunk of Yggdrasil emerge and begin to repopulate the
Earth.

After Odin was killed in a great battle in the myth of Ragnarök, the Earth was destroyed by a cataclysm of fire and flood, only to be created anew in a purified state. Such an account of a world catastrophe may have been based on an actual event, such as a volcanic eruption, but one of the functions of such an account was to explain fundamental human concerns.

Scholars have argued that at the simplest level this account of world catastrophe in a massive confusion of flood and fire describes allegorically the eruptions of the volcanic region of which Iceland is a part and by means of which

Iceland was created. Nowhere else in the world can a natural setting be imagined in which we find side by side earthquakes, sky-darkening dust and ashes, fire, ice, and tidal flooding. The 1963 volcanic eruption off Iceland that created the island of Surtsey has shown, in fact, the rise from the sea of new and eventually inhabitable land as a consequence of such violence in nature. Yet to treat this great saga of the world's destiny as simply an allegory of natural events would be to ignore some of the essential powers of great religious myths. Indeed, the extraordinarily beautiful, dramatic, and evocative myth of Ragnarök can be taken as an index to the extremes of the imaginative responses with which human beings meet natural catastrophes in an age of supernatural explanation. Many myths attempt to satisfy the human need to give nature an understandable and predictable order. Further, they serve to project onto nature human feelings, whether through simple models of human life or, as the Swiss psychologist Carl Jung argued, through natural symbols that give tangible form to unarticulated aspects of the unconscious mind. The story of Ragnarök thereby recreates within the context of a world disaster a number of mythological themes—including nature as providential, cyclical, and anthropomorphic—that satisfy universal human needs.

Nature as Providential

Like many other mythological stories, Ragnarök presents the natural world as a place sustained and explained by invisible dynamic forces in conflict with one another. In Greek mythology, and in many related Indo-European and Near Eastern myths, there is a connection between the conflict that exists among the gods in the invisible, mythical world and the violence of nature. In Greek mythology, for example, a succession of three generations of gods is punctuated by natural violence:

> *Ouranos (Heaven), the original male-sky-god, mates with his mother, Gaia (Earth). Out of jealousy Ouranos hides his children in the recesses of the earth (ambiguously conceived as both the natural earth and an anthropomorphic figure). With the help of Gaia, the youngest of these children, Kronos, obtains a sickle with which he attacks and castrates Ouranos. Kronos' rule follows, but he repeats the crime of Ouranos by swallowing his own children, including Hera, Demeter,*

and Poseidon. When Kronos' wife—Rhea, another earth goddess—is pregnant with Zeus, she succeeds in giving birth in secret, while presenting Kronos with a stone to swallow instead of the child.

In time Zeus fights and defeats Kronos, again with the help of Gaia. By bringing about Kronos' defeat Zeus becomes permanent master of the thunderbolt, a true weather god, and ruler of the Greek pantheon. But Gaia bears another child, this time the monster Typhon, a cross between man and animal, whose body is covered with the heads of snakes. A great fight takes place between Zeus and Typhon, one which Zeus nearly loses in some accounts. In the end Zeus triumphs, Typhon is confined in the volcanic hollow of Mount Etna in Sicily, and Zeus becomes undisputed ruler of the gods.

The imagined involvement of the natural world in these events can be seen in the account of the climax of the fight with the Titans, as given by Hesiod, the earliest Greek mythographer:

> *Then Zeus no longer restrained his strength, but at once his breast was filled with might. He displayed all of his force. At the same time he came forth from Heaven and Olympus. Thunderbolts flew from his mighty hand together with lightning and the crash of thunder. . . . Catching fire the life-bringing earth crashed, and the huge wood roared with fire. The whole land boiled and the streams of Ocean and the barren sea. The hot steam surrounded the earthborn Titans. Great flames rose to the sky. The glare was blinding. Unbelievable heat took hold of Chaos . . . it seemed as if Earth and Sky had met. . . . The winds stirred up dust and earthquake, thunder and lightning, and the gleaming thunderbolt. The unbearable roar of the terrible strife rose up.*

This myth of a series of cosmic conflicts between three generations of gods that culminate in the defeat of a monster figure has extremely close parallels in Hittite, Phoenician, Iranian, Norse, and Babylonian mythologies, and at least a loose relationship to the Vedic (ancient Indian) account of the creation and establishment of a world order. It is impossible to suggest a single, precise interpretation of these myths. In the Greek and other Indo-European stories there may be a common ancient social structure to which the evolution of the gods corresponds. A natural allegory has been argued for the Babylonian story in which salt and seawater and the formation of alluvial land are important. Motifs of castration and incest provide ground for Freudian interpretations. As the quotation from Hesiod shows, whatever else these stories express, one vital function is to make the natural world, particularly its violence, part of an order or cosmos.

The time in which mythological events occur cannot simply be divided into past, present, and future. In a sense mythical time is a dimension of the present, but conventional notions of time are probably inadequate. A cosmic war of the gods in which the order of nature, men, and gods is brought into being or destroyed has meaning for those who believe in it. Whether the events are imagined to occur in the past or in the future is unimportant. What is important is the relationship between the mythic catastrophe and present, visible nature. If mythical time is a type of fourth dimension, a war of the gods is not wholly "past" or "future" but a timeless and imperceptible aspect of the reality in which people live.

The temporal system of mythology is well illustrated by the Vedic account of the world's composition and origin. The wars of the Vedic gods, the Danavas and Adityas, result in the expulsion of the great world serpent Vritra. Somewhat like the serpent of Midgard, Vritra lies coiled beneath the earth in a place of terror and darkness, the *Asat*, or place of "not being." Like the Norse serpent he remains able to inflict injury on men if he escapes his bondage. Unlike his Norse counterpart, however, he is actively engaged in sending into the present-day world evil spirits whose purpose it is to torment men.

The sense of a mythological war constantly intruding into the present is also found in the Greek myth. Although the authority of Zeus is essentially unquestioned after the defeat of his enemies, those enemies are absorbed into a dynamic unseen world. The Titans are chained in Tartarus—a place much like the Vedic *Asat*. According to Hesiod:

> There, in order, are the springs and ends of dark earth and misty Tartarus and the barren sea and the starry heaven—mouldy and harsh—a place even the gods hate: a great chasm whose bottom a man who entered it could not reach in a year; but one cruel wind after another would carry him about.

The Titans in Tartarus are in an undifferentiated world of beginnings in which the real world is physically rooted. Conditions in Tartarus are like those in which the cosmos began. The Titans retain their potential to destroy the natural order, but at the same time they are not a part of the real world. The periodic eruption of Mount Etna in Sicily—one of the most impressive natural phenomena of the ancient Mediterranean world—is explained in Greek mythology as the activity of the last of Zeus's cosmic enemies, Typhon. Like the Loki of Ragnarök, as he lies bound and writhing in the depths of the Earth, Typhon gives regular evidence of his presence by the violence he is still able to produce on the Earth's surface.

There is a relationship between mythical events and the world. In these examples, as in many other religious and mythological systems, the mythic world has a paradoxical relationship with the real world. From the perspective of a person who accepts a timeless cosmic war underlying the instability of the world, a catastrophe is more than a sign of the unpredictability and malevolence of nature. As part of a larger cosmic system, such an event becomes tangible proof that the overall scheme of nature remains under control. Loki's subterranean movements or the eruptions of a Typhon may terrify and destroy, but they symbolize that the ultimate perils of the mythical wars are not at hand. Ragnarök is still to come, and Zeus still rules his enemies.

Nature as Cyclical

The descriptions of Tartarus and of Ragnarök suggest that the world order will someday return to a unity, to a point at which all things are one—whether it be water or a void like the Greek chaos. (Again one should remember the limitations faced by ordinary language in trying to describe such ideas. The "water" that precedes creation in Genesis, for example, may not mean that water is the original element but that water expresses a notion of primeval fusion for which there is no better terminology.) The world catastrophe myth places human beings in a providential relationship to nature through the feeling that the visible world is supported by an unseen dynamic order. Such myths also are part of the almost universal belief among mythmaking people in cycles in nature, human life, and the world order. Ragnarök is both a beginning and an end, a way of destroying or obliterating the present world and of allowing return to a renewed and purified world.

Thinking in terms of cycles distinguishes mythical or religious consciousness from historical consciousness. There is a human desire to pattern systems of belief on universal patterns of renewal and regeneration that exist in nature. There is also the desire of each person for life beyond death. Even the impulse to believe in personal immortality, however, fails to explain the full significance of the cycle of renewal, so powerful in world catastrophe stories.

Mythological accounts of reality, perhaps because they are communal in origin, or at least in belief, are attempts to account for self-contradictory or paradoxical feelings that are characteristic of human beings. Thus, a world catastrophe myth like Ragnarök or Zeus's battle with Typhon both frightens man and at the same time lends an element of order and stability to the world. The notion of cycles and recreation that such stories convey is both an expression of optimism for the continuity of the human race and a rejection of the concept of history. The symbolism of Tartarus and Ragnarök is rejection of the historical world man lives in in favor of a timeless world of mythical archetypes. As the Romanian-U.S. historian of religious symbolism Mircea Eliade has suggested, this impulse to reject historical time may be founded on the belief that time is meaningless unless its events conform to archetypes of a mythical world.

Eliade believes that concern with ritual in primitive societies is an attempt to enact mythical archetypes in the world. For example, the new year ritual of the ancient Babylonians, in which the great battle of Marduk (the weather god) and Tiamat (the primitive monster whose body is used to construct the cosmos) was annually recreated by choruses of men, represents movement from historical to archetypal time. The ritual represents an annual purging of the old year and its accumulated events, followed by the recreation of time. (The new year ritual continues in some forms today, for example, in the images of Father Time and Infant Time and in noisemaking, originally intended to drive out the demons of the old year.) The ritual also recreates the cosmic battle by which chaos was once transformed into order. Through the ritual man is returned to the point at which there is no time, no boundaries, no separation. Psychologically, the participants and observers of the ritual move out of the profane and temporary world into a sacred world.

World catastrophe myths offer a way of viewing the relationship between the mythical, timeless, unseen world and the visible, historical world. The state of the mythical world accounts for, and thus alleviates and stabilizes, the stresses of the visible world. The notion of a catastrophe that is cyclical, particularly one that can be reenacted through ritual, suggests that the vast scheme of human life—culture, sexuality, agronomy, and the like—has a basis in an archetypal world. The world of human life becomes a transformation of an original unity or oneness in nature, a greater reality underlying the reality in which men live.

There is a close parallel between the theme of cyclical events in myths and Leach's view of the significance of the expulsion from Eden. Human life after Eden is a dynamic process in which oppositions and contradictions must be faced. Paradise—because it opposes the world—must be a place in which all that exists is sufficient in and of itself. Whether they are leaving Eden, approaching Ragnarök, or celebrating ritually the triumphs of Zeus over Typhon and Marduk over Tiamat, human beings are imagining mythically and psychologically a crucial tension of all intelligent life. Through myths man asks some of the fundamental questions about life. What makes life real? How are the things that men do, that happen in life, and that are temporary related to the things that are not temporary and that man somehow must be in touch with if life is to continue? What relationship does the conscious self and the culture it creates bear to a "natural self" that is not burdened, or enriched, by the development of consciousness? The impulse to ask such questions is universal.

Nature as Anthropomorphic

World catastrophe myths are not simply justifications for punishing men for violations of a natural or social order. The catastrophes of a cosmic war, loss of paradise, or cyclical renewal of nature are ways of accounting for inescapable questions about human life. Yet, as the biblical account of the flood shows, such stories may emphasize moral themes. Although the story of the biblical flood can be understood as an exploration of social conventions, it is clear that the flood has a moral basis. According to Genesis 6:5–8, God places responsibility for the flood on man's general moral wickedness:

> *And GOD saw that the wickedness of man was great in the earth, and that every imagination of the thoughts of his heart was only evil continually. And it*

*repented the LORD that he had made man on the earth,
and it grieved him at his heart. And the LORD said, I
will destroy man whom I have created from the face of
the earth; both man, and beast, and the creeping thing,
and the fowls of the air; for it repenteth me that I have
made them. But Noah found grace in the eyes of the
LORD.*

A moral theme is also evident in other Mediterranean flood
stories. The U.S. scholar Joseph Fontenrose attempted to
derive the important Mediterranean flood stories from a
common source, the Babylonian-Sumerian flood myth. In his
view the chief motif of the stories is that all men and women
of a region or of the whole earth are destroyed, except for a
single pair who are saved because of their piety. In the Near
East these stories include Utnapishtim (where the piety is
not very clear or essential) and Noah. They also include the
story of Lot, whose piety in receiving and protecting the
angels from the advances of the Sodomites leads to his own
salvation (and very nearly that of his wife) while the cities
of the plain are consumed in a "flood" of fire and brimstone.

The group also includes the Greek myth of Deucalion
(Ovid's *Metamorphoses*), who survives the flooding of the
Earth in an ark, comes to ground on a mountaintop, and with
his wife restarts the human race. A clear moral emphasis is
also seen in the story of Philemon and Baucis (Ovid's *Metamorphoses*), in which Jupiter observes men's wickedness but
is moved to preserve one couple who piously give him hospi-
tality. After they have climbed a mountain to safety, Jupiter
grants them their wishes to serve as priest and priestess of
his temple and not to outlive one another. In Ragnarök moral
failure is also a cause of the final catastrophe. Both men and
the gods are at fault. The gods torture Gullveig, a goddess
who comes to them on a peaceful mission, in order to steal
the gold that she possesses. When the giant who builds their
palace comes to collect his promised bride, they use Loki to
cheat him of his payment. After these acts the moral and
natural orders of both men and gods begin to deteriorate.

That there is a moral dimension to the stories of world
catastrophes is clear. The mythic theme of cyclical regeneration, however, embodies the idea of the violation of nature on
a cosmic, not individual, level. Nature, in this view, does not
seek to punish human misdeeds but acts from a need to
purge itself. If there is evil in the mythic world, it is evil that

The Greek myth of Deucalion, as retold in Ovid's *Metamorphoses*, was only one of many accounts in ancient literature of a world flood.

is a necessary consequence of the good in creation, evil that must serve some purpose. The Stoics' view that cyclical destruction of the world is simply nature's inevitable process of self-correction arises directly from mythological stories.

Against this morally neutral view in which all forms of human life are violators of nature, men have felt compelled to introduce explicit moral guilt into their myths. In the biblical story moral guilt is so insistent that it eliminates, at least for Genesis, the whole notion of cyclical destruction and renewal. (The New Testament reintroduces belief in an end of the world and in Revelation does give the image of Armageddon, a world cataclysm the equal of Ragnarök.) In Genesis, Noah's goodness saves the seed of mankind, God repents, and the covenant of the rainbow ensures that He will never again bring about universal ruin.

A moral emphasis may seem to trivialize the deeper philosophical reasons for mythological belief in a world cataclysm.
Such moralism is, however, an expression of the human need
to explain punishment in terms of guilt. If nature or God
chooses to destroy mankind, men must have done something
to deserve the consequences.

The modern reader must also remain open to the logic that
transforms apparently negative expressions of guilt into
something more positive. In myths human acceptance of a
moral code imposed by a god is a two-way matter. Although
human beings are bound by the divine code, God, or the gods,
and nature itself are also bound to men. The admission of
human wrongdoing becomes a means of averting further
punishment. The expression of fear becomes an attempt to
ward off greater fear. Establishing a system of rules that
binds both gods and men and nature and men can prevent
the truly unimaginable, unredeemable extinction of life from
occurring. The effect of moralism in world catastrophe stories is not to provide trivial, after-the-fact reasons for what
has happened. Morality in myths shapes nature and the divine world in the image of man and provides a framework in
which man can amend his apparent helplessness. In this
context the value of the rainbow covenant granted by God to
Noah is clear: despite his omnipotence God is forever bound
to a contract with men.

One interesting aspect of the catastrophe myth is that it
places man at a juncture between rational and irrational
cosmic patterns. Myths insist, through their emphasis on
morality, that God is not mad (to borrow a memorable phrase
from U.S. anthropologist Clifford Geertz) and that His sanity
can be judged by human standards. Myths also express the
yearning—in the image of a cyclical return to chaos—for
participation in the oneness of mythical nature that precedes
all human civilization. The importance of these two functions of the catastrophe myth cannot be overstressed. They
help account for the astonishing appeal of catastrophe stories in popular culture today.

Insula Atlantis.

12.
The Atlantis Phenomenon

Belief that the history of the human race and of the Earth had been fundamentally altered by a worldwide cataclysm did not die easily, despite modern science's success at establishing the Earth's real age and prehistoric condition. Extraordinary efforts were made throughout the eighteenth and nineteenth centuries to sustain the biblical account of the creation and flood. These efforts, however, were directed at proving the authority of scripture and maintaining belief in the existence of a providential God. They had little to do with the subjective or psychological importance of belief in a world cataclysm myth. There was simply a need to reconcile widely held, ancient theological truths—from a text about whose interpretation actual wars had been fought—with modern scientific observation. A few representative titles of books on the subject, written in the quaintly verbose style of the past two centuries, illustrate their characters:

> W. Whiston (1714): "The Cause of the Deluge Demonstrated, Wherein It Is Proved that the Famous Comet of A.D. 1680 Came by the Earth at the Deluge and Was the Cause of It"
>
> L. V. Harcourt (1838): "The Doctrine of the Deluge, Vindicating the Scriptural Account from the Doubts Which Have Recently Been Cast upon It by Geological Speculations"
>
> S. Webb (1854): "The Creation and Deluge, According to a New Theory; Confirming the Bible Account, Removing most of the Difficulties Heretofore Suggested by Skeptical Philosophers, and Indicating Future Cosmological Changes Down to the Final Consummation and End of the Earth"

There has been, however, at least one attempt to preserve the myth of a world cataclysm in the face of modern science, which owes nothing to religious belief. No account of natural catastrophe myths would be complete without mentioning the legend of the lost continent of Atlantis. Equally important are the accompanying pseudoscientific theories of the 1800s and early 1900s that tried to justify belief in the myth.

A historical event may have been the basis for the story of Atlantis or at least of local legends that evolved into more complicated theories. Since 1885, when it was first proposed, with major revivals in the 1930s and 1960s, many archaeologists of classical Greece have accepted the theory that during the period from 1500 to 1450 B.C. the volcanic island of Thera, or Santorini—sixty miles north of Crete—exploded. The theory holds that the explosion was responsible for the sudden and otherwise inexplicable disappearance of the so-called Minoan civilization from coastal sites on Crete. Estimates of the quantity of material dispersed by the explosion have ranged as high as four times that involved in the Krakatoa eruption of 1883. (The sound of Krakatoa was recorded 3,000 miles away, heavy fall of volcanic ash as far as 900 miles away, and significant tidal flooding at a distance of about 4,500 miles.)

The effect of an explosion of such dimensions within a few miles of the Greek mainland, and just over the horizon from Crete, would have been stupendous. Such an explosion would possibly have been the single most dramatic natural catastrophe since the last Ice Age. It is possible that oral accounts of the event, if it indeed did occur, were passed down from generation to generation in the Greek world, telling not only of the massive eruption with its accompanying earthquakes and flooding but also of the destruction of the island civilization of Crete in its wake.

Local legends, however, would probably not have spread beyond the shores of the Eastern Mediterranean had it not been for the Greek philosopher Plato. In two of his dialogues, *Timaeus* and *Critias*, Plato created a commonwealth called Atlantis, an island continent colonized by descendants of the sea god Poseidon. These fortunate men and women, Plato says, lived in a magical, almost Edenlike world for a time but gradually succumbed to moral weakness and vice, losing touch with their divine heritage. The gods sent them into a war in which they tried but failed to enslave the nations living around the Mediterranean. As a final punishment for their wickedness the gods caused the island to sink into the sea in a massive natural cataclysm of earthquake, deluge, and conflagration.

There can be little doubt, despite the familiar mythological themes of moral decay and reabsorption by flood and fire, that all but the skeleton of Plato's story was a personal invention intended to serve his political, moral, and cosmological ideas. Like the imaginary city-state in the *Republic*, Plato's Atlantis was a place of exemplary qualities. Its people were blessed with a degree of wealth and power and with a lush and fertile natural environment that no Greek city-state could ever hope to achieve. It was Plato's point that wealth and ease did not corrupt them as long as they were able to retain their divine heritage. When their divinity was lost, they became like the Persians whose riches and corruption were proverbial in the Greek world. Plato's corrupted Atlanteans were no match for the self-discipline of relatively humble Greek city-states.

"Atlantomania"

The persistence of the Atlantis "myth" cannot be traced to any specific community feelings, any more than it can, like Genesis, to the strength of a religious tradition. Rather, Atlantis became in modern times a "home" for zealots and mystics in pursuit of private fantasies. In a reversal of Plato, mankind's expulsion from Atlantis was not regarded by such people as the act of a providential God punishing the human race for its misdeeds. Nor did the myth symbolize the existence of a dimension of the natural order to which man must periodically submit himself. Atlantis became instead a nostalgic, self-indulgent dream world like a child's fantasy of a royal home and parents from which he was secretly kidnapped at birth and to which he hopes someday to return.

Shorn of religious or genuine mythological values in the modern scientific world, this image of a natural catastrophe offered a fairy tale of a lost world, a world better or purer than the present one, from which man was cut off by an unfair or impersonal agency. For its enthusiasts Atlantis represented a means of correcting the flaws that they perceived in the world they lived in. For some the myth offered hope of nostalgic escape from the world and even fantasies of secret or occult weapons to be used against others. The claims were rather strong, but the "Atlantomania" that fascinated the European world from the late 1700s to the 1930s seemed to demand nothing less.

Looking back from a modern perspective of scientific skepticism, we may find it extraordinary that such vast energy was expended to document a myth that common sense must have identified as invention. Part of the enthusiasm was probably due to the Victorian passion for ancient authority.

Several areas of the world have been identified as the site of the lost
continent of Atlantis. Probably the most common theory has been
that Atlantis was an island or island continent in the Atlantic Ocean.

Consider, for example, the partially successful efforts of a
grandson of Heinrich Schliemann, the German entrepreneur
and archaeologist who discovered the site of Troy, to con-
vince the world that he had found among the Trojan treasures of his grandfather an inscription (in Phoenician
characters) from Atlantis itself.

Atlantis was identified in one study or another as North
America, South America, Algeria, Tunisia, Nigeria, the biblical Tarshish, Ireland, England, Sweden, the Arctic island of
Spitsbergen, the English Channel, and the submerged land
bridge between North Africa and Italy. The great age of
Atlantis theories began with the popularization in the late
1800s of the theory that Atlantis had been an island or island
continent in the Atlantic Ocean. Its existence and catastrophic submersion accounted not only for Plato's legend but also
for the biblical flood and for the distribution and "deteriora-
tion" of civilization. According to this theory the literary and
mythological history of the ancient world was a code to the
lost world that could be reconstructed. (The gods and god-
desses of the ancient world were simply the kings and queens
of Atlantis, memory of whom survived the destruction of
their continent.) Not only had Atlantis existed but also it had
contained, according to an influential study published in the
1880s, a miraculous civilization. Traces of its influence could
be seen in many parts of the world—Egypt, for example—
which were at one time mere colonies of the highly civi-
lized peoples of Atlantis. Atlantis was the ancestral home of
the Indo-Europeans, the Semites, and other major language
groups.

Such an attempt to document the Atlantean catastrophe allowed people to rewrite the history of civilization in favor of the West. Atlantis could "recall" European civilization from its traditional origins in Egypt and the Near East and place it closer to the shores of the nineteenth-century powers. This thesis received its most exhaustive exploration in Lewis Spence's *The History of Atlantis*, a definitive piece of Atlantis research and speculation written in the 1920s. According to the study, colonists from Atlantis arrived in Spain and Portugal from their Atlantic home (of which only the Canary Islands remain) in successive waves during the period 25,000 to 8000 B.C. From this beachhead they colonized the eastern Mediterranean, so that what is now known as European civilization was in fact due to the movement of Atlantean culture from the East back to the West.

Evidence for this theory, to put it mildly, was hard to come by. The animal paintings of primitive man found in the south of France, for example, had to be taken as forerunners of the bull-leaping friezes of Minoan Crete, as if similar art of animal cults could not have arisen independently. The cult of the Egyptian god Osiris was linked closely with Celtic religion and mythology on the grounds that the Arthurian legend is mysteriously like that of Osiris: both dedicate their lives to the defeat of evil and are murdered by their relatives. On these and other equally weak arguments, industrious authors built their texts. They convinced a good many otherwise rational people of the truth of an original migration of civilization from the West to the East.

As might have been predicted in the midst of the national rivalries of the nineteenth and early twentieth centuries, nationalism invaded the Atlantis myth. Welsh nationalists and nineteenth-century Frenchmen ardently defended a Celtic connection with Atlantis. In 1922 a German writer made the Atlanteans a wholly Aryan "race," whose integration into mainland tribes after the cataclysm had led to the degeneration of the pure "blond, blue-eyed" strain. Both themes—the ancient racial superiority of the Atlanteans and the modern nationalist superiority of the English-speaking peoples—were blended in a rather offensive excerpt from a science fiction work by the English novelist Arthur Conan Doyle (an enthusiast of the Atlantis myth). In Doyle's fantasy several intrepid British and American explorers find and live for a time with the surviving Atlanteans at the bottom of the ocean:

> *Every one of these things had been prepared by the skill and foresight of that wonderful far-away people [the Atlanteans] who seemed, from what we could learn, to have thrown out one arm to Central America and one to Egypt, and so left traces of themselves even upon this earth when their own land went down into the Atlantic. As to these, their descendants, we judged that they had probably degenerated, as was natural, and that at the most they had been stagnant and only preserved some of the science and knowledge of their ancestors without having the energy to add to it. They possessed wonderful powers and yet seemed to us to be strangely wanting in initiative, and had added nothing to that wonderful legacy which they had inherited. I am sure that Maracot [the British scientist] using this knowledge would very soon have attained greater results. As to Scanlan [the American], with his quick brain and mechanical skill, he was continually putting in touches which probably seemed as remarkable to them as their powers to us. He had a beloved mouth-organ in his coat-pocket when we made our descent, and his use of this was a perpetual joy to our companions, who sat around in entranced groups, as we might listen to Mozart, while he handed out to them the crooning coon songs of his native land.*

It would be useless to review further the pseudoscience and archaeology that have surrounded the Atlantis phenomenon for years. It would also be wrong to suggest that precisely the same imaginative impulses motivated people like the eighteenth-century English poet and mystic William Blake, for whom the world of Atlantis symbolized a miraculous dream of a prehistoric Eden that gave to ancient Israel and England a common lineage. The motives of some serious artists and scholars were not the motives of the occultists who waged verbal wars of the imagination replete with mysterious documentation and supernatural revelation as to the Atlanteans' height (as much as 27 feet), living habits (vegetarian), social organization (monarchical), and methods of transportation (levitating aircraft).

There were some aspects of the Atlantis phenomenon that pointed beyond narrow motives to something more general, however. The modern appeal of the myth was at least partly due to its similarity with the psychology of the fairy tale. The

Atlantis myth belongs among the stories that satisfy the desire of the childhood ego to compensate itself imaginatively for its inadequacies and suffering. The popularity of the Atlantis story in the nineteenth century may have been related to the appearance of fairy tales and children's literature in published form for the first time and to the development of popular literature in which the "lost world" theme was exploited. More important, the Atlantis myth satisfied the psychological craving for images of ecstasy, unity, and innocence in nature that characterized nineteenth-century Romanticism.

Like Mary Wollstonecraft Shelley's *Frankenstein*—a truly Romantic myth created at the beginning of the nineteenth century—Atlantis became a response to the feelings of self-alienation of people living in a world beginning to exalt intellect, science, and technology. Such people yearned for the satisfaction of a "natural self" having little to do with the modern world. The story of Frankenstein, however, is a myth in which a fundamental conflict is not fantasized away but symbolically explored and suffered in the love-hate relationship of master and creature. Atlantis, on the other hand, fantasized escape from conflict, and this was the secret of its appeal to the nineteenth century. It was unattractive escape, as the racist and nationalist tone of Doyle shows. Atlantis was not a myth that required man to accept loss or suffering in order to overcome the conflicts that preoccupied him in both his cultural milieu and his personal life. It was simply a place where such conflicts—whatever they might be—were wished away.

The meaning of the Atlantis myth around the start of the twentieth century was related to the collapse of the religious and rationalistic framework provided for man in previous centuries. Atlantis spoke to the crisis of human identity that followed. Atlantis, like Genesis, portrayed man as "fallen," although, like a typical fairy tale, the myth ignored the complication of guilt. It is difficult to think of a myth more useful to the late nineteenth century, confronted as it was with the English naturalist Charles Darwin's grim and radical new view of man.

The Atlantis phenomenon was partially a last-ditch effort to defend the importance and history of man against the implications of evolutionary theory. Although mankind might not be an object of interest to a closely watching God, the Atlantis myth protected human beings from the view that their history was entirely a matter of arbitrary biological development. Atlantis preserved an essential period of mystery in the history of mankind, a possibility for belief in a better, and perhaps divine, ancestral race whose spark remained alive in some of its descendants. It may seem devious, but Atlantis was an effective response to the shocking theory that human beings are simply a higher form of animal life. If the achievements of mankind no longer could be seen as God's selection of certain people to learn His word and imitate His intelligence, the lost world of Atlantis, from which modern culture derived, offered an evolutionary pattern that elevated, rather than degraded, man. Atlantis became a god itself—a fixed and unchangeable origin of power for certain people, an origin to which new access was denied.

A Fundamental Need

It is a long and winding path from Gilgamesh and Eden to the Atlantis myth in its nineteenth-century context. It would be wrong to suggest that the diverse ways in which people use and respond to their mythical images of natural catastrophe can be precisely defined or cataloged. It is as important to understand the diversity of human responses to catastrophes as it is to establish common bonds. Yet there are certain themes that seem to hold these myths, including Atlantis, together. There are recurring mythical motifs that attribute natural catastrophes to magical powers, to moral failure, or to human behavior on the part of natural forces.

Why do catastrophe images—whether in the form of the moral or social scheme of the biblical flood, the Wagnerian drama of Ragnarök, the pseudoscience of Atlantis, or the erupting volcanoes, tidal waves, and surreptitious sharks of contemporary films—have so profound a hold on the human imagination? The answer turns principally on the ability of such images to provide powerful and economical pictures of mankind's place in the order of nature. They provide a way for man to test his image of himself and of his cosmos. They also project man's greatest conflicts between rationality and the irrationality that he both fears and desires; between relevance and irrelevance to a divine order; between the social order that he creates and admires and the natural order that he fears to violate. The manner and depth of human responses to myths may vary greatly, from the genuine religious awe of Eden and Ragnarök, to the defensive rationalizations of Atlantis, to the titillation of the horror movie where disasters must satisfy the adolescent desire to view destruction for its own sake. Yet man's need to understand his place in the universe is always present. For many people scientific explanations of catastrophic events are unlikely ever to satisfy this fundamental need.

Appendix:
Recent Disasters (1938–1977)

Modern man prides himself on his ability to control his environment. Yet, before the elemental forces of nature, he can often do little more than stand in awe, as his primitive ancestors did before him.

The history of the Earth has been punctuated by a series of catastrophic events, and the processes of nature that cause such events continue. Mountains are thrust up, then worn away; canyons are cut deep, then refilled, the sun shines, winds blow, rains fall, oceans rise and fall, and the Earth's crust constantly shifts. All such occurrences are natural, necessary, and even advantageous, but they are also frequently devastating.

Modern man is not—as he sometimes chooses to believe—separated by time or distance from natural phenomena. They are occurring constantly and in all areas of the world. Many take no or few human lives, while others take many. During the past forty years alone more than a thousand catastrophes have been recorded in which ten or more deaths occurred. Chronologically, here is the record:

1938
Jan. 9
Smyrna, Turkey. At least 20 persons drowned in floods of the Gediz and Menderes rivers.

Feb. 9
Rio de Janeiro, Brazil. A violent windstorm with heavy rains contributed to the death of 15 persons.

Feb. 12
California. At least 16 persons were killed and about 2,000 made homeless in the Sacramento–San Joaquin River delta area after 18 days of almost continuous rain and storms.

Feb. 18
Rodessa, Louisiana. A tornado whirled through the town, killing at least 25 persons and causing extensive property damage.

March 2
Los Angeles, California. Floods and landslides in Los Angeles and 100 other communities in southern California caused the death of 95 persons, left nearly 100 others missing and

about 20,000 homeless; property damage was estimated at $60 million.

March 15

Midwestern United States. A series of tornadoes killed 22 persons in Illinois, Missouri, Iowa, Alabama, Georgia, Tennessee, and Arkansas.

March 30

Midwestern United States. A tornado that swept across parts of Arkansas, Oklahoma, Kansas, Missouri, and Illinois killed 36 persons.

April 7

Alabama and Georgia. A tornado and floods that followed caused the death of 27 persons.

April 20–21

Turkey. More than 300 persons were killed and at least 50,-000 made homeless by earthquakes in Central Anatolia in an area reaching from the Black Sea almost to the Mediterranean.

June 10

Clyde, Texas. A tornado killed 13, injured more than 40, and wrecked most of the houses in the village.

June 18

Honan Province, China. Extensive flooding of the Yellow River killed an estimated 2,000 persons and left about 700,-000 homeless.

July 1

Japan. Two days of rainstorms and earthquakes left 197 persons dead and nearly 300,000 houses destroyed or damaged.

July 6

Kobe, Japan. At least 870 persons were drowned or missing as a result of severe flooding.

July 20

Kweichow Province, China. More than 2,000 were killed or injured after several days of floods.

Sept. 1

Tokyo and vicinity. The worst typhoon in Japan since 1905 killed at least 175 persons.

Sept. 1

Portneuf and St. Gregoire, Quebec. Sixteen persons were killed and 38 injured during floods.

Sept. 21

Northeastern United States. A hurricane followed by floods and tidal waves killed almost 700 in several states; Rhode

Island was hardest hit with nearly 300 dead.

Sept. 29

Charleston, South Carolina. Thirty-one were killed and more than 200 injured in a tornado.

Oct. 4–5

British Isles. A severe storm with gale-force winds was responsible for 17 deaths.

Oct. 6

Philippine Islands. A typhoon and subsequent flooding caused the death of 18.

Oct. 21

Tokyo and Yokohama, Japan. A typhoon killed 226 persons, injured about 590, and left more than 35,000 homeless.

Nov. 2

Castries, St. Lucia, British West Indies. More than 200 persons were killed or missing in a series of avalanches.

Nov. 23

Southern England, Seventeen deaths were attributed to a severe storm.

Dec. 8

Philippine Islands. More than 300 persons were killed in a typhoon.

Dec. 17–18

Central Anatolia, Turkey. An undetermined number of persons were killed in an earthquake.

1939

Jan. 24

South central Chile. An earthquake devastated an area of approximately 50,000 square miles; the estimated death toll was close to 30,000, mostly in Concepción and Chillán; razed cities were evacuated by survivors.

March 25

Near Barèges, France. A series of avalanches in the Pyrenees Mountains killed 28 with many others missing and presumed dead.

April 15–16

Texas, Louisiana, Arkansas, Oklahoma. Tornadoes sweeping through these states left at least 40 dead.

June 18

Anoka, Minnesota. A tornado twisted through the community, killing 10 and injuring 63.

June 29

Bulgaria. Widespread flooding in the northern section of the country brought death to approximately 150 persons.

July 5

Northeastern Kentucky. At least 75 persons drowned and many others were reported missing as a result of flash floods in the area.

Aug.–Nov.

China. Floods inundated the northern provinces destroying all crops and most housing; at least 10,000,000 persons were homeless; the death toll from the floods and the famine that followed was estimated at 200,000.

Sept. 22

Smyrna, Turkey. A devastating earthquake brought death to at least 300 persons.

Sept. 24

Southern California coast. Eighteen persons were killed and 57 missing in a tropical storm.

Dec. 4

Masbate Island, Philippines. At least 20 persons were killed by a typhoon that swept the island.

Dec. 27

Northern Turkey. An earthquake demolished wide regions in eastern and northern Anatolia; more than 25,000 persons were killed, and thousands more were injured.

1940

Jan. 2

Kemal Pasha, Turkey. An estimated 5,000 persons drowned and another 1,000 were made homeless by a flood that swept over the region.

Jan. 18

Balcittoy, Turkey. About 50 persons were killed, nearly 160 injured, and more than 200 houses wrecked by an earthquake.

Feb. 10

Albany, Georgia. A tornado swept over the city, killing 17 and destroying property valued at $10 million.

Feb. 21

Turkey. More than 125 persons were killed and hundreds injured by an earthquake that wrecked Soysalli and three other villages in Kayseri Province.

March 12

Shreveport, Louisiana. Thirteen persons were killed, 37 injured, and hundreds made homeless by a tornado that swept over the city.

April 1–2
New York and Pennsylvania. Floods caused the death of 17 persons, made thousands homeless, and washed away many bridges.

April 30
Midwestern and southern United States. A series of tornadoes brought death to 9 persons and wrecked hundreds of buildings.

May 24
Peru. An earthquake that struck Callao, Lima, Chorrillos, and other cities killed approximately 350, injured at least 1,500, and caused widespread damage.

June 30
Southern Texas. Following heavy rainstorms, the Lavaca, Colorado, and Guadalupe rivers flooded many towns including Hallettsville and Cuero; at least 10 persons were drowned, and property damage caused by the floods was estimated at $5 million.

July 12.
Seoul, Korea. Fifty-two persons were killed, about 100 injured, and thousands made homeless by a typhoon.

The waterfront buildings of Beaufort, South Carolina, show the damage caused by a hurricane that struck the area on August 11.

July 13

Miyake-shima, Japan. More than 20 persons were killed by the eruption of the volcanic Mount Yuzan; many others were reported missing and presumed dead.

July 25

Chile. Storms in the northern provinces brought death to approximately 100 persons.

July 30

Anatolia, Turkey. More than 1,000 persons were killed by an earthquake.

Aug. 7

Texas and Louisiana. A hurricane swept inland over the Sabine River region, flooding towns and drowning 19 persons.

Aug. 11

Eastern United States. A hurricane swept from Savannah, Georgia, to Georgetown, South Carolina, flooding coastal islands and cities and killing at least 16 persons.

Sept. 30

Taiwan. A typhoon that struck the southern coast killed at least 50 persons, destroyed about 5,000 homes, and seriously damaged crops.

Oct. 18

Barcelona and Gerona, Spain. At least 182 persons were drowned by floods in these provinces.

Oct. 20

France. Widespread flooding in the southwestern region of the country caused the death of about 100 persons.

Oct. 26

Nicaragua. Fifteen or more persons were killed by a hurricane that swept over the Prinzapolca district.

Nov. 10

Romania. At least 400 persons were killed and another 800 injured by an earthquake that centered in Foscani.

Nov. 11

United States. A blizzard descending from Canada, accompanied by tornadolike winds and low temperatures, swept over the middlewestern and Rocky Mountain states and as far south as Louisiana, killing more than 100.

Nov. 18

Jamaica. At least 130 persons were drowned in a cloudburst in two provinces.

Dec. 7

Philippines. Eighty-one deaths were attributed to a typhoon that swept southeast of Manila.

Dec. 26
Bejucal, Cuba. About 40 persons were killed and more than 150 injured by a tornado accompanied by heavy rains.

1941

Feb. 16–18
Spain and Portugal. A violent hurricane lashed ports along the Bay of Biscay and Atlantic coast, killing 145 persons and starting a fire in Santander that left nearly 30,000 homeless.

March 1
Northern Greece. An earhquake rocked the town of Larissa, leaving thousands homeless and killing at least 25 persons.

March 15–16
Midwestern United States. Approximately 150 deaths were caused by severe storms in Minnesota and South Dakota.

April 15
Colima, Mexico. An earthquake followed by a seismic wave and eruption of Colima volcano brought death to 174 persons, injured about 175, and caused heavy damage.

May 21
Cape Girardeau, Missouri. A tornado swept through the city, killing 23 persons.

Mexico City and other cities such as Colima suffered heavy damage in an earthquake on April 15.

May 25
Ganges delta, India. An estimated 5,000 persons were drowned in a storm that struck a number of villages in the Barisal district.

July 22
Ashikaga, Shizuoka Prefecture, Japan. A typhoon following a week of heavy rains caused the death of 35 persons and left about 26,000 homeless.

Sept. 12
Agri, Turkey. An earthquake devastated the area, killing as many as 200 persons.

Sept. 29
Tegucigalpa, Honduras. A hurricane devastated the city and surrounding areas, killing as many as 100 persons and leaving thousands homeless.

Oct. 1
Kyushu and Honshu, Japan. At least 100 persons were killed in a typhoon that hit the two islands.

Oct. 26
Arkansas. Two tornadoes, six hours apart, killed 17 persons and injured many more.

Dec. 13
Huarás, Peru. A landslide wiped out the entire residential section of the city, killing more than 500 persons.

Dec. 17
Taiwan. The southern part of the island was demolished by an earthquake; about 300 persons were killed, and more than 400 were injured.

1942

Jan. 6
Rio de Janeiro, Brazil. Twenty-eight were killed and many others injured in a cloudburst over the city.

Feb. 1
Urubamba, Peru. Flooding from the Rímac River left at least 1,500 persons homeless and caused more than 100 deaths.

Feb. 5–6
Southern United States. A series of tornadoes hit six southern states, killing 23 persons.

March 15–16
Midwestern and southern United States. At least 136 persons were killed in a tornado that swept through the states of Mississippi, Alabama, Tennessee, Kentucky, Indiana, and Illinois.

April 27

Pryor, Oklahoma. A tornado brought death to nearly 100 persons, injured between 150 and 300, and caused damage estimated at $1 million.

May 13

Western Ecuador. About 200 persons were killed and more than $2.5 million in property damaged when a severe earthquake rocked several provinces.

May 23

Eastern Pennsylvania. Floodwaters caused by torrential rains took a toll of at least 30 lives and caused property damage estimated at several million dollars.

June 12

Oklahoma City, Oklahoma. Two tornadoes caused the death of 29 persons and injured 25 others.

July 15

Taiwan. More than 200 persons were drowned in a tidal wave that smashed the island.

Sept. 28

Shensi Province, China. As many as 3,000 deaths were attributed to flooding along the Yellow River; additional thousands were left homeless.

Oct. 16

Bombay, India. A cyclone rising from the Bay of Bengal swept inland, devastating a vast area in two Bengal districts and killing an estimated 40,000 persons.

Oct. 29

Berryville, Arkansas. At least 28 were killed and more than 200 others injured in a tornado.

Nov. 14

India. A cyclone and accompanying rains brought death to an estimated 650 persons near Calcutta.

Nov. 28

Kyushu, Japan. A tidal wave that hit the island killed about 60 persons and left thousands homeless.

Dec. 1

El Cobre, Venezuela, More than 30 persons were killed by a flash flood.

Dec. 19

Anatolia, Turkey. A severe earthquake killed 474 persons and injured 605.

Dec. 22

Aliquippa, Pennsylvania. An avalanche buried a bus loaded with workers, killing 22 of them.

1943

Jan. 25

Guacarí, Colombia. Twelve persons were killed when floods destroyed part of the town, sweeping away buildings and inundating fields in the Cauca valley about 15 miles northeast of Cali.

March 2

Yuramal, Colombia. River water flooded the nearby Sebastopol mines, killing 12 persons.

March 24

Boyacá Province, Colombia. Ten persons died in a flash flood that inundated many buildings and caused heavy damage to property.

April 6

Ovalle, Chile. An earthquake rocked nearly 2,000 miles of the country's coast and killed 11 persons in the northern provinces, primarily in the area near the town of Ovalle, located on the Limari River.

June 21

Turkey. A devastating earthquake hit several small towns east of Istanbul, killing more than 1,300 persons.

Aug. 4

Rajputana, India. As many as 10,000 persons were reported drowned or missing when the Khari River flooded the area.

Aug. 5

West Virginia. A flash flood in the central part of the state claimed 21 lives.

Sept. 10

Tottori, Japan. An estimated 1,400 persons were killed by an earthquake that demolished the city.

Oct. 9

Mexico. More than 50 persons were killed by a hurricane that struck the Pacific coast; at least 100 were injured.

Nov. 26

Ankara, Turkey. As many as 1,800 persons were killed and nearly 2,000 others injured in a series of earthquakes that rocked northern Turkey.

Dec. 14

Sinaloa State, Mexico. At least 30 deaths were attributed to widespread flooding.

1944

Jan. 15

San Juan, Argentina. A severe earthquake rocked the Andes

Mountain Province in west central Argentina causing heavy damage in San Juan and neighboring villages; about 900 people were killed, and nearly 70,000 left homeless.

Feb. 1

Ankara, Turkey. A devastating earthquake centering in Gerede brought death to an estimated 1,400 persons.

March 21

San Sebastiano, Italy. The town was engulfed by a stream of molten lava flowing down the sides of erupting Mount Vesuvius; at least 100 persons were killed.

April 9

Buenos Aires, Argentina. Heavy rains caused flooding that killed about 60 persons.

April 16

Southeastern Georgia and western South Carolina. At least 38 persons were killed and more than 500 others injured by a tornado that swept through the two-state area.

June 10

Parícutin, Mexico. An eruption of Parícutin volcano buried two villages and killed at least 3,500 persons.

Following a tornado on April 16 that killed 11 persons in Royston, Georgia, alone, survivors in the community examine the damage left by the storm.

June 23

Eastern United States. A tornado sweeping through parts of Pennsylvania, West Virginia, and Maryland killed at least 145 persons, injured hundreds of others, and impaired communication facilities.

Sept. 10

Mexico. At least 50 deaths were attributed to floods throughout the country.

Sept. 14

East coast, United States. A hurricane ripped along 1,500 miles of the Atlantic coast between the Carolinas and Canada, killing at least 27 persons, injuring many more, and causing property damage estimated at $50 million.

Oct. 20

U.S. South Atlantic coast and Cuba. A hurricane swept through Cuba and up to the Carolinas coast, bringing death to at least 35 persons and causing heavy property damage.

Dec. 17–18

Near the Philippines. Several American ships east of Luzon were caught in a typhoon that claimed as many as 750 lives.

1945

Jan. 29

Chavin, Peru. Heavy rains caused the collapse of a dike near the city; at least 150 deaths were attributed to the flooding.

Feb. 8–9

New England. At least 20 deaths were attributed to a severe blizzard that piled up huge drifts in most of New England; property damage was extensive.

Feb. 12

Mississippi-Alabama. At least 43 persons were killed and hundreds injured by a tornado that swept across parts of the two states; property damage was extensive.

March 7

Cincinnati, Ohio. The Ohio River rose above flood stage and floodwaters of other midwestern rivers spread into Ohio, Pennsylvania, West Virginia, Kentucky, and Indiana, causing heavy damage and taking a toll of more than 10 lives.

March 28

Petrópolis, Brazil. A flash flood claimed the lives of at least 30 persons.

April 12

Oklahoma-Arkansas-Missouri area. A tornado slashing through the tristate region caused more than 100 deaths and substantial property damage.

Oct. 9

Okinawa. Forty-three persons were killed, 30 were listed as missing, and 49 were injured in a typhoon that swept the island.

Oct. 19

Media Luna, Cuba. About 20 persons were killed in a flood that also ruined crops.

Nov. 30

Northeastern United States. A raging storm accompanied by heavy gales and snow caused the death of at least 34 people and inflicted heavy property damage in New England, New York State, and New Jersey.

Nov. 30

Pasni, India. More than 400 deaths were attributed to an earthquake and tidal wave.

Dec. 24–25

North and South Carolina. Approximately 25 deaths were attributed to a two-day ice storm.

1946

Jan. 4

Eastern Texas. Thirty-three persons were killed by a tornado that struck Nacogdoches and nearby areas.

Feb. 13

Constantine Department, Algeria. At least 276 persons were killed in earthquakes that hit the Setif and Batna regions.

April 1

Alaska-Hawaii area of Pacific Ocean. A series of tidal waves that started off Alaska and the Aleutian Islands spread to the Hawaiian Islands, causing about 150 deaths and leaving 5,000 homeless in Hawaii alone; damage was estimated at several million dollars.

April 18

Betania, Colombia. At least 20 persons were killed by a landslide.

May 12

Turkey. Widespread flooding devastated several villages and killed an estimated 2,000 persons.

May 28

Susquehanna River Valley, New York-Pennsylvania. A Susquehanna River flood, aggravated by heavy rains, caused widespread damage; 12 persons were killed, and several others were missing and presumed dead.

May 31

Mus and Erzurum provinces, Turkey. At least 1,330 persons were killed in an earthquake in eastern Turkey that leveled many villages.

June 17

Detroit-Windsor. Fourteen persons were killed and many others injured by a tornado that swept the U.S.-Canada border area.

June 29

Southern Korea. Heavy rains left as many as 2,000 homeless and caused at least 40 deaths.

Aug. 4–10

West Indies. A violent earthquake accompanied by a seismic wave on August 4 in the northern provinces of the Dominican Republic brought death to at least 73 persons; minor tremors were felt in Puerto Rico, Haiti, and Cuba.

Oct. 9

Off Portugal. A hurricane that swept over Madeira and the Azores resulted in the death of 27 persons.

Oct. 22

Northern Italy. At least 20 deaths were attributed to severe storms over a wide area.

Oct. 27

Sardinia, Italy. A raging storm caused more than 40 deaths.

Nov. 3

India. Between 300 and 400 persons were killed in earthquakes that struck Muzaffarpur in Bihar Province.

Nov. 12

Philippines. A typhoon that struck Negros Island killed about 260 persons.

Nov. 13

Northern Peru. More than 500 persons were killed in a series of earthquakes over a 72-hour period in the Andes Mountain area; the first quake had occurred on November 10.

Nov. 15

Colorado. At least 18 persons died in a two week-long period of snowstorms that paralyzed communications over a large area of the state.

Dec. 21

Southern Japan. A severe earthquake that started six seismic waves devasted an extensive area of Honshu Island; official figures indicated 1,088 persons dead, 165 missing, 142 injured, and 94,669 left homeless; 21,846 houses were ruined or damaged.

Residents of Wakayama, Japan, leave their village after an earthquake and seismic wave on December 21 destroyed or damaged nearly all of the homes.

1947

Jan. 12
Cerro Negro, Nicaragua. An eruption of the Nicaraguan volcano devastated an extensive area and killed scores of people.

Jan. 30
Southern United States. At least 20 persons were killed by a tornado that swept through Georgia, Alabama, Arkansas, Tennessee, and Missouri.

Jan. 30–Feb. 8
Germany. At least 250 deaths were attributed to a 10-day cold wave.

April 9
Western Texas and Oklahoma. A tornado whipping through southwestern U.S. communities killed 167 persons and injured 1,305; 70 percent of the town of Woodward, Oklahoma, was destroyed.

April 29
Worth, Missouri. A freak windstorm razed every building on the city's main street, killed 16 persons, and injured 25 others.

June 1
Pine Bluff, Arkansas. A tornado sweeping through rural communities in the region killed 35 persons, injured scores more, and caused heavy property damage.

June 22
Cambridge, Nebraska. Sixteen persons were killed in a flash flood that inundated the city at dawn.

July 5
St. Louis, Missouri. Floods in the Missouri and upper Mississippi valleys brought death to 16 persons, left 34,812 others homeless, and caused damage totaling at least $850 million.

Sept. 17–19
Gulf of Mexico. A violent hurricane that cut through southern Florida and struck Louisiana and Mississippi caused widespread property damage; casualties were put at 84 dead or missing.

Sept. 20
Honshu Island, Japan. Five-day floods borne in the wake of a typhoon caused widespread damage in Kanro and Tohoku districts; final casualty figures were 999 persons killed, 984 missing, and 1,616 injured.

Sept. 21
New Orleans area, Louisiana. Floodwaters coming in the wake of a hurricane inundated vast areas, caused heavy crop damage, and resulted in a casualty toll of 55 dead with many others listed as missing.

Oct. 5
Eastern India. A disastrous flood in eastern Bengal destroyed about 100,000 tons of rice and thousands of cattle; about one million persons were left homeless.

Oct. 7
Hong Kong. An estimated 2,000 persons were drowned in a typhoon that destroyed a fishing fleet off the coast.

Nov. 2
Andes Mountain region, Chile. An earthquake that struck east of Lima killed 233 persons and caused extensive property damage.

Dec. 2
Near Portuguese coast. A hurricane killed at least 160 persons at sea.

Dec. 26
New York City and north Atlantic states. The greatest snowfall in recorded history blanketed the city under 26.8 inches of snow; 55 deaths were attributed to the storm.

1948

Jan. 15

Europe. Gales and floods from France to Hungary accounted for the deaths of 12 persons and caused the evacuation of thousands from along the rivers.

Jan. 24–31

Southern United States. Thirty-eight deaths were attributed to an ice storm that hit Arkansas, Mississippi, and South Carolina.

Jan. 25–27

Panay Island, Philippines. At least 27 persons died in a series of earthquakes.

Jan. 26

Réunion Island. At least 300 persons were killed and tens of thousands on this Indian Ocean island were left homeless by a hurricane that also destroyed many crops.

Feb. 17

Southern Turkey. Hundreds of persons were drowned when the Seyhan and Ceyhan rivers burst their dikes.

March 19

Area from Texas to New York. Forty-two persons died and more than 300 were injured in tornadoes ranging over this wide area; at least 25 died in the communities of Bunker Hill and Fosterburg, Illinois.

March 26

Midwestern and southern United States. Storms in eight states killed a total of 23 persons, 11 of them in Indiana.

May 30

Vanport City, Oregon. As a climax to floods that caused the deaths of at least 40 persons in Washington and Oregon, a Columbia River dike gave way, flooding a housing development; thousands were left temporarily homeless, although only 15 persons were known to have lost their lives.

May 30

Iyang district, southwest of Hankow, China. A reported 330 persons were drowned in floods of the Yangtze River.

June 6

Amasyz, Turkey. Floodwaters destroyed many homes, leaving 92 dead and about 40 missing.

June 7

Tungting Lake area, China. A typhoon killed nearly 200 persons, injured about 100, and caused vast damage to rice fields.

June 29

Foochow, China. Approximately 1,000 persons were drowned and nearly 200,000 made homeless by a three-day flood.

July 1

Fukui, Japan. At least 3,200 persons died and 7,500 were injured in a series of earthquakes that began June 28; the fires that followed damaged great sections of the city.

Aug. 7

China. Official estimates were that 3,000,000 persons were homeless and 1,000 dead as a result of floods in the Yangtze and Yellow river valleys and in southern China.

Sept. 5–6

Northwestern Italy. Storms and floods brought death to about 80 persons and caused extensive property damage.

Sept. 16–17

Tokyo, Japan. A typhoon left 541 persons dead, at least 200 injured, more than 600 missing, and damage estimated at $55 million.

After a series of earthquakes that struck the Fukui area of Japan ended on July 1, residents of the northern town of Kanozu evacuate their homes.

Sept. 18
Assam, India. An estimated 500 persons were killed by a landslide.

Sept. 20
Havana, Cuba. Ten persons were killed in Havana and Matanzas provinces by a hurricane; damage was estimated at more than $3 million.

Sept. 27
Leichow, China. More than 100 fishing boats sank during a typhoon, killing an estimated 800 persons.

Oct. 2
Hainan Island, China. A typhoon swept the island, killing at least 30 persons and causing $6 million damage.

Oct. 4
Kagi, Formosa. At least 1,200 persons were killed and about 2,000 injured by an earthquake; an estimated 6,000 homes were destroyed.

Oct. 5
Ashkhabad, Iran. An earthquake demolished the city, killed about 600 persons, and injured as many as 6,000.

Oct. 5
Cuba. A hurricane caused 11 deaths and damage estimated at more than $10 million.

Oct. 18
Southern Chile. At least 40 and possibly 100 died as a result of the eruption of the Villarrica volcano and the flash floods that followed when mountain snows melted from the heat of the eruption.

Nov. 1
Posillipo, Italy. Twenty-five persons were buried by a landslide that covered a house.

Nov. 17–20
Southwestern United States. Twenty-nine persons died in a blizzard that blanketed parts of Colorado, Kansas, and Nebraska.

Nov. 22
Bombay, India. An estimated 35 persons were killed in a typhoon.

Dec. 16
Rio de Janeiro State, Brazil. About 200 persons died and more than 1,000 were injured or left homeless in floods caused by cloudbursts in the states of Rio de Janeiro and Minas Gerais.

Dec. 19–20
Northwestern United States. Twenty-four deaths were at-

tributed to storms that dumped about 20 inches of snow on the area.

1949

Jan. 3
Louisiana and Arkansas. Fifty-nine persons were killed and more than 250 injured as tornadoes lashed a dozen communities; 54 of the fatalities occurred in Warren, Arkansas.

Feb. 15
Sondondo, India. At least 70 persons were killed in a landslide that buried as many as 200 houses.

March 1
Germany. At least 30 persons died as the result of gales that struck Germany near Essen and Düsseldorf.

March 24–26
Midwestern United States. Tornadoes left 28 persons dead in Oklahoma, Texas, Tennessee, Kentucky, Mississippi, and Arkansas.

April 7
Telkief, Iraq. About 50 persons were killed in floods precipitated by a sudden cloudburst.

April 20
Central Chile. Fifty-seven persons were reported killed and 89 injured when an earthquake that caused damage estimated at several million dollars shook several cities.

May 20
Maceió and vicinity, Brazil. More than 100 persons died and at least 200 were injured as the result of a 60-hour torrential rain.

June 20
Kyushu, Japan. Hundreds were killed in a typhoon that swept through the city.

June 25
Pachuca, Mexico. A flash flood inundated the area and brought death to about 45 persons.

July 17
Yangtze and Yellow river valleys, China. The worst floods in half a century, aggravated by incessant rain, were reported to have left 20,000,000 persons homeless; in Hunan Province alone, at least 57,000 persons were reported drowned, and 5,000,000 homeless; 5,000,000 acres of rice fields were destroyed.

July 23
Okinawa. Thirty-eight persons died and 252 were injured

while at least 40,000 buildings were damaged or destroyed by a typhoon; 55 fishing craft were sunk and most of the U.S. installations of the island were damaged.

Aug. 5–7

Central Ecuador. An earthquake that virtually demolished four towns and destroyed sections of many others killed more than 8,000 persons and left an estimated 100,000 homeless; property damage was at least $86 million.

Aug. 7

China. A death toll of 1,000 persons was reported following a typhoon.

Aug. 18

Erzurum, Anatolia, Turkey. Forty-five villages were devastated, nearly 6,000 persons left homeless, 437 were killed, and 355 injured as the result of an earthquake.

Sept. 1

Japan. A typhoon followed by landslides and floods killed 123 persons, left 51 missing, 419 injured, and approximately 150,000 homeless.

Oct. 8

Oberschlema, Thuringia, Germany. At least 100 miners were reported killed in a flood in a mine.

Oct. 13–14

Guatemala. Torrential rains followed by floods that did $23 million worth of damage to crops caused an estimated death toll of 4,000 persons.

Oct. 27

Southeastern India. As many as 1,000 persons were killed in a cyclone that also caused extensive property damage.

Oct. 31–Nov. 2

Philippine Islands. The central Philippines' worst typhoon in 12 years left a total of 975 persons dead or missing, at least 20,000 homeless, and property damage calculated at $25 million.

Nov. 17

Goa, India. A landslide buried much of the village, killing more than 30 persons.

Nov. 22

Cyprus. The worst flood in 20 years hit the island, killing 20 persons.

Nov. 28

Northwestern United States and southwestern Canada. Storms that swept across a thousand-mile front left 34 persons dead.

Dec. 8

Korea. A devastating typhoon hit the eastern coastal area, killing a reported total of 1,000 persons.

1950

Jan. 15

Pacific northwest, United States. Violent storms were responsible for at least 30 deaths in the United States and 4 in Canada.

Feb. 11–12

Louisiana, Texas, Arkansas. Tornadoes killed 38 persons, injured about 200 others, and caused extensive property damage.

April 2–7

Southern Ecuador. Floods of the Tomebamba River left at least 50 persons dead or missing and caused property damage estimated at $1.5 million.

May 21

Cuzco, Peru. At least 83 persons died and more than 200 were injured, while an estimated 30,000 were rendered homeless, when the 900-year-old city was rocked by an earthquake.

June 1

Khorassan Province, Iran. Thirty-six persons were drowned and 16 others were reported missing in floods that washed away 932 houses in an area around Meshed, the provincial capital.

June 9–11

Near Tokyo, Japan. Floods and landslides caused widespread damage with 30 known dead and 20 injured among 70 railway workers buried in one slide; hundreds of houses were swept away by high waters.

June 10–16

Darjeeling area, India. Heavy rains caused floods and landslides that resulted in the death of more than 100 persons.

June 25

North central West Virginia. Flash floods sent streams over an area nearly 100 miles wide roaring out of their beds, leaving 33 known dead and property damage of several million dollars.

July 9–11

Northeastern Colombia. An estimated 150 persons died in a series of violent earthquakes that wrecked numerous mountain villages.

Aug. 3

El Tocuyo, Venezuela. Severe earth tremors virtually demolished the community of 7,000, causing nearly 100 deaths.

Aug. 6

Eastern Japan. At least 40 persons were missing in severe floods in Ibanki Prefecture; 19 were killed, 58 were missing, and 196 were injured in all of eastern Japan.

Aug. 14

Anhwei Province, China. Nearly 10,000,000 persons were reported affected by floods of the Hwai River that killed 489 persons, damaged or destroyed at least 890,000 houses, and ruined crops on 3,700,000 acres.

Aug. 15–27

Assam Province, India. A severe earthquake, followed by lesser tremors and floods, devastated large areas of northeastern India; 574 persons were killed, nearly 5,000,000 left homeless; crop and property damage was extensive.

Sept. 4

Japan. The worst typhoon in almost 20 years swept Japan's four home islands, leaving nearly 250 persons dead, 236 missing, 5,648 injured, and tens of thousands homeless.

Sept. 15

Camiguin Island, Philippines. A sudden eruption of the volcano Hibok Hibok left 84 persons dead of burns or suffocation from hot ashes and gases.

Sept. 20

Punjab, India. As many as 200 persons were killed in floods that inundated the northern part of the state.

Oct. 21

Santa River, Peru. About 30 persons were killed, at least 100 were unaccounted for, and 28 were injured in a landslide of mud and water that resulted when the Pisococha lagoon collapsed.

Nov. 25–28

Northeastern United States. Snowstorms that blanketed the area caused damage estimated at about $400 million and resulted in the deaths of 295 persons; Canadian damage was estimated at $3 million and deaths at 10.

1951

Jan. 3

Morocco. Floods that swept the Rharb plain area of Morocco left 71 persons known dead and nearly 60 missing and presumed dead.

Jan. 4

Comoro Island, between Madagascar and Africa. A two-day tornado left an estimated total of 500 persons dead.

Jan. 4

Peru. A construction project in the Andes Mountains triggered a landslide that killed at least 130 persons.

Jan. 18–21

Mount Lamington, New Guinea. As many as 4,000 persons were reported killed when the volcanic mountain erupted in a series of explosions that destroyed 20 villages.

Jan. 19–24

The Alps of Switzerland, Italy, Austria, and France. Avalanches precipitated by record snowfalls killed about 300 persons during this period.

May 6–7

El Salvador. Earthquakes killed at least 375 and left as many as 25,000 homeless; the greatest losses occurred in the cities of Jucuapa and Chinameca.

May 12

Faridpur District, East Pakistan. More than 200 persons were reported killed or injured in a tornado.

May 19

Taiwan. Flash floods over most of the island claimed an estimated total of 300 lives.

July 1

Kyushu, Japan. At least 13 persons were killed and widespread property damage was inflicted by a typhoon that struck Japan's southernmost island.

July 12–14

Western Japan. Floods caused the deaths of nearly 100 persons, while leaving more than 200 persons injured and 200 missing.

July 11–25

Kansas, Oklahoma, Missouri, and Illinois. The Missouri River and its tributaries, swollen by unseasonable rains, roared through a succession of cities; about 1,000,000 acres of farmland were covered with muck and debris, nearly 200,-000 persons fled their homes, and as many as 40 persons lost their lives.

Aug. 3

Potosi, Nicaragua. Earthquakes split the sides of a dormant volcano, sending water from its crater down to inundate this coastal port, which was reported virtually destroyed with heavy casualties among its population of 1,000.

Aug. 1–22

Central Texas. At least 44 persons died in a prolonged heat wave that also caused heavy damage to crops.

Aug. 13

Changra, Turkey. Earthquakes that centered in northern Turkey caused 54 deaths and injuries to at least 150 persons.

Aug. 15–25

Caribbean and Gulf of Mexico areas. A prolonged hurricane swept from Jamaica across the Yucatán Peninsula and into Tampico, Mexico, killing an estimated 260 persons and injuring scores more; damage was estimated at nearly $1 billion; among the deaths in Mexico were many caused by floods from storm-swollen rivers, including 42 persons who were drowned when a dam crumbled at Cardenas.

Aug. 20

Manchuria. Floods were reported to have killed as many as 1,800 persons, with 3,000 others reported missing and feared dead.

Sept. 26–27

Pescadores Islands and Taiwan. More than 100 persons died in a typhoon.

Sept. 26

Wisconsin, Illinois, and Michigan. Storms and tornadoes killed 12 persons.

Oct. 4

Southern Japan. After a typhoon, 448 persons were reported dead.

Oct. 21

Calabria Province, Italy. Week-long storms virtually wrecked the province; 109 deaths were attributed to the storms, and thousands were left homeless.

Oct. 22–23

Taiwan. As many as 45 persons were killed and scores injured in a series of earthquakes that shook the island.

Nov. 14

Iran. Floods near the Caspian Sea demolished the village of Roodsar, leaving about 225 dead or missing.

Nov. 1–20

Po River Valley, Italy. Three weeks of storms and floods left an estimated total of 150 persons dead and about 150,000 homeless.

Nov. 22

Central Philippines. At least 60 persons were killed in a typhoon.

Dec. 4–13

Camiguin Island, Philippines. Repeated eruptions of the volcano Hibok Hibok killed at least 248 persons and left about 500 missing and caused destruction that left as many as 20,000 homeless.

Dec. 10–13

Central Philippines. Reports indicated that as many as 724 persons were killed during typhoons that swept through the area.

Dec. 25

Epi Island, New Hebrides. A hurricane killed nearly 100 persons.

1952

Jan. 3

Eastern Turkey. Sixty-two persons were killed and as many as 250 injured in an earthquake.

Jan. 12–19

California and Nevada. Snowstorms and floods killed more than 20 persons; a train with more than 200 aboard was snowbound in the Donner Pass, Sierra Nevadas, for three days.

Jan. 22–23

Minnesota, North Dakota, South Dakota. More than 20 persons died in blizzards.

Feb. 11–13

Melkoede, Austria. Seventy-eight persons were killed during a three-day series of avalanches.

Feb. 18–19

New England. As many as 50 deaths were attributed to severe snowstorms.

March 4

Hokkaido Island, Japan. An earthquake followed by tidal waves killed approximately 30 and injured nearly 200 persons.

March 21–22

Southern United States. Tornadoes killed almost 250 and injured an estimated 2,500 in Missouri, Arkansas, Tennessee, Kentucky, Mississippi, and Alabama; more than 45 were killed in Judsonia, Arkansas, which was almost completely razed.

March 24

Java, Indonesia. A landslide near the city of Lebang killed 28 persons.

Judsonia, Arkansas, lies in ruin following a series of tornadoes that struck the southern United States on March 20–21.

April 24

Menton, France. Twelve persons were killed in floods and landslides that destroyed more than 20 houses.

June 24

Japan. At least 65 deaths were attributed to a typhoon.

July 2–3

Philippines. About 85 persons were reported dead and more than 100 missing in typhoons; at least 10,000 were left homeless.

July 6–12

Western Japan. Eighty-four persons were reported killed, 92 missing, and 94 injured in rainstorms and landslides.

July 21

California. An earthquake with its epicenter near Tehachapi, California, killed 12 and injured several hundred persons.

Aug. 16

Lynmouth, England. A flash flood killed 34 persons.

Aug.–Sept.

Southeastern Mexico. Month-long floods left more than 100 dead and caused $25 million damage.

Aug. 31

Philippines. Two days of rain left at least 70 persons dead in Zamboanga Province.

Sept. 6

Near Chamba, Himachal Pradesh State, India. A postmonsoon storm in the Himalaya Mountains was reported to have taken the lives of as many as 350 religious pilgrims.

Sept. 21

Tebessa, Algeria. A flash flood caused about 25 deaths.

Oct. 15

Tabasco State, Mexico. More than 40 persons were reported dead in floods that also destroyed $35 million worth of crops.

Oct. 20–22

Indochina. Typhoons and an ocean wave killed more than 500 persons along the coast; about 350 of the casualties were in Panthiet port.

Oct. 21–22

Philippines. A typhoon struck the central Philippines killing more than 400; at least 350 others were reported missing.

Oct. 22

Southern Turkey. An earthquake that shook the region around Adana killed at least 18 persons.

Nov. 14

Southwestern Taiwan. A typhoon killed at least 67 persons,

injured an estimated 530, and inflicted heavy property damage.

Nov. 30

Albertsville, Union of South Africa. A tornado killed an estimated 35 persons and injured more than 400.

Dec. 22

Near Langen, western Austria. An avalanche hurled a bus into the river and killed 28 passengers.

Dec. 30

Near San José, Costa Rica. Twenty-one persons were reported killed by an earthquake.

1953

Jan. 8–11

New England, New York, and New Jersey. Thirty deaths were attributed to heavy storms that also caused extensive property damage.

Jan. 31–Feb. 5

United Kingdom and Low Countries. North Sea storms and tides flooded lowlands of the Netherlands and Belgium and battered coasts of Great Britain, France, and Germany. The greatest toll was in the Netherlands where 1,794 persons died, many were missing, and as many as 100,000 were left homeless.

Feb. 9

North Sumatra, Indonesia. Eighty-two persons were reported drowned and 32 missing in floods.

Feb. 12

Turud, Iran. An earthquake caused 531 deaths in Turud and 25 additional in neighboring villages.

March 12

Jaramijo, Ecuador. The flooding Bravo River left 26 persons dead, 45 reported missing, and hundreds homeless.

March 13

Texas and Oklahoma. Tornadoes caused at least 16 deaths and extensive property damage.

March 18

Canakkale and Balikesir provinces, Turkey. An earthquake caused an estimated death toll of at least 1,000.

April 18–19

Arkansas, Alabama, Georgia. Tornadoes killed at least 10 persons and injured more than 200.

April 30–May 2

Southern United States. A series of tornadoes that struck

from Texas to Georgia killed 41 persons.

May 6

Chile. An earthquake that centered near Chillán killed 20 persons.

May 11

Texas. Tornadoes killed 114 persons and injured 600 in Waco, killed 11 and injured more than 100 in San Angelo, and caused millions of dollars of property damage in the two cities.

May 19–21

Southwestern Louisiana. Floods in the wake of tornadoes caused estimated property damage of $200 million, killed 12 persons, and left more than 25,000 homeless.

May 20–21

Colombia. Floods and storms caused 18 deaths and left 2,000 families homeless.

June 5–8

Southern and Western Japan. A typhoon followed by floods killed 29 persons, injured about 40, and caused damage estimated at $20 million.

June 8

Michigan and Ohio. Tornadoes killed 17 persons in Ohio, left 116 known dead and approximately 850 injured in the Flint, Michigan, area, and caused extensive property damage in the two sections.

June 9

Central Massachusetts. A tornado struck Worcester and neighboring towns, killing 97 persons and injuring approximately 1,250; property damage from the storm was estimated at $52 million.

June 22

Near Hyderabad, India. An estimated total of 80 persons were reported drowned as a result of floods on the Sabari River.

June 25–30

Kyushu Island, Japan. A flood caused by torrential rains left as many as 700 persons dead, about 2,000 injured, at least 1,000,000 homeless, and many missing.

July 7

Chile. A party of 23 hikers were killed by an avalanche of snow in the Andes Mountains.

July 19

Honshu, Japan. A flood in the Wakayama Prefecture left a reported 638 persons dead, 386 missing, and 5,709 injured.

Aug. 1

Khurtrudbar, Iran. Flash floods drowned as many as 470 persons.

Aug. 4

Vaz, Iran. Flash floods destroyed the village and drowned at least 265 persons.

Aug. 9–Sept. 3

Ionian Sea islands. A series of earthquakes killed 424 persons and caused an estimated $100 million property damage; hardest hit were the islands of Cephalonia, Zante, and Ithaca.

Aug. 16

Near Kyoto, Honshu, Japan. The rain-swollen Yodo River burst the dam at Taisho, leaving 377 persons dead or missing and about 170 injured.

Aug. 18

Central India. Flood waters of the Godavari River left approximately 1,000,000 persons homeless, hundreds dead or reported missing, and property damage estimated at $100 million.

Aug. 21

South central Chile. Floods left 15 persons dead, 7 missing, and property damage estimated at $20 million.

Aug. 31

Argentina-Chile. A severe snowstorm in the Andes Mountains caused the death of 72 persons.

Sept. 10

Southwestern Cyprus. An earthquake killed about 40 persons and injured more than 100.

Sept. 25

Central Vietnam. A typhoon left an estimated total of 1,000 persons dead and many homeless; hardest hit was the Hue area.

Sept. 25

Southern Japan. A typhoon killed 115 persons, injured 259, and left 288 missing.

Oct. 15

Northern Spain. Floods caused the death of nearly 50 persons and property damage estimated at $20 million.

Oct. 28

Southern Italy. A two-week storm caused floods that killed 62 persons.

Dec. 5

Vicksburg, Mississippi. A tornado killed 38 persons, injured 230, and caused property damage estimated at $25 million.

1954

Jan. 3–9
Southern Europe. Fifty-eight deaths were attributed to snowstorms throughout Europe; Baltic Sea floods caused the death of at least 20 persons in East Germany.

Jan. 12
Austria, Switzerland, West Germany. Avalanches in the Alps Mountains caused extensive damage and left 198 persons dead or missing; hardest hit was the Blons, Austria, area.

Jan. 18
Near Jokjakarta, Java. An eruption of Mount Merapi brought death to 37 persons and injured 79.

Feb. 27
Manchil, Kashmir. At least 30 persons were reported killed in an avalanche.

April 16
Western Austria. Thirteen tourists froze to death during a snowstorm on Dachstein Mountain.

April 30
Central Greece. An earthquake caused the deaths of 31 persons, injured nearly 200, and caused damage estimated at $10 million.

June 27–July 1
Texas-Mexico. Floods along the Rio Grande River left a death toll estimated at between 62 and 100 persons; hardest hit was the Piedras Negras, Mexico, area.

July 8–12
Central Europe. Danube River floods killed 36 persons in Austria, Hungary, Czechoslovakia, and Germany; property damage was estimated at nearly $100 million.

July 12
Near Medellín, Colombia. Landslides in the Andes Mountains killed at least 140 persons.

July 26
Southeastern Tibet. Week-long floods reportedly killed between 300 and 1,000 persons.

July 28
Taegu, South Korea. Floodwaters undermined an ancient stone wall that collapsed, killing 14 persons and injuring 64.

July 28–31
Kazvin District, Iran. Nearly 150 persons were killed and another 100 missing in floods caused by torrential rains.

Aug. 1
Central China. The heaviest rainfall in 100 years brought

disastrous floods along the Yangtze and Hwai rivers; 40,000 persons were reported drowned.

Aug. 1

Terai, Nepal, area. An estimated total of 60 persons died as a result of floods.

Aug. 17

Farahzad, Iran. A flash flood in a gorge killed nearly 2,000 religious pilgrims at a Moslem shrine.

Aug. 17–18

Kyushu and Shikoku islands, Japan. A typhoon that struck the islands killed 46 persons.

Aug. 21

Dacca, East Pakistan. Week-long floods caused the deaths of at least 300 persons.

Sept. 1

New England and Long Island, New York. Hurricane Carol killed 68 persons and caused property damage estimated at $500 million.

Sept. 9

Northern Algeria. An earthquake killed an estimated total of 1,460 persons; hardest hit was the Orléansville area.

Sept. 10–11

North Atlantic coast. Hurricane Edna struck northward from Cape Hatteras, North Carolina, to Nova Scotia, killing at least 22 persons and causing property damage estimated as $50 million; hardest hit was the Maine area.

Sept. 13–14

Kyushu Island, Japan. A typhoon left nearly 80 persons dead.

Sept. 19

Japan. A typhoon killed 27 persons and caused property damage estimated at more than $10 million.

Sept. 23

Lahore, Pakistan. Flash floods killed 46 persons and injured about 150.

Sept. 26

Hakodate Bay, Japan. A typhoon resulted in the death of as many as 1,600 persons; the Japanese ferryboat "Doya Maru" ran aground and turned over in the Sea of Japan.

Oct. 11

Chicago, Illinois, area. An unusually severe rainstorm caused the deaths of 19 persons and property damage estimated at $50 million.

Oct. 12–16

Southwest Haiti, U.S. Atlantic coast, southern Canada. Hurricane Hazel struck Haiti where at least 410 and as many as 1,000 persons were killed, nearly 5,000 injured, and property damage was severe; a landslide destroyed the town of Berly killing about 260 persons; following a clockwise course it caused 99 deaths in the United States and then veered northeastward into Canada where estimates of deaths ranged up to 250; property damage in the United States and Canada was estimated in excess of $100 million.

Oct. 26

Near Naples, Italy. Floods and landslides caused the deaths of 272 persons, left 50 others missing; hardest hit were Salerno and surrounding towns.

Nov. 12

Zagora, French Morocco. Floods caused the deaths of about 30 persons.

Nov. 28

Fujiyama, Japan. An avalanche on Mount Fujiyama swept 16 persons to their death.

Dec. 11

Parasia, India. The accidental flooding of a coal mine caused a cave-in that killed 64 miners.

Dec. 23

North Sea. Storms struck England, Germany, Denmark, and the Low Countries, killing 74 persons.

Dec. 28

Near El Carmen, Colombia. A series of landslides killed 47 persons.

1955

Jan. 5

Leyte, Philippines. A storm and subsequent floods killed 51 persons.

Feb. 1

Tunica, Mississippi. Tornadoes touched down in the area, killing 31 persons and injuring at least 100.

Feb. 18

Western United States. Eighteen deaths were attributed to a severe snowstorm.

Feb. 21

Japan. A blizzard killed 18 persons and left about 180 others missing.

Feb. 26

Western New South Wales, Australia. Floods left at least 70 persons dead; hardest hit was the Maitland area.

March 22–23
Western United States. Blizzards, tornadoes, and floods hit Colorado, Idaho, and Montana, killing 47 persons and injuring 200 others.

March 27–28
Eastern United States. Storms and freezing temperatures in the eastern two-thirds of the country caused 41 deaths; crop losses in the South were estimated at $50 million.

April 1
Southern Philippines. There were 432 persons killed and more than 2,000 injured by earthquakes; hardest hit was the Mindanao area.

April 14
Kangting, Sikang, China. Earthquakes killed a reported total of 39 persons and injured 113.

April 16
Sasebo, Japan. At least 73 persons were reported dead in a landslide.

May 25
Santa Catarina, Brazil. A tornado killed 22 persons and left 2 others missing and presumed dead.

May 25–27
Kansas, Oklahoma, Texas, and Missouri. A series of tornadoes caused at least 125 deaths, injured more than 700, and left heavy property damage; hardest hit was Udall, Kansas, where at least 80 were killed.

June 23
Near Patani, Thailand. An ocean wave brought death to approximately 500 persons.

Aug. 17–19
Northeastern United States. Floods and winds caused by Hurricane Diane in Connecticut, Pennsylvania, Massachusetts, New Jersey, Rhode Island, and New York resulted in 191 deaths, 6,992 injuries, and property damage estimated as high as $1.6 billion.

Aug. 30
Kalu, India. A reservoir burst causing floods that killed nearly 180 persons and injured 200 others.

Sept. 12
Near Cairo, Egypt. An earthquake killed approximately 20 persons and injured 28 others.

Sept. 19
Tampico–Vera Cruz, Mexico, area. Hurricane Hilda killed an estimated total of 250 persons and injured nearly 1,000.

In Udall, Kansas, National Guardsmen inspect damage incurred when a series of tornadoes struck several states on May 25–27.

Sept. 23
Caribbean Sea. Hurricane Janet battered the area, killing approximately 150 persons in the Windward Islands, 125–200 on Grenada, and 24 on Barbados.

Sept. 28
Mexico. Hurricane Janet devastated the Yucatán Peninsula; several towns were virtually destroyed, at least 200 persons killed, and more than 100,000 were left homeless.

Oct. 1
Kyushu, Japan, area. Typhoon Louise caused the deaths of 31 persons, injured 241, left 41 missing, and caused property damage estimated at $30 million.

Oct. 13
Volos, Greece. Twenty-three persons were killed and 15 injured in floods.

Oct. 13

Punjab, Patiala, and Delhi, India. Floods killed an estimated total of 1,700 persons and caused property damage of at least $63 million.

Oct. 17

Northeastern United States. Torrential rains and floods killed 42 persons and inflicted property damage estimated as $21 million.

Nov. 30

Mindanao, Visayan area, Philippines. At least 90 persons were killed in rainstorms.

Dec. 2

Madras, India. Rainstorms and resultant three-day floods killed approximately 120 persons.

Dec. 18

Lebanon. The worst flood in a century devastated a wide area, killing 140 persons and leaving another 200 missing and presumed dead; hardest hit was the Tripoli area.

Dec. 27

Northern California–Oregon area. Nine-day rains and resulting floods killed 80 persons and caused property damage estimated at more than $225 million; hardest hit was the Yuba City, California, area.

1956

February

Europe. Snowstorms and intense cold gripped the entire continent, killing more than 900 persons and causing crop damage estimated at more than $2 billion.

Feb. 4

Texas. Eighteen deaths were attributed to a snowstorm that swept the entire state.

Feb. 9

Toyama, Japan. An avalanche killed approximately 60 persons.

March 2

Near Seoul, Korea. A snow avalanche engulfed the South Korean army barracks; 79 persons were killed, 36 injured, and another 24 listed as missing.

March 2

Santos, Brazil. A cloudburst and resultant floods and landslides killed at least 30 persons.

March 16

Southern Lebanon. A series of earthquakes killed 145 persons and injured more than 200.

March 20

Northeastern United States. A four-day snowstorm extending from West Virginia to Maine killed 162 persons and caused property damage of more than $150 million.

March 25

Santos, Brazil. For the second time in less than a month the port city was hit by heavy rains and landslides; 36 persons were killed.

April 2–3

Midwestern and southern United States. Tornadoes striking a 13-state area killed 45 persons, injured 375, and caused property damage estimated at more than $15 million.

April 11

Nampula-Niassa districts, Portuguese East Africa. A cyclone swept the area killing 107 persons.

April 15

Near Birmingham, Alabama. A tornado killed 22 persons and injured more than 800 others.

May 12

Michigan and Ohio. Heavy wind, rainstorms, and tornadoes killed 10 persons and injured more than 135; hardest hit was the Cleveland, Ohio, area.

June 10–17

Kabul, Afghanistan. There were at least 2,000 persons injured and about 100 dead following a week-long period of earthquakes.

July 6

Central Philippines. A tropical storm killed 39 persons; 11 others were missing and presumed dead.

July 9

Thera, Greece. An earthquake that precipitated a seismic wave and a volcanic eruption killed 48 persons and injured 92.

July 21

Kutch area, India. An earthquake killed 113 persons and injured 219; the city of Anjar was devastated.

July 23–24

Kashan and Isfahan area, Iran. Floods killed at least 450 persons and caused property damage estimated at $60 million.

July 26

Kandahar area, Afghanistan. Fifty-one deaths were attributed to floods that followed unusually heavy rains.

Aug. 1–7

Chekiang, Hopeh, and Honan provinces, China. Floods following typhoon Wanda killed more than 2,000 persons and injured thousands more.

Aug. 4–5

Southwestern Pennsylvania. Fifteen deaths were attributed to violent rainstorms and subsequent floods.

Aug. 17–18

Northern Japan and Okinawa. Typhoon Babs killed 30 persons, injured 168, and left 16 others missing.

Aug. 22

West Pakistan. The flooding of several villages resulted in the death of at least 70 persons, with hundreds of others missing.

Aug. 22–23

Adiejaman Province, Turkey. Flash floods caused by heavy rains killed 138 persons.

Sept. 10

Okinawa, Japan, South Korea, and Philippines. Typhoon Emma killed 55 persons and caused property damage estimated at more than $2 million.

Sept. 17

Nemours, Algeria. A cyclone killed at least 21 persons and injured about 40.

Sept. 23–25

Florida, Georgia, and Louisiana. Twenty-four persons were reported dead or missing after Hurricane Flossy devastated the area; most of the $2 million damage was to oil rigs in the Gulf of Mexico.

Sept. 26–27

Okinawa-Japan area. Typhoon Harriet ripped through the area killing 23 persons.

Sept. 27

Near Anasol, India. A flood in a coal mine trapped and killed 28 workers.

Sept. 30

Darbhanga, North Bihar, India. Flash floods along the Gandak River killed an estimated total of 100 persons.

Oct. 11

Near Manizales, Colombia. Twenty truck drivers died when landslides buried their trucks.

Oct. 14

Near New Delhi, India. Floods on the Jumna River killed at least 50 persons and caused property damage estimated at more than $30 million.

Oct. 20

Bampa, Garhwal, India. Avalanches killed 27 persons.

Oct. 30

Honshu, Japan. Rainstorms contributed to the deaths of a reported 44 persons.

Nov. 3

South Dakota, Montana, Nebraska area. Thirteen deaths were attributed to a two-day snowstorm.

Nov. 3–11

Southeastern Iran. Earthquakes killed an estimated 350 persons.

Nov. 12

Southwestern Vietnam. A hurricane caused the death of a reported 56 persons.

Dec. 2–8

Eastern Java. A week of typhoons and floods brought death to about 300 persons.

Dec. 13

Philippines. Typhoon Polly killed 79 persons.

Dec. 15

New York, New Jersey, Connecticut, Massachusetts. Twenty-five deaths were attributed to a snowstorm that blanketed the area.

1957

Jan. 17

Palma Island, Canary Islands. Twenty-six persons were killed during a rainstorm.

Jan. 22

Louisiana, Oklahoma, Missouri area. Tornadoes killed 11 persons and injured 16.

Feb. 3

Kentucky, Virginia, West Virginia. Week-long floods in the Cumberland Valley brought death to 15 persons.

March 26

Western United States. Blizzards in 13 states contributed to the death of 13 persons and severely hampered transportation and communication.

April 2

Dallas, Texas. A tornado ripped through the city killing 10 persons, injuring about 175, and causing extensive property damage.

April 8

Southern United States. Tornadoes in six states killed 22

persons and injured at least 100.

April 23

Kejur Mesqal, Iran. Earthquakes and floods killed an estimated 44 persons.

April 28

Fethiye, Turkey area. An earthquake killed 23 persons and injured more than 100.

May 16

Silverton, Texas. Twenty-one persons were killed and 58 injured by a tornado that hit the area.

May 20

Kansas City, Missouri. A tornado killed 39 persons and injured nearly 100.

May 21

St. Louis, Missouri, area. Thirteen persons were killed in a tornado and at least 70 others injured.

May 26

Seben-Bolu, Turkey, area. An earthquake killed a reported total of 53 persons and injured 119.

June 14

St. Louis, Missouri, area. Seventeen persons were killed and four others missing and presumed dead as a result of flash floods.

June 16

France, Germany, Italy, Switzerland. Storms and a tornado in the Alps killed 17 persons, injured at least 60, and caused property damage estimated at more than $150 million.

June 20

Fargo, North Dakota. Ten persons were killed and 75 others injured when a tornado struck a residential area.

June 27

Lake Charles, Louisiana, area. Hurricane Audrey and a subsequent seismic wave caused the death of 534 persons; approximately 190 persons were missing and presumed dead.

June 27

Japan and Formosa. Eighty-six persons were killed in Typhoon Virginia.

July 2

Northern Iran. An earthquake that struck an extensive area killed more than 1,500 persons, injured scores of others, and caused extensive damage.

July 2–Aug. 27

South Korea. A series of typhoons and subsequent floods

Dead cattle lie in the streets of Cameron, Louisiana, after Hurricane Audrey on June 27 and a following seismic wave destroyed much of the town.

caused the deaths of 208 persons and left at least 30 others missing and presumed dead.

July 17

Mabini, Philippines. Fifty-four persons were killed in a typhoon and floods, with another 35 presumed dead.

July 21

Shantung Province, China. Heavy floods along the Yi, Shu, and Yellow rivers caused the death of at least 560 persons.

July 27

Northern Kyushu Island, Japan. Heavy rains killed an estimated 592 persons, leaving another 408 missing and presumed dead.

July 28

Mexico City area, Mexico. An earthquake caused at least 200 deaths, including 68 in the capital.

Rescue workers search for bodies in the rubble of a building in Mexico City after an earthquake struck the area on July 28.

Aug. 3–10
Near Kupo, South Korea. Floods along the Naktong River killed 198 persons; 49 others were missing and presumed dead.

Aug. 25
West Pakistan. Torrential rains and resulting floods on the Ravi, Chenab, and Jhelum rivers killed 75 persons.

Sept. 11
Ankara, Turkey. Eighty-seven deaths were attributed to a flood of the Bent River; 12 others were missing and presumed dead.

Sept. 14–19
Tabriz, Iran, area. Floods caused the deaths of a reported 122 persons.

Sept. 22
Uttar Pradesh, India. Floods killed as many as 92 persons.

Sept. 26
Okinawa–Ryukyus Island area. Typhoon Faye killed at least 60 persons, injured 146, left 49 missing and presumed dead; property damage was estimated at more than $10 million.

Oct. 14

Valencia, Spain. Heavy floods on the Turia River killed 77 persons.

Nov. 8

Louisiana, Texas, Mississippi. Thirteen persons were killed and more than 200 injured in a tornado.

Nov. 9

Nellore, Andhra, India. Floods resulting from monsoon rains brought death to 53 persons.

Dec. 4–8

Rio de Janeiro state, Brazil. Floods killed 52 persons and left about 60 missing.

Dec. 13

Outer Mongolia. An earthquake killed an estimated total of 1,200 persons.

Dec. 13–15

Western Iran. Two successive earthquakes killed 1,392 persons and injured at least 5,000 others.

Dec. 19

Missouri, Illinois, Arkansas. Tornadoes killed at least 20 persons, 10 of them in Illinois.

Dec. 26

Central Ceylon. At least 250 persons died in floods following a cyclone that left more than 400,000 homeless.

1958

Jan. 15

Arequipa, Peru. An earthquake and resultant landslides brought death to 128 persons.

Feb. 15–16

Northeastern United States. More than 170 deaths were attributed to blizzards that hit several states.

Feb. 26

South central Mississippi. Tornadoes killed 13 persons, injured 70 others, and caused extensive property damage.

March 19–21

Northeastern United States. A three-day snowstorm reaching from Virginia to Maine caused the death of 56 persons.

March 31–April 4

Northern California. Floods caused the death of 13 persons and property damage estimated at $12 million.

April 29

Northeastern Afghanistan. Widespread flooding in Badakhshan Province killed 49 persons.

June 4

Northwestern Wisconsin. A tornado killed at least 30 persons and injured about 350; property damage was estimated at more than $1.5 million.

June 7

Northeastern India. Fifty-two persons died in a landslide.

June 10

El Dorado, Kansas. A tornado caused the death of 13 persons and injured 57 others.

June 10–13

North central Indiana. Floods of three days' duration left 13 persons dead, at least 5,000 homeless, and property damage of more than $35 million.

July 2

Audubon, Iowa, area. A rainstorm killed 13 persons; 6 others were missing and presumed dead.

July 7

South Korea. At least 40 deaths were attributed to heavy rains and flooding.

July 17

Eastern Taiwan. Typhoon Winnie brought death to 31 persons and injured 53.

July 23

Hokkaido, Japan. Typhoon Alice and resulting floods killed 41 persons, injured 61, and left 8 others missing and presumed dead.

July 28

Buenos Aires, Argentina. Floods brought death to an estimated total of 60 persons and injured about 25; approximately 300 other persons were reported missing and were presumed dead.

Aug. 16–21

Teheran, Iran. A three-day series of earthquakes killed 191 persons and injured 984.

Aug. 26

Tokyo, Japan. Fifteen persons were killed and 39 injured in Typhoon Flossie; at least 30 others were missing and presumed dead.

Sept. 18

Japan. A typhoon caused the death of 24 persons, injured 108, and left 44 others missing.

Sept. 27–28

Tokyo, Japan, area. Typhoon Ida left 579 persons dead, 495 injured, and nearly 500 persons missing and presumed dead.

Sept. 30

Alès-Nîmes area, France. Flash floods killed 36 persons when the Gardon, Vidourle, and Cèze rivers overflowed; 4 others were missing.

Nov. 5

East Pakistan. At least 500 deaths were attributed to violent storms that occurred during the week ending November 5.

Nov. 17

Western and central United States. A severe snowstorm left 34 persons dead, 12 or more injured, and 19 reported missing.

1959

Jan. 9

Rivaldelago, Spain. The dam of Vega de Tera reservoir burst drowning 123 persons.

Jan. 21–23

Eastern and midwestern United States. Floods, sleet, and snowstorms caused 71 deaths in 15 states; thousands were left homeless.

Feb. 10

St. Louis, Missouri. At least 21 persons were killed and more than 300 injured in a tornado.

Feb. 11

Near Tehran, Iran. An avalanche on a mountain road caused the death of 15 persons and injured 14 others.

April 6

Malagache Republic (Madagascar). Heavy rains and floodwaters during a two-week period killed 305 persons.

April 21

Buenos Aires, Argentina. The flooding of the Rio Negro and Uruguay rivers caused an estimated 124 deaths in Argentina, Brazil, and Uruguay.

April 29

Port-au-Prince, Haiti. An estimated 25 to 50 persons were killed and about 700 injured in a flash flood brought on by heavy rains.

May 21

Natal and Cape Provinces, Union of South Africa. Flooding of the Umzikulu River caused 51 deaths.

May 23

Northeastern Turkey. Floodwaters killed 12 persons.

June 1

Jaipur, India. A cyclone killed 11 persons.

June 15
Hong Kong. Three days of torrential rains killed 43 persons.
June 21
Newcastle, New Brunswick. Twelve Canadian fishermen were lost and 22 reported missing in a North Atlantic gale.
June 24
Canton, China. Severe floods in the area brought death to 187 persons.
June 24
Assam state, India. Floods and a landslide killed 12 persons and left more than 100,000 homeless.
June 30
Las Juntas, Colombia. A flash flood killed 184 persons.
July 15
Tokyo, Japan. Floods following torrential rains caused the death of 41 persons.
July 15
West Pakistan. More than 100 persons were reported dead in floods.
July 17
Srinagar, Kashmir, India. Floods killed 104 persons.
July 18
Pusan, Korea. A sudden torrential rain killed 62 persons and injured 40.
Aug. 8
Taiwan. Violent thunderstorms created floods that brought death to 649 persons.
Aug. 15
Southern Brazil. Fifty-nine deaths were attributed to high winds.
Aug. 15
Central Japan. A typhoon killed 139 persons.
Aug. 16
Hungchun, Formosa. Sixteen persons were killed and more than 80 others injured in an earthquake.
Aug. 18
West Yellowstone, Montana. A series of earthquakes created landslides that killed 28 persons.
Aug. 20
Fukien Province, China. Typhoon Iris devastated a wide area, killing as many as 2,300 persons.
Aug. 26
Vera Cruz state, Mexico. An earthquake brought death to at least 28 persons.

Sept. 14

Fukien Province, China. A tidal wave and floods killed an estimated total of 47 persons.

Sept. 17

Korea. Typhoon Sarah struck the country and claimed 432 lives.

Sept. 18

Surat, India. At least 500 persons were killed when the Tapti River burst a dike and flooded the area.

Sept. 26–27

Central Honshu, Japan. Typhoon Vera, the worst in Japanese history, killed 4,464 persons; property destruction was severe and widespread and more than 400,000 persons were left homeless.

Sept. 28

Rio Grande do Sul, Brazil. Flash floods from the Pardo River killed at least 100 persons.

Sept. 30

Near Charlottesville, Virginia. A tornado ripped through the area, killing at least 10 persons.

Oct. 3–4

West Bengal and Orissa, India. A cyclone and resulting floods killed 22 persons.

Oct. 17

Okinawa. Landslides caused by Typhoon Charlotte killed at least 27 persons.

Oct. 25

Eastern Turkey. An earthquake killed at least 17 persons.

Oct. 29

Colima and Jalisco states, Mexico. A hurricane and resulting floods killed 1,452 persons.

Dec. 16

Near Peshawar, Pakistan. An avalanche brought death to 49 persons.

Dec. 18

Philippines. Typhoon Gilda caused the death of 29 persons.

1960

Jan. 22

Mindanao Island, Philippines. A landslide struck a school, burying 40 children alive.

Jan. 24

Carangola and Divino, Brazil. Twenty persons perished in floods resulting from a cloudburst.

Feb. 21

Melouza and Beni Illmane, Algeria. Forty-seven persons were killed in an earthquake.

Feb. 27

Mauritius Island, Indian Ocean. Winds reaching 160 mph caused 42 deaths.

Feb. 29–March 1

Agadir, Morocco. Two earthquakes, a seismic wave, and fires destroyed 95 percent of the city; the death toll was estimated to be as high as 20,000 persons.

March 7–14

Bahia and Pernambuco states, Brazil. Flash floods caused the death of as many as 100 persons.

April 24–28

Lar, Iran. The death toll from an earthquake was estimated at 700 persons.

May 5–6

Southeastern Oklahoma and Arkansas. Tornadoes and storms killed 23 persons.

May 21–June 30

Chile. Earthquakes, volcanic eruptions, and seismic waves desolated 10 provinces, leaving an estimated 10,000 persons dead and causing hundreds of millions of dollars damage.

May 24

Hawaii, Okinawa, and Japan. Seismic waves, the result of earthquakes in Chile, killed at least 240 persons.

May 28

Luzon, Philippines. Rainstorms touched off floods that left more than 166 dead.

June 9

China. Typhoon Mary battered Fukien Province, claiming approximately 1,600 lives; at least 90 others were dead or missing in Hong Kong.

June 27

Luzon, Philippines. Typhoon Olive with winds up to 170 mph left about 109 persons dead and hundreds missing.

July 4

Gujarat region, India. Floods caused at least 30 deaths in the Kathrawa peninsula.

Aug. 2

Taiwan. Typhoon Shirley and ensuing floods killed 104 persons; 95 others were missing and presumed drowned.

Aug. 6

Southern Philippines. As a result of two days of storms, 33

persons were reported missing and were presumed drowned.
   Aug. 13–14
Central Japan. Torrential rains following Typhoon Wendy killed 18 persons.
   Aug. 25
Orissa, India. Floods, the worst in the state's history, left 47 persons dead and 1,500,000 homeless.
   Aug. 31
Southern Japan. Typhoon Della killed 41 persons.
   Sept. 3–5
Northern India. An estimated total of 155 persons were drowned as the result of floods.
   Sept. 6
Puerto Rico. Floods and high tides following Hurricane Donna left 102 dead.
   Sept. 9–12
Caribbean Sea area and U.S. east coast. Hurricane Donna ravaged the area killing 138 persons and causing property damage in excess of $1 billion.
   Sept. 15–19
Italy. Heavy rains and flash floods caused the death of nearly 50 persons.
   Oct. 10
East Pakistan. A cyclone and resultant tidal wave killed about 6,000 persons in East Pakistan, Ramgati and Hatia islands, and the coastal area of the Bay of Bengal.
   Oct. 13
Philippines. Typhoon Lola caused the death of an estimated 32 persons and damage of more than $10 million.
   Oct. 20–Nov. 1
Nicaragua. Floods brought on by torrential rains left 325 persons dead and about 5,000 families homeless.
   Oct. 31
East Pakistan. A cyclone hit Chittagong and the surrounding coastal area, killing an estimated total of 6,000 persons.
   Dec. 12
Atlantic seaboard from Virginia to Nova Scotia. The worst snowstorm in several years caused the deaths of at least 127 persons.

1961
   Feb. 3–4
Northeastern United States. Severe snowstorms swept the region, causing at least 100 deaths.

Feb. 21–28
Georgia, Alabama, Mississippi, Louisiana. Torrential rains caused rivers to overflow, killing 12 persons.

March 13
Kiev, U.S.S.R. A mud slide at a reclamation project reportedly caused the death of 145 persons and injured 143 others; many houses and public buildings were demolished.

March 19
East Pakistan. A tornado struck four districts, killing 266 persons and injuring nearly 800 others.

May 5
Howe and Reichert, Oklahoma. A tornado killed 14 persons and injured 57 others.

May 8
East Pakistan. A seven-hour cyclonic storm claimed the lives of about 430 persons.

June 11
Dehkuyeh, Iran. An entire village was destroyed by an earthquake; at least 60 persons were killed and hundreds more injured.

June 28–30
Honshu, Japan. Floods in the western and central parts of the island took at least 265 lives.

July 12
Seoul, South Korea. Floodwaters burst through a dam at Namwon sweeping 119 persons to their deaths; about 130 others were missing and presumed dead.

July 20
Charleston, West Virginia. Flash flood caused by a five-inch rainfall brought death to 21 persons; nearly 1,500 homes were destroyed.

Sept. 11–13
Texas-Louisiana. Hurricane Carla and accompanying tornadoes lashed a broad area of the Gulf of Mexico coastline and penetrated far inland; because of orderly evacuation only 40 persons were killed; damage was estimated at $400 million.

Sept. 12–13
Taiwan. Typhoon Pamela swept across northern Taiwan, killing 106 persons and injuring 913 others; property damage was extensive.

Sept. 16–17
Japan. Typhoon Nancy plowed through central Japan, killing 185 persons, injuring 3,879, and leaving about 15 others

missing; property damage was estimated at $230 million.

Oct. 7

Bihar State, India. A 25-inch rainfall in a 48-hour period resulted in floods that drowned about 1,000 persons.

Oct. 26–28

Western Japan. Heavy rains and landslides brought death to 64 persons; an estimated 80 others were injured, and 30 were reported missing.

Nov. 1

Belize, British Honduras. Hurricane Hattie with 200-mph winds and tidal waves completed two days of destruction throughout the colony; about 250 persons died, and more than 15,000 others were left homeless; damage was estimated at $150 million.

Nov. 6

Athens, Greece. A four-hour cyclone followed by floods devastated a large area of the city and left 43 persons dead, more than 350 injured, and at least 4,500 homeless.

Nov. 11–13

Acapulco, Mexico. Hurricane Tara struck north of the city and swept 120 miles along the coast, destroying the seaside village of Tuxco; about 430 persons died, and hundreds were missing.

Nov. 18–25

Lower Juba Province, Somalia. Heavy unseasonal rains caused flooding of the Juba and Webi Shebeli rivers over a 60,000-square-mile area; about 200 persons were reported dead and more than 300,000 homeless.

Dec. 20

Central Colombia. A 45-second earthquake centering in Caldas state caused damage as far east as Bogotá, the capital; at least 20 persons were killed and scores injured.

1962

Jan. 10

Mt. Huascarán, Peru. A huge avalanche dropping from the 22,205-foot extinct volcano buried at least 16 villages; the death toll was estimated at more than 4,000 persons.

Feb. 8–12

Southern California. Five-day torrential rains caused floods and mud slides that killed 20 persons.

Feb. 17

North Sea coast, Germany. A storm with raging seas and winds of hurricane force brought death to at least 343 persons; the worst of the storm was centered about the port of Hamburg, but the coasts of the Netherlands, Denmark, Sweden, and England were lashed; a total of about 17,500 persons were left homeless, and damage was estimated at $250 million.

Feb. 28

Conchucos, Peru. Heavy rains caused a mud slide that buried the village; about 60 persons were reported dead or missing.

Feb. 28

Mauritius and Réunion islands. A hurricane with 156-mph winds whipped in from the Indian Ocean, killing at least 27 persons; several hundred others were injured, and more than 8,000 were left homeless.

March 5–9

East coast, United States. A heavy storm with high winds and racing tides swept in from the Atlantic; at least 40 persons died, about 1,250 others were injured, and property damage was estimated at $160 million.

March 10

Pensilvania, Colombia. A landslide brought on by heavy rains killed 23 persons.

March 15

Lima, Peru. Two landslides near Paucartambo hydroelectric station 125 miles northeast of Lima killed 41 persons.

March 18

Southern Albania. A severe earthquake shook the districts of Fier and Vlore, leaving 15 dead; another 154 persons were injured, and at least 1,000 homes destroyed.

April 7

Tapanuli district, Sumatra. A landslide killed 12 persons and left more than 2,500 homeless.

April 30

Qbour-el-Beidh, Syria. Floods surging across the Syrian-Turkish border brought death to 23 persons and destroyed about 100 homes.

May 6

Northeastern Afghanistan. Floods caused heavy property damage and brought death to 17 persons.

May 22

Between Petare and Guarenas, Venezuela. A landslide buried a farmland area; at least 30 persons were missing and presumed dead.

June 23–24

Western Turkey. Heavy rains flooded coastal areas and

caused the deaths of at least 15 persons.

July 9

Kyushu Island, Japan. A weekend of torrential rains resulting in floods and landslides brought death to 51 persons; about 20 others were reported missing, 58 were injured, and more than 40,000 were left homeless. (Unusually heavy seasonal rains had accounted for a total of 75 deaths in Japan earlier in July.)

July 26

Luzon Province, Philippines. Floods caused by Typhoon Kate that struck north and central areas of the province brought an eight-day death toll of 41 persons; property damage was estimated at $12 million.

July 30

Central Colombia. The worst earthquake to strike Colombia in 10 years caused 47 deaths; 65 persons were missing, and at least 300 others injured.

Aug. 5

Yilan, Taiwan. Typhoon Opal with 170-mph winds lashed inland, killing at least 87 persons; about 20 others were missing and another 1,400 injured.

Aug. 9

Central Philippines. Typhoon Patsy roared in from the sea, leaving at least 23 persons dead and 133 missing.

Aug. 18

Florencia, Colombia. A flash flood propelled an avalanche of water, trees, and boulders through the town; 135 persons were killed or missing.

Aug. 21

Avellino, Italy. An earthquake centered in the Ariano Irpino area left 18 persons dead, more than 200 others injured, and several thousand homeless.

Aug. 25

North Sikkim, India. Floodwaters poured down the Tista River causing two bridges to collapse; about 100 roadworkers were washed away to their deaths.

Aug. 28

Sunchon, Korea. Several dikes on the rain-swollen Nam River broke, and floodwaters poured through the town leaving 242 persons dead and 48 missing.

Sept. 1

Hong Kong. Typhoon Wanda with 180-mph winds swept out of the South China Sea, leaving about 175 persons dead, 515 injured, and at least 52,000 homeless.

Sept. 1

Northwestern Iran. A violent earthquake shook a 23,000-square-mile area centered at Danesfahan; the death toll was officially set at 12,403 persons; another 10,000 persons were injured, and more than 25,000 homes were destroyed in 200 towns and villages, leaving 100,000 homeless.

Sept. 4

Northeastern India. As a result of 10-day floods 73 persons perished; in the states of Assam, Bihar, and Uttar Pradesh nearly 38,000 homes were destroyed.

Sept. 7

Philippines. Typhoon Amy dumped heavy rain on the islands and caused the death of 16 persons.

Sept. 7

Sfax region, Tunisia. Flash floods brought death to at least 22 persons.

Sept. 24–27

Barcelona, Spain. Devastating flash floods ripped through

His wife having been killed by an earthquake on September 1, an Iranian father and his daughter share a meager meal beside their salvaged belongings.

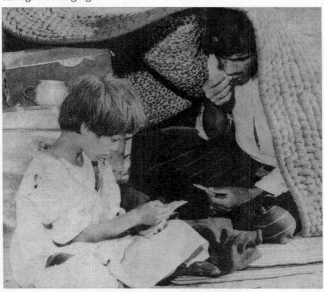

industrial centers around the city area; the death toll was estimated at more than 800 persons with about 1,000 more injured; property damage was around $80 million.

Oct. 6

Lower California. The Mexican coast suffered heavy damage as Typhoon Doreen swept across the peninsula, killing at least 25 persons.

Oct. 11–13

Pacific northwest, United States. The west coast area was lashed by 120-mph winds as a severe storm moved in from the ocean; at least 46 persons died, and property damage in California, Oregon, Washington, and British Columbia was estimated as high as $150 million.

Oct. 27

Southern Thailand. Tropical Storm Harriet ravaged three southern provinces, killing at least 769 persons, including as many as 500 who perished when an entire village disappeared into the sea; 142 others were missing and 252 seriously injured; damage amounted to about $20 million.

Nov. 9

Port de Paix, Haiti. Severe floods caused by heavy rain brought death to at least 26 persons.

Nov. 11

Guam. Typhoon Karen, the worst storm in Guam's history, left the territory devastated by its 178-mph winds; because of the early warnings and orderly evacuation of the inhabitants, only 6 deaths were reported although hundreds of persons were injured and more than 25,000 homeless; damage was estimated at $100 million.

Nov. 18

Western Europe. Gale winds and heavy snows caused at least 13 deaths in England.

Nov. 27

Southern Tunisia. A flooded oasis on the edge of the Sahara drove thousands from their homes and brought death to at least 40 persons.

Nov. 28

Central Philippines. Typhoon Lucy ripped through the islands and into the South China Sea; 11 persons were killed, and damage amounted to about $3 million.

Dec. 13

Eastern and mid-United States. Week-long winter storms brought subnormal temperatures and snow to much of the nation; at least 112 deaths were attributed to the cold wave;

heavy damage struck the Florida citrus crops.

1963

Jan. 1

Northeastern United States. An intense storm with 100-mph winds, subzero temperatures, and heavy snowfall moved out to sea, leaving in its wake at least 26 dead.

Jan. 2

Great Britain and Western Europe. A week-long cold wave accompanied by snowstorms and fog brought death to at least 800 persons.

Jan. 10

Rharb Valley, Morocco. Three weeks of torrential rains brought death to more than 100 persons and left about 100,-000 homeless.

Jan. 24

Katsuyama, Japan. A sudden avalanche destroyed seven houses and killed 19 persons.

Jan. 24

Eastern United States. Frigid cold spreading from the midwest engulfed the eastern seaboard as far south as Florida; the subzero blast was blamed for at least 150 deaths.

Feb. 2

Western Japan. Blizzards of 21 days' duration piled up 16-foot snowdrifts and accounted for 86 deaths.

Feb. 19

Bali, Indonesia. The eruption of the 10,308-foot Agung volcano, dormant for 100 years, killed 17 persons.

Feb. 21–22

AlMarj (Barce), Libya. Three severe earthquakes accompanied by torrential rains demolished the ancient city, leaving nearly 15,000 inhabitants homeless; an estimated 300 persons were killed and at least 500 others injured.

March 16

Eastern United States. Week-long floods caused great havoc in ten Atlantic seaboard and Ohio Valley states; 21 persons died, about 5,000 others were left homeless, and damage was estimated at more than $50 million.

March 18

Mymensingh district, East Pakistan. A cyclone brought death to 18 persons; damage to houses and crops amounted to an estimated total of $2 million.

March 21

Bali, Indonesia. Four days of continuous lava and hot ash

eruptions from Agung volcano killed 1,584 persons and left another 78,000 homeless; about 123,000 acres of cropland were destroyed.

April 8

Petra, Jordan. A flash flood entrapped and drowned a group of 25 tourists and guides, killing all of them.

April 18

Bulongwa, Tanganyika. A 100-foot-wide avalanche of mud oozed down a mountainside engulfing a cluster of homes and killing 10 sleeping persons.

April 19

Eastern India. Two cyclones struck areas in the states of Assam and West Bengal; at least 112 persons were killed and 500 others injured; about 1,500 houses were destroyed, leaving almost 10,000 villagers homeless.

April 25

Herat, Afghanistan. Floods in the western part of the country killed 107 persons.

May 4

Mascara, Algeria. A cyclone hit the city, killing at least 10 persons and injuring 29 others.

May 19

Bali, Indonesia. Mount Agung erupted for the third time in three months, killing another 106 persons.

May 29

Chittagong, East Pakistan. A two-day storm and a 15-foot tidal wave hit the city and the Bay of Bengal coastal areas; at least 22,000 persons perished, several islands were completely swept away, 5,000 small boats sank, and the entire rice crop was destroyed.

June 19

Southern Ecuador. A landslide caused by tropical storms in the Masaca region killed 18 persons.

June 27

Pusan, Korea. Eight days of heavy rains in the Pusan area and on Koje Island caused flooding and landslides that buried four villages; 186 persons died and 176 others were injured.

July 1

Kyushu and Honshu islands, Japan. Three days of violent rainstorms, cloudbursts, and flooding caused 24 deaths; another 23 persons were missing, and several thousand were homeless.

July 15

Chittagong, East Pakistan. Monsoon rains flooded the rivers

and drove thousands from their homes; at least 30 persons died.

July 20

Pahalgam, India. Tumbling rock loosened by flash floods swept away two mountain resort hotels and many tourists' tents, killing at least 200 persons.

July 24

Pontianak, Indonesia. Lightning struck a home occupied by a group enjoying an afternoon feast; 16 persons were reported killed.

July 26

Skopje, Yugoslavia. A rapid series of devastating earthquakes leveled four-fifths of the city, killed 1,011 persons, and injured about 3,350 others; damage was estimated at about $80 million.

Aug. 10

Western Nepal. Landslides caused by heavy rains completely destroyed one village and partially covered several others; at least 150 persons were killed.

Sept. 2

Kashmir valley, India-Pakistan. A severe earthquake rocked a 50-mile area causing damage to 56 villages; about 100 persons were killed and another 500 injured.

Sept. 15

Eastern Asia. Typhoon Gloria brought five days of devastation to the Philippines, the Ryukyus, Taiwan, Japan, and mainland China; 239 persons died, 89 were missing, and 93 injured.

Sept. 20

Northwest India. Week-long rains caused heavy floods, especially in western Uttar Pradesh; at least 237 persons died.

Sept. 30–Oct. 8

Caribbean area. Hurricane Flora made a nine-day, 140-mph sweep of destruction through the islands of the Caribbean, killing a reported total of more than 6,000 persons in Tobago, Grenada, and Trinidad (36 dead), in Jamaica (9), Haiti (5,000), and Cuba (1,000); damage was estimated in the millions of dollars.

Oct. 7

East Pakistan. A cyclonic storm caused heavy crop damage and brought death to 79 persons.

Oct. 9

Longarone, Italy. An avalanche of earth and rock rumbled into the artificial lake behind Vaiont Dam and forced a more

In Longarone, Italy, hundreds of wooden crosses wait to be placed over a grave for victims of the Vaiont Dam disaster of October 9.

than 75-yard-high wall of water down the Piave River valley, destroying the town of Longarone and several hamlets; more than 2,600 persons were killed.

    Nov. 16
Northern Haiti. Three days of floods and landslides brought death to at least 500 persons; crops in the Grande Rivière du Nord area were completely destroyed, and damage was estimated in the millions of dollars.

1964
    Jan. 14
Eastern seaboard, United States. A four-day storm moved out to sea leaving in its wake deep snow, freezing temperatures, and heavy crop damage over the midwest and northeastern section of the United States; a death toll of 140 persons was reported.

    Jan. 18
Taiwan. Earthquake tremors were felt throughout the island with heavy damage centered in the area of the towns of Paibo

and Tungshan; an estimated 100 persons were killed.

Jan. 20
Eastern Brazil. Heavy rains and extensive floods in the São Francisco and Jequitinhonha river valleys brought death to more than 100 persons and left at least 100,000 homeless.

Jan. 24
Harpersville, Alabama. A tornado struck the town, demolished a number of houses, killed 10 persons, and injured 9 others.

Jan. 31
Northern Morocco. A series of floods left 76 persons dead and more than 83,000 homeless.

Feb. 6
Southwestern United States. Heavy blizzards piling up 20-foot snowdrifts blocked highways and killed thousands of cattle; 10 persons died in the storms.

March 2
Tamuco, Chile. Nearby 9,325-foot Villarica volcano erupted burying the village of Conaripe; 24 persons perished.

March 4
Southern United States. Tornadoes and windstorms left a six-state area heavily damaged by floods, winds, and lightning; 11 persons died, and at least 40 others were injured.

March 10
Midwestern United States. Flooding of the Ohio River valley brought great destruction to Pennsylvania, Ohio, West Virginia, Kentucky, and Indiana with damage set at $100 million; 15 deaths were reported.

March 27
Alaska. A devastating earthquake struck the southern part of the state, destroyed the central business section of Anchorage, and heavily damaged the cities of Seward, Valdez, Cordova, Kodiak, and Chenega; giant seismic waves wrecked coastal areas in Canada, Oregon, and California and were felt in Hawaii and Japan; the Alaska Civil Defense Office estimated damage at $750 million and listed 131 persons as dead.

April 12
Central United States. Tornadoes, dust, and sandstorms raged through a five-state area, inflicting the worst damage on Garnett, Kansas; Pleasant Hill, Missouri; Yorktown, Iowa; and Lake Tawakoni, Texas. Property losses were about $5 million; 13 persons were killed.

April 12
Jessore District, East Pakistan. Cyclonic storms hit with 150-

mph gusts that obliterated 25 villages, killed hundreds of cattle, and flattened the rice crop; official figures listed more than 400 persons dead, about 1,000 missing, and at least 700 injured.

May 8

Southeastern Michigan. A tornado slashing through Chesterfield township demolished or seriously damaged about 500 homes and endangered the U.S. Air Force base at Selfridge; 11 persons died, and about 100 were injured.

June 8

Northeastern Italy. Sudden cloudbursts with hail, rain, and wind swept away the buildings of several large tourists resorts on the northern Adriatic coast; many inland farm crops were a total loss; at least 10 persons died.

June 8

Northwestern Montana. Rain and melting snow sent flash floods swirling down the mountain valleys to break through dams and wash out bridges; 34 persons perished, and 30 others were missing; damage was estimated at more than $62 million.

June 13–14

Hyderabad, West Pakistan. Blanketing rains and high winds leveled hundreds of homes, killed at least 332 persons, and destroyed 60,000 head of cattle.

June 16

Northern Japan. Violent earthquakes jarred the prefectures of Niigata, Yamagata, and Akita; exploding oil tanks at the oil-processing center of Niigata set off raging fires that burned uncontrolled for three days; floodwaters overflowed the banks of the Shinano River; property damage was estimated at $280 million with almost 30,000 buildings in ruins; 27 persons died, 5 were missing, and another 377 were injured.

June 18

Denizli Province, Turkey. Rain-loosened boulders rumbled down the mountainside, crushed a small village, and killed 21 persons.

June 30

Northern Philippines. Typhoon Winnie, striking with 118-mph winds, brought death to 107 persons before drifting on to the Asian mainland; property damage exceeded $30 million.

July 6

Guerrero State, Mexico. An earthquake jolted a coastal area

and destroyed several mountain villages; 36 persons died, and another 65 were injured.

July 7

Near Chamonix, France. An avalanche rumbling down from the 13,540-foot Aiguille Verte peak of the Mont Blanc Range in the French Alps engulfed a party of instructors and students from the National School of Skiing and Mountain Climbing; all 14 climbers were killed.

July 19

Central and western Japan. Several days of torrential rains caused floods and landslides that killed 106 persons, injured at least 220, and left 44,000 homeless, and 30 missing.

Aug. 3–10

Philippines, Taiwan, and Hong Kong. Typhoon Ida, with winds of up to 140 mph, lashed from the China seas, killing at least 75 persons; thousands of others were homeless.

Aug. 21–28

Caribbean and east coast of Florida. Hurricane Cleo swept Guadeloupe and hit the southern tip of Haiti and the central port of Cuba before bearing down on the Florida coast; of the 138 persons killed, none was from Florida, but damages there were estimated at more than $100 million.

Aug. 23

Kyushu Island, Japan. Typhoon Kathy slashed through southwestern Japan, leaving 13 persons dead, 25 injured, and more than 4,000 homeless.

Sept. 4

Punjab State, India. Floodwaters pouring from the Punjab swept into New Delhi; 51 persons throughout the area died.

Sept. 5

Hong Kong and Kwangtung Province, China. Typhoon Ruby, with 120-mph winds, raked across the colony and swung up the Pearl River estuary of mainland China; more than 730 persons perished, and hundreds were injured.

Sept. 14

Central South Korea. Violent rainstorms battered the Seoul area and Kyonggi Province, flooding the village of Nagakni and drowning all 96 of its inhabitants; a reported total of 563 persons were dead, more than 250 injured, and at least 28,-000 homeless.

Sept. 25

West coast of Japan. Typhoon Wilda slammed southern and western port areas leaving 42 persons dead or missing and 459 injured.

Sept. 29

Andhra Pradesh State, India. Monsoon rains burst an upland reservoir pouring a 10-foot wall of water down upon the town of Macherla; 36 persons drowned and about 2,000 head of cattle were washed away.

Oct. 4–7

Louisiana. Hurricane Hilda hit the coast of Louisiana with winds up to 120 mph, spinning off two tornadoes that killed 21 persons in the towns of Larose and Erath; 15 other deaths brought the total to 36; property damage amounted to $100 million.

Oct. 6

Western Turkey. A series of earthquakes jolted the provinces of Bursa and Balikesir; 30 persons were killed and 52 injured.

Oct. 13

Hong Kong. Typhoon Dot, the colony's fourth severe storm of the year, left at least 36 persons dead or missing and presumed dead; 85 others were injured.

Nov. 1

Tunis, Tunisia. Rampaging rivers swollen by heavy rains flooded towns and villages; at least 35 persons died or were missing and presumed dead.

Nov. 12

Northern areas of South Vietnam. Typhoons Iris and Joan brought the most devastating floods in 60 years to inundate 5,000,000 acres in ten provinces (mainly Quang Ngai, Quang Nam, and Quang Tin); one million persons were homeless; roads, bridges, and railways were washed away; the final death toll was placed at 7,000.

Nov. 20

Central Philippines. Typhoon Louise, with winds of 93 mph, swept across the central islands, leaving an estimated 250 persons dead and about 100,000 homeless.

Dec. 13

Central South Vietnam. The provinces of Ninhthuan and Khanhhoa were heavily flooded and suffered great crop and livestock losses; about 400 persons drowned, and at least 2,000 were left homeless.

Dec. 19–31

Pacific Northwest. Drenching rain and melting snow flooded the rivers of Washington, Oregon, and northern California, driving thousands of persons from their homes; subsequent freezing and heavy snows checked the flooding but added to the suffering of isolated communities in the three states and in Idaho and Nevada; at least 42 persons died; damage was estimated at $7 million.

Dec. 22–23

India-Ceylon. A powerful 150-mph cyclone, followed by a huge tidal wave, bore down upon the Indian islet of Dhanushkodi and the Ceylonese fishing village of Myliddy (both on the Gulf of Mannar), marooning the inhabitants on small patches of land or washing them into the sea; an entire train and its 150 passengers were also swept from Rameswaram Island; estimates placed the total death toll caused by the storm at 1,800.

1965

Jan. 24

Indonesia. A violent earthquake and seismic wave struck areas in Celebes and the islands of Mangole, Sanana, and Buru, killing 40 persons.

Feb. 9

Fiji. Floods caused by a two-day typhoon covered dozens of villages in the islands and brought death to at least 25 persons.

Feb. 18

Stewart, British Columbia. An avalanche from a nearby glacier buried a mining camp and trapped 20 workmen in an 11-mile tunnel at the Le Duc copper mine site; they survived but 27 men who were on the surface died.

Feb. 19

Puerto Montt, Chile. The nearby hamlet of Cabrera was crushed by an avalanche that killed all but one of the 27 inhabitants.

Feb. 18–24

Sanana Island, Indonesia. A series of earthquakes destroyed almost 3,000 buildings and 14 bridges; 71 islanders were killed.

Feb. 24–25

Central and eastern United States. Snowstorms and blizzards blanketed a 21-state area in the country's midsection before moving eastward to the Atlantic Coast states; at least 17 persons were reported dead.

March 2

Near Obertauern, Austria. An avalanche thundering down upon a mountain road buried a tourist bus and killed 14 of the 39 skiers aboard.

March 22–23

East Pakistan. Four districts were hit by a 50-mph cyclone that killed 15 persons and injured 25 others.

March 28

Central Chile. The provinces of Aconcagua, Valparaíso, Coquimbo, and Santiago took the full force of an intense earthquake that broke a 230-foot dam above the mining village of El Cobre and sent seas of mud and rubble down the valley to destroy or damage 45,000 buildings; more than four hundred persons died; property loss was near $200 million.

March 31

Cabo Delgado District, Mozambique. Ten days of torrential rains and flooding brought death to 24 persons and left 2,000 homeless.

April 5

Megalopolis, Greece. Four nearby villages were completely destroyed by a series of three earthquakes that killed at least 32 persons, injured 200 others, and left 20,000 homeless.

April 11

Midwestern United States. The six-state area of Ohio, Michigan, Indiana, Illinois, Wisconsin, and Iowa was severely damaged by a series of violent tornadoes; Indiana's death toll was the heaviest, with 141 of the 270 total; at least 5,000 other persons were injured, and property damage was estimated at more than $250 million.

May 3

San Salvador, El Salvador. A major earthquake was felt in the capital city with the heaviest damage suffered in the outlying villages; at least 125 persons died, more than 500 others were injured, and about 48,000 were left homeless.

May 6

Minneapolis, Minnesota. A string of tornadoes twisted through 15 of the city's suburbs, wrecking hundreds of homes, killing 13 persons, and injuring about 400 others.

April 16–May 7

Mississippi Valley, United States. The month-long rampage of the Mississippi River, from St. Paul–Minneapolis to St. Louis, was recorded as the greatest flood in the river's history; the cresting waters drove more than 40,000 persons from their homes, caused 15 deaths, and resulted in a property loss of more than $200 million.

May 11–12

East Pakistan. A cyclone, striking the densely populated southern and Barisal coastal areas with deadly force, was followed by gigantic ocean waves; more than 17,000 persons died, at least 600,000 were injured, and 5,000,000 others were homeless.

June 1–2

East Pakistan. The second violent cyclone within a month struck the Bay of Bengal coastal area, killing an estimated 30,000 persons.

June 11

Sanderson, Texas. A cloudburst sent a 15-foot wall of water through the town, drowning 16 persons and causing property damage of about $3.5 million.

June 13

Pernambuco State, Brazil. Heavy rains caused landslides and floods that killed at least 20 persons and left an estimated 20,000 others homeless.

June 9–16

Northern India. A week-long heat wave, with temperatures ranging from 108° F in New Delhi to more than 120° F in Bihar State, brought death to at least 100 persons.

June 19

Taiwan. Typhoon Dinah destroyed or damaged more than 5,000 houses, killed 31 persons, and injured 89 others.

June 18–26

West central United States. Violent rain and thunderstorms in Montana set off flooding in the Arkansas and South Platte river valleys through Wyoming, Colorado, Nebraska, Kansas, and New Mexico; at least 20 persons died in the six-state area, and property damage in the five states was estimated at $100 million.

June 26

Kawasaki City, Japan. Rain-loosened mounds of coal cinders and mud buried 13 buses and killed 24 of the occupants; 14 others were injured.

July 5

Northern Italy. Hot winds ended a 10-day series of tornadoes and hailstorms during which 37 persons died.

July 12–13

Philippines. Floods churned up by Typhoon Freda swept through Cotabato Province and the northern Luzon area, leaving at least 37 persons dead.

July 21

South Korea. Countryside week-long floods accounted for 207 deaths; another 89 persons were missing, and more than 220,000 were left homeless.

July 20–24

Western Japan. Torrential rains caused floods and landslides and brought death to 28 persons.

Aug. 6

Southern Japan. Typhoon Jean with 110-mph winds battered through the island leaving 26 persons dead and at least 40 others injured.

Aug. 9–16

Central Chile. Mid-coastal areas along a 1,000-mile front suffered a week of violent storms that killed at least 58 persons, left more than 70,000 others homeless, and damaged 40 percent of the country's farmlands.

Aug. 16

Near Mendoza, Argentina. Snow and rock avalanches in the Andes rumbled down on the village of Las Cuevas and buried at least 45 persons.

Aug. 19

Taiwan. Typhoon Mary, hitting hardest across the southeastern end of the island, left 24 persons dead or missing and 77 injured.

Aug. 21

Western and central Mexico. Drenched by three weeks of heavy rain, swollen rivers flooded vast areas of the country and brought death to 27 persons; damage was estimated at more than $8 million.

Aug. 30

Saas-Fee, Switzerland. Million of tons of ice splintered from Allalin Glacier and crashed down upon the Mattmark Dam hydroelectric construction site burying 90 workers.

Sept. 2–6

Southern Italy. Torrential rains and floods from Rome southward through Sicily left 55 persons dead, 46 others missing and presumed dead.

Sept. 7–10

Southern Florida and Mississippi River Delta. Hurricane Betsy struck Miami and the Keys area with 150-mph winds, then sped across the Gulf to New Orleans. The final death toll stood at 74; damage in Florida amounted to $100 million, in Lousiana $1 million.

Sept. 10

Central Japan. Typhoon Shirley roared across Shikoku Island and southern Honshu before hitting Hokkaido; 39 persons were killed and 21 missing; about 730 others were injured.

Sept. 18
Southern Japan. Swirling waters gathered by Typhoon Trix flooded nearly a million homes and brought death to at least 114 persons; ancient national treasures at Kyoto suffered damages estimated at $60 million, and the national railway about $30 million.

Sept. 24
Khemis Nagua, Morocco. Heavy rains produced floods that swept through the village on a crowded market day and killed at least 75 persons.

Sept. 25–26
Honduras. Torrential rains and flooding left 22 persons dead and more than 4,000 others homeless.

Sept. 28
Near Manila, Philippines. Taal volcano, lying but a few feet above sea level on a small island in Lake Taal, erupted with a great roar and shooting flames; casualty figures ranged from an estimated thousands to the officially reported toll of not more than 208 persons.

Oct. 28–29
Central Burma. Cyclonic storms and rains lashed wide areas and killed at least 100 persons.

Nov. 10
Northern Burma. Heavy floods inundated Yamethin District and destroyed 12,000 acres of rice; at least 34 persons died in the floods.

Nov. 27
Manizales, Colombia. Drenching rains caused a landslide that buried several houses and killed 32 persons.

Dec. 15
East Pakistan. Chittagong-Cox's Bazar coastal area was hit by a devastating 100-mph cyclone (the third to hit the region within seven months) and tidal wave; the toll of dead and missing was reported to be more than 10,000 persons.

Dec. 17
Rila Mountains, Bulgaria. An avalanche swept down from Malyvitza Peak and killed 11 students from a nearby mountaineering school.

Dec. 22
Lake Carhuacancha, Peru. Spring rains flooded the lake, which broke over its banks and washed down upon three small Andean villages, killing about 60 persons.

Dec. 24
Tipuani, Bolivia. Floodwaters from the swollen Tipuani River

inundated the village, killing 31 persons.

1966

Jan. 3–8

Southwestern Africa. Flash floods in the Umbeluzi River followed in the wake of a cyclone that roared through Mozambique, Rhodesia, and South Africa; more than 150,-000 persons were left homeless; at least 30 died, including 7 crewmen of a helicopter attempting rescue operations.

Jan. 11

Rio de Janeiro, Brazil. Floods caused by Rio's heaviest recorded rainfall triggered landslides that covered several hillside shantytowns and brought death to 239 persons.

Jan. 29–30

Samoa Islands. The islands were swept by a violent hurricane that left at least 90 persons dead.

Jan. 31

Eastern coast, United States. A severe winter storm lashed the coastal areas from Maine to Florida, killing 166 persons.

March 3

Mississippi. Tornadoes slashed across the central part of the state and on into Alabama, killing 61 persons and injuring more than 500 others.

March 4

Upper middle west, United States. A raging blizzard with 100-mph winds whipped snow into huge drifts over the northern plains and along the Great Lakes; hundreds of persons were marooned and at least 20 died.

March 9

Northern China. A major earthquake, registering 6.7 on the Richter scale, struck densely populated regions in Hopeh Province. Casualty figures were not made public, but it was believed that several thousand persons perished.

March 20–22

Western Uganda. A succession of earthquakes centered in the Ruwenzori foothills killed at least 79 persons.

March 28

Rio de Janeiro, Brazil. Torrential rains paralyzed the city and inflicted heavy damage in the slum areas of nearby Petrópolis; 40 persons were reported dead and at least 200 injured.

March 29

Indonesia. Floods in the Solo River led to the evacuation of 500,000 persons; an estimated 9,000 homes were destroyed, and at least 123 persons drowned.

April 3

Central Florida. Tornadoes cutting a swath from Tampa to Cape Kennedy caused damage estimated at $29.4 million; 11 persons died, and at least three hundred others were injured.

April 24

East Java. Volcanic eruptions from 5,678-foot Mount Kelut demolished the village of Margomlujo and killed 90 persons.

April 26

Tashkent, U.S.S.R. A violent earthquake destroyed nearly 28,000 buildings and left at least 100,000 persons homeless; Pravda reported "approximately 10 persons were killed."

May 14

Near Quito, Ecuador. Landslides rumbled down upon a cluster of roadworkers' huts, killing 52 persons.

May 18

North Kivu Province, the Congo. Violent earth tremors centering on the town of Beni toppled hundreds of houses and killed about 90 persons.

June 4–10

Honduras, Cuba, and southeastern United States. Hurricane Alma poured drenching rains on western Honduras, swept through Havana Province in Cuba, then crossed the Gulf of Mexico to strike the Florida panhandle, Georgia, and the Carolinas; a total of 51 persons were killed.

June 8

Kansas. A devastating tornado left a path of wreckage through the northeastern part of the state with Topeka taking the brunt of the $100 million damage; 17 persons died, and more than 300 others were injured.

June 11–15

Hong Kong. Several consecutive days of heavy rain flooded the entire colony and set off a series of landslides; more than 80 persons died or were missing and presumed dead.

June 27

Nepal. An earthquake in the western mountains killed between 80 and 100 persons.

June 28

Honshu Island, Japan. Typhoon Kit flattened the east central coastal areas with 78-mph winds and torrential rain that caused floods and landslides; 44 persons died, 22 were missing, and 80 others were injured.

July 12

Sangi Talaud Island, Indonesia. A volcanic eruption of Mount Awu spewed lava and rocks over farms and villages; 28 persons were killed; 60 children, buried under molten rock that covered their schoolhouse, were listed as missing; 2,000 islanders were injured, and more than 20,000 were left homeless.

Aug. 19–20

Eastern Turkey. A series of violent earthquakes shook 19 mountain provinces, leveling at least 139 villages; according to the official count, at least 2,394 persons were killed, another 1,494 injured, and thousands left homeless.

Sept. 13

Northwestern Iran. Drenching rains and flooding destroyed 30 villages and killed 42 persons; about 70 others were injured.

Sept. 24–Oct. 12

Caribbean area. Hurricane Inez struck the Dominican Republic, Haiti, Cuba, the Bahamas, and southern Florida, turned again upon Cuba, then headed for Mexico to dump torrential rains on the Tampico area; the unofficial international toll was 293 dead, including 44 Cuban refugees who were drowned while attempting to escape in a small open boat.

Sept. 25

Japan. Twin typhoons struck at nearly the same time in two separate areas; more than 300 persons were dead or missing, and at least 700 others were injured.

Oct. 2

East Pakistan. Chittagong and the coastal areas were lashed by cyclonic winds that left nearly 100,000 persons homeless; the official death toll was 845 persons.

Oct. 17

Lima, Peru. A 40-second earthquake jolted the capital city and port at Callao bringing death to 110 persons and injuring more than 3,000 others; damage was estimated at $35 million.

Oct. 21

Aberfan, Wales. A rain-soaked slag heap avalanched down upon a mining village, burying a school and 20 homes; 144 persons were killed.

Nov. 4

Eastern United States. Heavy snow, blizzards, and record cold covered the Midwest eastward to the seaboard and deep into the South, causing 37 deaths.

Nov. 4–6

Northern Italy. Torrential rains flooded and battered the

country from the Alps to Sicily inflicting the greatest havoc upon the cities of Venice and Florence where thousands of art treasures were ruined; at least 113 persons died.

Dec. 18
Khamolane, Lesotho. Lightning struck and killed 14 persons as they sat enjoying a feast.

1967

Jan. 12
Northern Mexico. The worst winter storm in Mexican history dumped snow on Mexico City for the first time in 26 years; 34 deaths were attributed to the storm.

Jan. 18–24
Eastern Brazil. Tropical rains and cloudbursts caused flooding of the Paraíba and Maracaña rivers in Rio de Janeiro and São Paulo states; added to the fatalities from landslides and flooding streams was the heavy loss of life resulting from dozens of cars and buses being washed off the President Dura Highway; at least 894 persons died.

Jan. 26–27
Lower Great Lakes region, United States. A sudden heavy snowfall covered Chicago with a record breaking 23 inches; surrounding areas reported up to 26 inches with drifts of 12 feet; at least 80 persons died in Illinois, Indiana, Michigan, Ohio, and Wisconsin.

Feb. 7–8
East coast, United States. Blizzards and intense cold invaded the New England states and as far south as Washington, D.C.; 74 storm-connected deaths were reported.

Feb. 9
Huila Department, Colombia. A series of jarring earthquakes, centered in the Upper Magdalena Valley, destroyed the village of Guacamayas, damaged buildings in Bogotá, killed at least 100 persons, and injured more than 420 others.

Feb. 17–23
Rio de Janeiro, Brazil. Torrential rains loosened the earth on the city's hillsides and caused hundreds of slum dwellings to slide into the valleys below; at least 224 persons died, and more than 30,000 were left homeless.

Feb. 23
Northern Europe. Destructive storms brought huge flood-tides to the Elbe estuary area and wind damage to Denmark, Germany, and Sweden; many small ships were lost in the North Sea; more than 40 persons perished.

March 19
Rio de Janeiro, Brazil. The third major landslide of the season caused by pounding rains buried the seaside resort of Caraguatatuba; at least 436 persons were killed.

April 21
Northern Illinois. Violent twisters whipped through heavily populated areas, including Belvidere and the Chicago suburb of Oak Lawn, killing 56 persons; at least 1,500 others were injured, and property damage amounted to $20 million.

April 30
Southern Minnesota. Tornadoes lashed through rich farmland, killing 16 persons and injuring nearly 100 others.

May 2
Dacca, East Pakistan. A cyclone swept over the city and destroyed seven surburban villages; about 50 persons died, and at least 200 others were injured.

July 9
Southern Japan. Typhoon Billie roared out of the Pacific with torrential rains that triggered extensive floods and landslides on Honshu and Kyushu islands; 347 persons were dead or missing, and 395 others were injured.

July 22
Northwestern Anatolia, Turkey. A devastating earthquake collapsed most of the buildings in Adapazari and razed 456 other towns and villages; hundreds of residents were buried in rubble and debris with 97 known dead and 147 injured.

July 26
Erzican and Tunceli provinces, Turkey. The second series of major earthquakes in five days struck along the Anatolia Fault, destroyed thousands of buildings, and killed 112 persons.

July 30
Caracas, Venezuela. Three earthquakes within an hour rocked the capital city and surrounding communities; many high-rise apartment buildings were knocked down and shantytowns leveled; the death toll reached 277, nearly 2,000 persons were hospitalized, and more than 110,000 homeless; damage was estimated at $100 million.

Aug. 31
Niigata and Yamagata prefectures, Japan. Week-long rains and flooding brought death to 53 persons; 83 others were missing and 34 injured.

Sept. 5–9
Northern and central India. Monsoon rains fed swollen wa-

terways and flooded land, leaving more than 300 persons dead and possibly 1,000,000 homeless.

Sept. 5–23
Caribbean Islands, Mexico, and Texas. Hurricane Beulah swept across several Caribbean islands, ripped through the Yucatán Peninsula, and slammed into the Texas coastline at Brownsville with 170-mph winds; 54 persons died (43 in the Caribbean and Mexico, 11 in Texas); damage was estimated at $1 billion.

Oct. 3–11
Buenos Aires, Argentina. Prolonged rains caused heavy flooding, left at least 59 persons dead and at least 70,000 others homeless.

Oct. 11
Bay of Bengal. A severe storm swept the bay and coastline, killing nearly 50 persons; almost 300 fishermen were missing.

Oct. 17
Taiwan. Typhoon Carla, leaving a path of death and destruction through the Philippines, lashed into Taiwan with high winds and heavy rain; at least 69 persons were killed, 32 missing, and 67 others injured.

Oct. 28
Central Japan. Rains from Typhoon Diana caused landslides and flooding that brought death to 27 persons; 11 others were missing and 34 injured.

Nov. 26
West central Portugal. Unusually heavy rainfall swamped the Lisbon area surrounding the mouth of the Tagus River; waters were 6 feet deep within the capital city itself, and many towns, villages, roads, and railways were inundated or washed away; the official death toll stood at more than 450.

Nov. 30
Central Java, Indonesia. An irrigation dam collapsed and flooded the villages and rice fields in the valley below; at least 160 persons died.

Nov. 30
Yugoslav-Albanian border. A severe earthquake shattered a wide area on both sides of the frontier but centered on the Yugoslav town of Debar; more than 20 persons were killed and at least 200 injured.

Dec. 11
West coast, India. Intense tremors struck up and down the coast from Bombay to Bangalore, inflicting the heaviest dam-

age on the town of Koyna Nagar; 172 persons perished and at least 1,600 others were injured.

Dec. 12–20

Southwestern United States. Dual blizzards struck with unabating fury, piling snow into six-foot drifts and carrying freezing rain and sleet over much of the Great Plains region; the Navaho Indian Reservation near Window Rock, Arizona, was isolated without food, fuel, or medical supplies; at least 8 Navahos were numbered among the more than 50 deaths resulting from the storms.

1968

Jan. 7

Johore state, Malaysia. Week-long monsoon rains falling on the southern lowlands drove almost 10,000 residents from their homes and brought death to 21 persons.

Jan. 14

Eastern United States. Weekend snow, sleet, and icy rain falling along the Atlantic coastline caused the death of 55 persons.

Jan. 14–15

Scotland. Winds of 125 mph raged through most of the country, damaging buildings and farmlands; 20 persons died, at least 700 others were homeless, and damage amounted to about $2.5 million. Elsewhere in Europe, storms, avalanches, and high seas caused extensive damage and the death of more than 21 persons.

Jan. 15–16

Sicily. A series of earthquakes struck the western tip of the island, destroyed the towns of Gibellina, Partanna, Salaparuta, and Montevago, as well as many villages; 235 bodies were recovered, at least 1,500 persons were missing, 1,500 others injured, and more than 83,000 were left homeless; damage was estimated at $320 million.

Jan. 16

Mindanao Island, Philippines. Floods and landslides caused by nine days of heavy rain brought death to at least 29 persons.

Jan. 28

Swiss Alps. Avalanches occurring over the weekend accounted for the death of about 20 persons; 2 others were missing.

Feb. 20

Aegean Sea. A severe earthquake rocked several small Greek islands, killing 19 persons on Ayios Efstratios and Lemnos;

39 others were injured and many left homeless when more than 500 houses collapsed.

March 8

Eastern Congo (Kinshasa). Earth tremors caused a landslide on the slopes of Mandwe Mountain that swept away the village of Luhonga and killed about 150 persons.

April 4

Central United States. Freezing temperatures, snow, and tornadoes hit the Midwest, bringing death to 18 persons.

April 12

East Pakistan. A cyclone ripped through Faridpur District, ruined numerous towns, and killed at least 100 persons; more than 1,000 persons were injured, and hundreds were left homeless.

April 23

Midwest United States. The four-state area of Ohio, Kentucky, Michigan, and Tennessee bore the brunt of a chain of tornadoes; 12 persons died, and at least 200 were injured.

April 29

Western Iran. An earthquake jolted the area between Maku and Rizaiyeh, killing more than 50 persons; nearly 250 were injured, and many were left homeless.

May 16

Northern Japan. Northern Honshu Island and southern Hokkaido Island were severely damaged by an earthquake that left 47 persons dead and 281 others injured; damage amounted to at least $131 million.

May 16

Midwest and lower Mississippi Valley, United States. Twisters snaked through an 11-state area, causing extensive damage to Arkansas, Iowa, Illinois, and Indiana; known dead stood at 70, with more than 1,000 injured and thousands homeless.

June 19

Northern Peru. An earthquake severely damaged the town of Moyobamba; 16 persons were killed and at least 100 others injured.

July 15

Northwestern and southeastern India. Monsoon floods swirled through six states and caused the deaths of at least 80 persons.

July 28

Southern Japan. A typhoon swept across the land and piled up floodwaters that killed 22 persons.

July 29–31

San José, Costa Rica. Eruption of 5,249-foot Mount Arenal, the first in about 500 years, hurled rocks and lava over a 30-mile area and killed 52 persons; 112 others were missing; damage amounted to millions of dollars.

Aug. 2

Manila, Philippines. A sharp earthquake hit the city at dawn and toppled a five-story apartment building; more than 300 died, most of them residents of the apartment building.

Aug. 7–14

Gujarat and Rajasthan states, India. Week-long flooding claimed the lives of more than 1,000 persons.

Aug. 10–24

Celebes Island, Indonesia. Earthquakes and seismic waves in the Donggala area caused the disappearance of Tuguan Island and killed 293 persons; 23 others were missing.

Aug. 31–Sept. 4

Northeastern Iran. A series of devastating earthquakes shook several areas in the province of Khurasan and centered upon the village of Kakhk; official estimates of the disaster were 30,000 dead, 17,000 injured, and 100,000 homeless.

Sept. 25

Chiapas state, Mexico. A 26-second earth tremor brought death to 15 persons; more than 500 others were injured.

Oct. 2–5

Sikkim. A three-day, 30-inch rainfall caused flooding of the Tiesta River that washed out villages, roads, and bridges and brought death to at least 267 persons.

Oct. 7

Sub-Himalayan region, India. Four days of torrential rain caused floods and landslides around the Darjeeling and Jalpaiguiri areas; at least 560 persons died, and many others were homeless.

Oct. 24

South Korea. Rainstorms and heavy snowfall swept the east coast, bringing death to at least 18 persons; landslides caused an estimated $3 million damage.

Oct. 28

Caspian Sea coast, Iran. Weekend floods along the coastal regions killed at least 30 persons.

Nov. 2–3

Northeastern Italy. Floods and landslides wrought great destruction to the Piedmont countryside; at least 113 persons died or were missing.

Nov. 12

New England and Eastern Canada. High winds, heavy tides, and snow struck the east coast of North America as far south as Long Island, N.Y.; at least 25 persons perished.

1969

Jan. 3

Khurasan Province, Iran. An earthquake of moderate intensity struck along the Iran–U.S.S.R. border bringing death to about 50, injuring at least 300 others, and destroying about 800 homes.

Jan. 18–26

Southern California. Nine days of torrential rains left the area a sea of mud and debris with a death toll of at least 100 persons; more than 9,000 homes were destroyed or damaged, and property loss was estimated at more than $60 million.

Jan. 23

Southern Mississippi. Slashing a mile-wide swath through the hill country at dawn, tornadoes killed 31 persons, injured hundreds of others, and leveled at least 35 buildings.

Feb. 9–10

Northeastern United States. A two-day storm dumped 15 inches of snow along the eastern seaboard causing a total of 166 deaths (New England 73, New York City 43, New York State 37, New Jersey 11, and Pennsylvania 2); damage was estimated at about $25 million.

Feb. 23

Celebes Islands. An earthquake rocked Madjene and the surrounding area killing 64 persons, injured 97 others, and destroyed more than 1,200 buildings.

Feb. 23–26

Southern California. The second downpour of drenching rains within four weeks caused renewed mudslides and flooding; more than 12,500 residents were driven from their homes, with many of the houses sliding down the muddy hillsides; 18 persons died, others were unaccounted for and thought to be buried under mud and debris.

Feb. 24–27

New England-Virginia coast. Heavy two- to three-foot deep snows covered the eastern states for the second time in a month; 40 deaths in New England and 14 in New York City were attributed to the storm.

Feb. 28

Straits of Gibraltar. An earthquake of great magnitude was

felt along the coasts of Portugal, Spain, and Morocco; 13 persons died.

Feb. 28

Central Sulawesi, Indonesia. Striking without warning, an earthquake killed 64 persons; about 100 others were injured, and property damage was at least $1.5 million.

March 17

Alagôas State, Brazil. A flash flood sweeping through the Mundaú Valley, a drought-stricken area, reportedly killed 218 persons and left nearly 50,000 others homeless.

March 28

Western Turkey. A strong earthquake rumbled through an area near Alasehir, killing at least 53 persons and injuring about 350 others; at least 2,500 homes and 2 mosques collapsed.

March 29

Northeastern Ethiopia. A major earthquake completely destroyed the town of Sardó; 24 persons perished, another 165 were injured, and property damage was estimated at $320,-000.

April 4–6

Azerbaijan Province, Iran. Torrential rains caused flooding that brought death to at least 20 persons.

April 14

East Pakistan. The cities of Dacca and Comilla suffered most heavily as a 90-mph tornado struck the area; at least 540 persons died, and more than 1,000 others were injured.

May 17–21

Southern India. Windstorms and tidal waves struck villages along the Bay of Bengal, killing 618 persons in the city of Vijayawada and leaving an estimated 20,000 others homeless; hundreds of cattle died in the floodwaters of the Krishna River in Andhra Pradesh, and crop damage in the rich ricelands was estimated at $40 million.

July 4

Northern Ohio. A sudden violent storm caused high choppy waters on Lake Erie and heavy flooding; 41 persons died.

July 6

Northern French coast. Resorts in Brittany and Normandy were scourged by 100-mph winds off the Atlantic; most of the 23 victims of the storm were vacation sailors.

July 7

Kyushu Island, Japan. Week-long rainstorms brought death to 72 persons.

A grief-stricken woman stands amid the rubble of Gediz, Turkey, one of the towns damaged by an earthquake on March 28.

July 22

Kannaman, India. Torrential rains and strong winds striking the village caused the collapse of a new elementary school, killing 15 children and injuring 92 others.

July 27

Northern Philippines. Typhoon Viola with 100-mph winds caused rough seas, landslides, and swollen rivers that contributed to the death of 11 persons; 17 others were missing and presumed dead.

Aug. 6

Northern Minnesota. Eight separate twisters writhed through the vacation resort country leaving the heaviest destruction in the Roosevelt Lake area; 14 persons were killed and at least 40 others injured.

Aug. 6–8

South Korea. Heavy monsoon rains pelting the countryside caused landslides centered about Hwachon in the north; 85 persons perished, 15 others were missing, and about 12,000 were left homeless.

Aug. 17–20

Gulf of Mexico. The states of Mississippi, Louisiana, Alabama, and Virginia were ravaged by Hurricane Camille, spawned off Cuba on August 15 and finally dissipating off the Virginia coast; at least 400 persons were dead or were reported missing and were presumed dead; damage was estimated at $1 billion.

Sept. 14

Southern Mexico. Month-long torrential rains and flooding brought death to at least 58 persons.

Sept. 14

South Korea. The southern coastline was heavily battered by the most severe rainstorms in 10 years; flooding caused most of the 475 deaths; 407 persons were injured, 78 others missing; property damage was about $61 million.

Sept. 28

Taiwan. Typhoon Elsie raged across the island, killing 102 persons; 24 others were missing and 227 injured; crops were heavily damaged.

Sept. 28–Oct. 8

Tunisia. After five years of drought the country was deluged by 10 days of torrential rain and flooding, leaving half of the land under mud and water; nearly 500 persons were listed as dead; at least 500,000 homes were destroyed, as were highways, railroads, bridges, and whole villages.

Sept. 30

Cape Province, South Africa. A major earthquake leveled three villages, killing 11 persons and leaving about 1,000 others homeless.

Oct. 1–5

Taiwan. Typhoon Flossie, striking within a week of Typhoon Elsie, left 75 dead and nearly 31,000 homeless; damage amounted to millions.

Oct. 13

Biskra, Algeria. Continuing flooding over a wide area brought death to 68 persons; 218 others were injured and more than 100,000 homeless; outbreaks of typhoid, dysentery, and measles added to the misery of the sufferers.

Oct. 19

Morelia, Mexico. Workmen assisted by a number of school-children were toiling to rebuild a damaged village church when an earth slide rumbled down to cover half of the building; 18 children were buried alive.

Oct. 27

Banja Luka, Yugoslavia. A series of three powerful earth-quakes hit the city and surrounding area, leaving 22 persons dead, at least 700 injured, and more than 60,000 others homeless in the midst of thousands of ruined buildings.

Nov. 11

Bay of Bengal, India. A cyclone and tidal wave swept the coastline tearing up huge trees; at least 23 persons died; 30 others were injured.

Dec. 4

Tunisia. Countrywide seasonal rains of unusual intensity over a two-month period left 542 persons dead, more than 300,000 homeless, and property damage of more than $40 million.

1970

Jan. 4

Mendoza, Argentina. Waters released from a collapsed earth-en dam on the Mendoza River poured over the Andean city in a three-foot-high wave, leaving masses of slime and mud; at least 36 persons perished, hundreds were injured, and many more were left homeless; property damage was around $25 million.

Jan.16

Northern Morocco. Two weeks of torrential rain turned the Sebou Valley into an inland sea and completely inundated the city of Kenitra; at least 15 persons died, and nearly 100,000 others were left homeless; crop damage alone was estimated at $26 million.

Jan. 27–28

Northeast of Teheran, Iran. Avalanches of snow tumbled down from the Elburz Mountains onto a highway, sweeping 150 vehicles into a deep ravine; a 50-hour entombment in snow and near-zero weather brought death to at least 43 persons (including 39 in one bus); of the 1,000 others rescued, 100 were injured.

Feb. 10–12

Val d'Isère, France. A landslide thundered off the 7,000-foot crest of Le Dôme to cover an Alpine resort chalet where 200 young skiers were lodged; 43 persons were killed.

Feb. 24

Reckingen, Switzerland. A single giant avalanche swept over the small village and an army training camp; of the 48 persons buried beneath the tons of snow, at least 30 were known to have perished.

March 28–31

Kutahya Province, Turkey. Registering over 7 on the Richter scale, severe earthquakes that centered in Kutahya Province destroyed the town of Gediz and several villages in the Anatolia region; 1,087 persons died, at least 1,500 were injured, and 90,000 were left homeless.

April 7

Manila, Philippines. A destructive earthquake shook the Manila area, killed 15 persons, and injured 200 others.

April 13

Near Dacca, Pakistan. A vicious tornado ripped through six villages, killing 17 persons and injuring about 110 others.

April 16

Plateau d'Assy, France. The third major avalanche of the year plunged down an Alpine slope, killing 72 persons.

April 18

Northern Texas. Tornadoes ripped through a 200-mile area in the Panhandle region, killing at least 25 persons; hundreds more were injured, and property damage was estimated in the millions.

May 11

Lubbock, Texas. A second series of tornadoes in less than a month struck the Texas plains, hitting hardest at Lubbock; 26 persons perished, about 300 others were seriously injured, and property damage amounted to more than $200 million.

May 14–31

Romania. The worst floods in centuries, triggered by torrential rains and melting snow, inundated 37 of Romania's 39 districts, laying waste 1,000 villages and about 2,000,000 acres of choice farmland in the valleys of the Danube River and its tributaries; at least 226 persons died.

May 31

Peru. A devastating earthquake registering 7.75 on the Richter scale centered in northern Peru and levelled towns and cities along the coastal mountain areas; the official toll reached 66,794 dead or missing, with at least 800,000 persons homeless.

July 3–8

South Korea. Five days of ceaseless rain caused the deaths of at least 39 persons; 36 others were injured, and 2,500 were left homeless; property damage was estimated at $5.1 million.

July 22

Pernambuco State, Brazil. Torrential rains caused floods that killed 47 persons.

July 22

Near Badrinath, India. A flash flood poured over a highway, engulfed a cluster of vehicles caught in a narrow gorge, and swept away 25 buses carrying Hindu pilgrims from "the Home of the Gods," as well as 5 taxis and an army truck; nearly 500 persons were killed.

July 30

Northeastern Iran. A strong earthquake left scores of villages in ruins throughout a rugged area of more than 20,000 square miles; known dead numbered at least 176, with 483 persons seriously injured and about 10,000 homeless.

Aug. 1–9

Dacca, Pakistan. Floodwaters spread over vast areas of East Pakistan to affect 10,000,000 persons; at least 100 persons died, and property damage amounted to $150 million.

Aug. 4

Southern Texas. Hurricane Celia swept through the Caribbean off the tip of Florida and struck the Corpus Christi area with a devastating force of 160 mph; of the 32 persons killed, 5 died in Cuba, 14 in Florida, and 13 in Texas; damage in Texas alone was estimated at more than $300 million.

Aug. 11–12

Recife, Brazil. Floods caused by heavy rains brought death to at least 123 persons.

Aug. 19

Eastern Caribbean Sea. Tropical Storm Dorothy lashed the islands of Martinique, Dominica, and Guadaloupe; 43 persons perished, and hundreds were left homeless.

Aug. 20

Ontario, Canada. A freak storm with 90-mph winds roared through the Lake Huron region almost destroying the town of Lively; 10 persons died, and hundreds were left homeless.

Sept. 2

Central Luzon, Philippines. Three days of torrential rains caused flooding over much of Luzon Island; 24 persons died, and thousands were left homeless.

Sept. 8

Near Pyinmana, Burma. A flash flood raced down a river and caught a crowd of 90 persons watching construction work on a bridge; all were drowned.

Sept. 9

Central Arizona. Floods in Maricopa County caused 15 deaths and more than $1 million in damage.

Sept. 11

Venice, Italy. A sudden cyclone with a 125-mph wind spun across the city and killed 35 persons; more than 200 others were injured, and damage amounted to about $3.2 million.

Sept. 11

Northern Luzon, Philippines. Typhoon Georgia raged inland along the northern coast, ravaged the town of Casiguran, and killed as many as 300 persons.

Sept. 15–17

South Korea. Torrential rains lashed the countryside, flooding more than 3,000 homes, killing 28 persons, injuring 35, and leaving 7,000 homeless.

Sept. 27

Lete, Nepal. A landslide engulfed the Himalayan village of Lete and killed 21 persons.

Sept. 30

Mexico City, Mexico. A week of heavy rain caused eight rivers to overflow, forcing thousands from their homes and killing 35 persons.

Oct. 3–10

Puerto Rico. A week-long stationary tropical depression deluged the country with heavy rainfall; at least 60 persons died and property damage amounted to about $100 million.

Oct. 5–9

Italian Riviera. Driving rains triggered floods that swept

through the heart of the port city of Genoa, inundated villages for 50 miles up and down the coast, and brought death to at least 30 persons.

Oct. 12

Philippines. Typhoon Joan roared across the islands, killing at least 525 persons; 169 others were missing and 912 injured.

Oct. 19

Philippines. Typhoon Kate, the second typhoon to hit the islands in a week, left 501 persons dead, 312 missing, and 76 injured.

Oct. 23

East Pakistan. Hurricane winds of 90 mph slashed across nine districts, and accompanying tidal waves washed over the districts on the Bay of Bengal; 100 persons were believed dead.

Oct. 26–30

South Vietnam. Severe floods swept five northern provinces with Quang Ngai suffering the heaviest destruction; at least 237 persons were killed, and more than 204,000 were left homeless.

Nov. 12

Northern Colombia. Month-long storms followed by an earthquake took the lives of more than 200 persons; 460 others were reported missing.

Nov. 12–13

East Pakistan. Possibly the greatest catastrophe of the century came in the wake of gigantic 30-foot cyclone-driven sea waves that hurtled in from the Bay of Bengal to pound the Ganges-Brahmaputra delta, its dozens of offshore islands, and four coastal districts, affecting 3.3 million persons in a 3,000 square mile area. The official death toll was close to 200,000 persons, with another 100,000 missing, but it was believed as many as 500,000 might have perished. Property damage was estimated at more than $2 billion.

Nov. 20

Luzon, Philippines. A violent typhoon with winds of 125 mph raged through the heavily populated island, wrecking the harbor and airport facilities at Manila; 120 persons died, 60 others were missing, and more than 1,000 were injured; property damage reached $80 million.

Dec. 9

Peru-Ecuador border. An earthquake registering 7.6 on the Richter scale struck the Andes border area with such force that many towns and villages were shattered; at least 28 persons were killed, and about 600 others were injured.

Dec. 12

Caldas, Colombia. Avalanches of mud and rocks tumbled down the northwestern slopes of the Andes to block the rain-swollen Cauca River between the towns of Pintada and Supia; the ensuing floodwaters killed more than 100 persons.

1971

Jan. 4

Midwestern United States. A storm piled snow into 12-foot drifts, stranding thousands of motorists; 37 deaths were attributed to the storm.

Jan. 7

Temerloh region, Malaysia. Nine days of rain and flooding isolated an estimated 150,000 victims who perched on rooftops and roads awaiting relief; at least 60 persons were believed dead.

Jan. 29

Zambézia region, Mozambique. Torrential rains accompanying a cyclone inundated lowland areas and threatened the half-million trapped residents with starvation; estimates of the death toll ranged from 500 to 1,000 persons.

Feb. 6

Toscana, Italy. Twin earthquakes struck within hours to destroy the ancient city of Tuscania; the city and 23 surrounding small towns suffered at least 22 fatalities; 120 other persons were injured, the homeless numbered 4,000 and property damage in Tuscania alone was estimated at $41.6 million.

Feb. 9

Eastern Australia. More than a week of heavy rains and flooding caused by Cyclone Sheila swamped New South Wales, Queensland, and Victoria; at least 27 persons died, and damage amounted to about $20 million.

Feb. 9

San Fernando Valley, California. An earthquake of moderate intensity struck the Los Angeles area, killing 65 persons, injuring about 1,000 others, and causing an estimated $1 billion in damage.

Feb. 21

Louisiana and Mississippi. Twisters ripped through the ill-famed "Dixie Tornado Alley," hitting Mississippi with violent fury; 115 persons died and about 500 others were injured;

property damage amounted to more than $7.5 million.

March 9.

Near Quito, Ecuador. Tons of earth tumbled off a mountainside, blocking a major road and killing nearly 30 persons; 6 others were injured.

March 18

Near Canta, Peru. An earthquake triggered an avalanche that roared down the Andes, overran the remote mining camp of Chungar, and buried as many as 600 persons.

March 21

Telefomin, New Guinea. A landslide in the Telefomin area buried about 100 villagers.

April 26

Central Philippines. Tropical Storm Wanda brought heavy rains and violent winds that killed at least 25 persons; more than 100 others were missing.

April 28

Central United States. Tornadoes slashed Kentucky, touched on Illinois and Tennessee, and killed at least 11 persons; more than 100 others were injured.

April 29

Salvador, Brazil. Three days of heavy rain, floods, and landslides left more than 150 persons dead, 10,000 others homeless, and damages amounting to around $6 million.

May 4

St. Jean de Vianney, Quebec. Excessive rains led to an earth cave-in that dumped 35 homes, several cars, and a bus into a crater 70 feet wide and 100 feet deep; 31 persons perished.

May 12

Burdur, Turkey. A severe earthquake shook the Burdur area in southwest Turkey, killing 57 persons.

May 22

Bingöl, Turkey. Turkey's second quake within ten days centered in the eastern province of Bingöl, destroying 90 percent of the capital city of Bingöl and wreaking havoc on more than 300 mountain villages and hamlets; the official death toll stood at 1,000 persons.

June 16

Acapulco, Mexico. Tropical Storm Brigitte with 95-mph winds and torrential rains struck the west coast resort area, leaving a reported 17 persons dead or missing.

June 26

Salgar, Colombia. A rain-swollen mountain stream swept through dozens of village homes, claiming the lives of at least

15 persons; another 36 were reported missing.

July 8

Central Chile. A major earthquake caused heavy damage to the oil and copper refineries of the central coastal area; at least 82 persons died, and about 450 others were injured.

July 20

Seoul, South Korea. A cloudburst dumped 7 inches of rain on the city and caused 45 deaths.

July 27

South Korea. Torrential rains brought on floods and landslides throughout the central and southwestern regions, killing at least 64 persons; 5 others were missing and about 45 injured.

July 28

Khinjan Pass, Afghanistan. A landslide occurring near the pass in the Hindu Kush mountains opened a natural reservoir, allowing floodwaters to sweep through a village below, killing 100 persons.

Aug. 3

Baltimore County, Maryland. Several days of heavy rain and swollen rivers caused 13 deaths.

Aug. 5

Western Japan. Typhoon Olive swept across the western part of Kyushu Island, leaving at least 135 persons dead or missing and presumed dead.

Aug. 17

Hong Kong. Typhoon Rose, with 130-mph winds, drenched Hong Kong and the harbor areas with 12 inches of rain, capsized about 40 fishing boats and a ferry (drowning 85 persons), and grounded another 26 oceangoing vessels; official death toll stood at about 90 persons; another 200 were injured.

Sept. 9

Uttar Pradesh, India. The worst floods in 11 years forced the evacuation of 35,000 persons from Lucknow, the capital city; the official death toll was 300.

Sept. 9

Central America. Hurricane Edith, with 175-mph winds, slammed into the coast of the Nicaragua-Honduras border and eastern areas of British Honduras, killing at least 23 persons.

Sept. 14

Southeastern Pennsylvania. A four-day downpour caused flooding and left 13 persons dead or missing; damages in

Chester, Delaware, and Montgomery counties were estimated at $14 million.

Oct. 23

South Vietnam. Typhoon Hester tore into five northern provinces, flattening 17,000 homes and damaging another 40,000 buildings with its 140-mph winds; 89 persons perished.

Oct. 29–30

Eastern India. Preceded by a cyclone, a 15-foot ocean wave devastated a wide area of eastern Orissa State; officials estimated that possibly 10,000 to 25,000 persons died, with tens of thousands left homeless.

1972

Jan. 4

Buenos Aires, Argentina. A scorching 10-day heat wave with a steady temperature of 100° F settled over the capital city and resulted in a death toll of about 100 from dehydration, traffic accidents, and drownings.

Jan. 4

Philippines. Typhoon Kit left an official death toll of 67, although 200 was considered a more realistic figure.

Jan. 26

San Josecito, Colombia. Triggered by heavy rains, a landslide killed an estimated 70 villagers.

Feb. 4

Istanbul, Turkey. A two-week wave of snowstorms and subfreezing temperatures brought death to at least 30 persons.

Feb. 10

Iran. Two weeks of heavy blizzards and freezing temperatures with up to 26 feet of snow killed at least 60 persons.

Feb. 26

Buffalo Creek, West Virginia. The collapse of a dam released millions of gallons of water and sludge to wreak havoc in the narrow valley below; 118 persons died; at least 4,000 others were homeless.

March 14

Peru. Flooding from a month-long deluge of rain brought death to at least 40 persons and left another 200,000 homeless in 41 cities and villages.

March 26

Herat Province, Afghanistan. Floods in the province were reported to have claimed 118 lives.

April 2

Mymensingh District, Bangladesh. A tornado with winds of

160 mph struck the area and killed at least 200 persons, leaving another 25,000 homeless.

April 10

Southern Iran. A devastating earthquake centering on the village of Ghir in Fars Province caused great destruction over an area that included some 60 towns and villages; an estimated 4,000 persons died; thousands of others were injured.

April 29

Mymensingh District, Bangladesh. The second tornado in less than a month lashed the district, killing more than 200 persons; crop and property damage were extensive.

May 3

Mexico City, Mexico. Violent thunderstorms caused flash floods that swept rocks, mud, and tree trunks from the hills and onto the city; 37 persons died, at least 70 others were injured, and more than 100,000 were left homeless.

May 14

New Braunfels, Texas. A two-inch rainfall along the Guadalupe River brought the river over its banks to reach nine feet above flood stage; 17 persons drowned in the swirling waters.

May 31

India. A month-long heat wave and drought affected 50 million persons, killing at least 800, and destroying an estimated $40 million worth of crops.

June 9–10

Rapid City, South Dakota. A cloudburst in the Black Hills triggered runoff floods that roared down Rapid Creek, swelling it to a width of 400 feet, inundating the city and surrounding countryside, and washing out the earthen dam of Canyon Lake; the death toll was 235, with nearly 500 homes destroyed and total property damage estimated at about $100 million.

June 15–25

Caribbean-Eastern United States. Hurricane Agnes slashed Cuba, the Florida Keys, and central Florida and then struck the eastern seaboard with deadly torrents of rain that flooded the six-state area of Virginia, West Virginia, Pennsylvania, Maryland, New Jersey, and New York; the final death toll was 134; at least 128,000 homes and businesses were destroyed with damage estimated at more than $60 billion.

June 18

Hong Kong. Three days of torrential rain caused landslides that killed at least 100 persons; 69 others were missing, and about 1,000 were left homeless.

June 25
Sylhet District, Bangladesh. Devastating floods destroyed hundreds of homes and about 80,000 acres of crops; at least 50 persons were killed.

July 5
Oimawashi, Japan. Rescue workers attempting to find a family buried in a previous landslide set off a second slide that pushed a local train into a river; 80 persons buried in the debris were presumed dead.

Aug. 6
Philippines. Month-long floods brought on by incessant rains devastated Luzon Island, causing shortages of food, medicine, and fuel, and threatening outbreaks of cholera; the death toll reached 427.

Aug. 19–20
South Korea. A two-day deluge poured 18 inches of rain on Seoul and lesser amounts on the provinces of Kyonggi and Kangwon; flooding and landslides killed 467 persons; at least 100 others were missing, about 400 injured, with 326,000 homeless; property damage was estimated at $17 million.

Aug. 31
During the month of August, a severe drought caused starvation conditions in the state of Bihar, India, which resulted in at least 250 deaths.

Sept. 14
South Korea. A second round of rains and floods in Korea in less than a month inundated the southern part of the peninsula, bringing death to 101 persons; 29 others were missing and 59 injured.

Sept. 16
Japan. Typhoon Helen hit Honshu Island, killing at least 50 persons, destroying about 400 houses, and damaging or sinking 75 ships.

Oct. 21
Srinagar, Kashmir. Strong winds accompanying a severe snowstorm hurled 75 mountain porters down the mountainside where 50 of them perished.

Nov. 13
Northern Europe. High winds and torrential rains hit the Netherlands, Belgium, West Germany, and the British Isles, leaving at least 25 dead.

Nov. 14
Midwestern and northeastern United States. A severe storm battered the Great Lakes area before passing through New

England; at least 24 deaths were recorded.
Dec. 5
Philippines. Tropical Storm Theresa slashed the Philippine Islands; at least 169 persons died, and more than 2,500 were left homeless.
Dec. 23–24
Managua, Nicaragua. Earthquakes, with the strongest tremor registering 6.25 on the Richter scale, leveled the capital city; an estimated 6,000–7,000 persons were believed dead, 20,000 injured, and 300,000 left homeless.

1973
Jan. 1–6
Sicily. Storms lashing the island of Sicily and southern Italy with high winds and torrential rains claimed 24 lives and left 5,000 persons homeless; damage amounted to more than $360 million.
Jan. 5
Uttar Pradesh and Bihar states, India. A bitter two-week cold wave brought death to at least 115 persons.
Jan. 10
San Justo, Argentina. A three-minute tornado with 100-mph winds wrecked buildings in the town and surrounding farmland, killing 60 persons and injuring more than 300 others.
Jan. 17
Iberian Peninsula. A severe 70-mph storm hit the coasts of Spain and Portugal, stirring up 45-foot waves that sank dozens of boats, leveled harbor installations, and left at least 10 persons dead or missing.
Jan. 31
Tecomán, Mexico. An earthquake struck Mexico's Pacific coastal area, killing 17 persons and injuring hundreds of others.
March 26
East central Brazil. Flooding along the Caratinga River caused at least 20 deaths; thousands of persons were left homeless, and damage amounted to $16 million.
April 7
Tunisia. Late March and early April floods devastated a wide area of the country, leaving 86 persons dead and 33 missing; an estimated 6,000 homes were destroyed and 10,000 head of cattle lost.
April 9
Midwestern United States. A 24-hour storm battered a three-

state area and churned up Lake Michigan into huge waves that pounded 28 miles of lakefront, causing nearly $600,000 in damage to breakwaters and shorelines; 26 deaths were recorded.

April 12
Faridpur District, Bangladesh. More than a dozen villages were struck by a 90-mph wind and rainstorm that killed up to 200 persons, injured about 15,000 others, and left 10,000 more homeless.

April 14
Guanacaste Province, Costa Rica. An earthquake centering near the village of Tilarán killed at least 16 persons.

April 29
Mississippi Valley, United States. Flood waters from the Mississippi River and its tributaries flooded 11,000,000 acres, washing out farms and homes, bridges, roads, and levees; flood-related accidents caused at least 16 deaths.

May 26–28
South central United States. Severe weekend rainstorms and tornadoes wreaked havoc over 11 states; 48 persons died, hundreds were injured, and damage to buildings and crops was in the millions of dollars.

June 26
San Antonio de Prado, Colombia. Rubble from a landslide buried homes in which 16 persons perished.

July 8
Near Guadalajara, Mexico. A cloudburst in the mountains poured floodwaters over the fishing towns of Ocotlán, San Pedro Itzican, and Mazcola on the shores of Lake Chapala; at least 30 persons died, and 27 others were injured.

July 14–15
Northern Italy. Heavy weekend rainstorms drenched the Italian Riviera area, touching off floods and landslides that resulted in 14 deaths.

August
Northern Indian subcontinent. Prolonged monsoon rains along the entire Himalayan mountain range caused rampaging rivers to overflow their banks and engulf entire towns in Pakistan, Bangladesh, and the Indian states of Uttar Pradesh, Assam, and Bihar; thousands died, millions were made homeless, and property damage was estimated in the hundreds of millions of dollars; thousands of square miles of farmland were inundated, huge quantities of stored crops were washed away, and numerous bridges, railroad tracks,

and roads were destroyed.

August

Iripuato, Mexico. Severe flooding caused by prolonged rains that fell over wide areas of Mexico killed an estimated 200 persons and made 150,000 homeless; crop losses were valued at more than $100 million.

Aug. 28

States of Puebla, Veracruz, and Oaxaca, Mexico. An earthquake measuring 6.4 on the Richter scale occurred along the Zacomboxo Fault in central Mexico, killing at least 600 persons (the highest such toll ever recorded in Mexico), injuring about 4,000, and destroying or severely damaging nearly 10,-000 buildings.

Oct. 12

Central United States. Unusually heavy rains and severe flash flooding from Nebraska to Texas took the lives of at least 11 persons; at least 35 others were reported missing.

Oct. 19–21

Southern Spain. Torrential rains that caused widespread flash flooding in the provinces of Granada, Almería, and Murcia brought death to at least 500 persons; damage was estimated at $400 million.

Nov. 10–11

South Vietnam. Typhoon rains pouring down on Binh Dinh and neighboring provinces washed out bridges, destroyed homes, and damaged crops; at least 60 persons died, and about 150,000 were forced to flee their dwellings.

Nov. 18–24

Philippines. A typhoon and heavy monsoon rains flooded Cagayan Valley and many towns in the southern islands, bringing death to 54 persons and damaging crops, roads, bridges, and thousands of homes.

Dec. 9

Bangladesh. A cyclone striking the southern coast capsized at least 200 fishing boats; many of the 1,000 missing fishermen were feared drowned.

Dec. 13

Qafsah, Tunisia. Surging floodwaters brought on by torrential rains smashed into a school and swept 45 children to their deaths.

Dec. 17

Atlantic seaboard, United States. A severe weekend snow and ice storm stretching from Maine to Georgia cut off power supplies to hundreds of homes and left at least 20 dead.

Dec. 23

Eastern and northern India. A cold wave that continued for several weeks in the state of Bihar claimed 146 lives; similar fatalities were reported in Delhi and neighboring areas.

1974

Mid–Jan.

Australia. Floodwaters in eastern Australia claimed 17 lives and left an estimated 1,000 persons homeless; in New South Wales and Queensland tens of thousands of sheep and cattle were killed.

Mid–Jan.

Situbondo, Indonesia. Heavy rains and ocean waves in East Java destroyed homes, washed out bridges, and ruined rice crops; 19 died, and about 2,000 were made homeless.

Jan. 21

Tatra Mountains, Czechoslovakia. Three avalanches, brought on by a sudden temperature rise, brought death to 12 Czechoslovak ski students, their instructor, and a mountaineer.

Late Jan.

Eastern Australia. Prolonged storms caused record flooding over vast areas of the eastern half of Australia; Queensland, the most devastated region, reported at least 15 deaths and damage to crops, cattle, and homes well in excess of $100 million.

February

Northwestern Argentina. Torrential rains inundated half of Santiago del Estero Province, virtually destroying the entire cotton harvest; similar destruction occurred in ten other provinces; at least 100 persons were killed, and more than 100,000 were forced to evacuate their homes.

Feb. 10

Natal, South Africa. Rivers, swollen by an intense rainfall, overflowed their banks in northern Natal and swept away huts and shacks during the night; more than 50 persons were believed dead, many of them children.

Late March

Tubarão, Brazil. After months of drought, torrential rains poured into the Tubarão River, which rose 36 feet within hours, overflowed its banks, and virtually destroyed the city; reports estimated that between 1,000 and 1,500 persons died and about 60,000 of the city's 70,000 people were made homeless.

Early April

Grande Kabylie, Algeria. Several days of torrential coastal rains caused severe flooding; at least 50 persons were reported killed and 30 injured.

April 3

United States and Canada. A series of tornadoes, nearly 100 of which struck during an eight-hour period, caused more than $1 billion in damage in 11 southern and midwestern states and in Ontario; the final death toll was 323.

April 16

Okuura, Japan. A storm-triggered landslide buried about 80 homes in mud in an area of old mine tunnels about 190 miles north of Tokyo; 8 bodies were recovered but 9 other persons were missing and believed killed.

April 25

Central Andes, Peru. Heavy rains and earth tremors caused parts of three mountains to shear loose in gigantic landslides that virtually obliterated several villages; in all, more than 1,000 persons were killed.

Early May

Northeast Brazil. Heavy rains caused landslides that reportedly brought death to 91 persons; all told, floods claimed about 200 victims, mostly in the state of Ceará.

May 9

Izu-hanto, Japan. A powerful earthquake, striking 90 miles southwest of Tokyo, damaged or destroyed hundreds of homes, killed more than 30 persons, and injured 102.

June 8

Oklahoma. A series of tornadoes swept through Oklahoma, killing 14 persons and injuring hundreds; 6 others were killed in Kansas and 4 in Arkansas.

June 17

Near Acapulco, Mexico. Torrential rains carried by Hurricane Dolores devastated an area on the outskirts of Acapulco; at least 13 persons were killed and 35 injured; the fate of 16 others was unknown.

June 28

Quebradablanca, Colombia. A huge avalanche of rocks and mud thundered onto a highway, engulfing 6 crowded buses and more than 20 other vehicles, some of which were hurled into a ravine; officials estimated the death toll to be in excess of 200 and the injured to number about 100.

July 6–7

Japan. A typhoon that dumped as much as 12 inches of rain

on some areas of western and southern Japan killed 33 persons; 50 others were injured, and 15 were reported missing.

July 11

Japan. Prolonged rains in various parts of the country brought death to at least 108 persons and caused damage estimated at nearly $400 million.

Mid–Aug.

Bangladesh and northeastern India. Two Himalayan rivers, at flood stage for several weeks, were reported to have caused at least 800 deaths in Bangladesh and 100 deaths in seven states of northeastern India.

Mid–Aug.

Luzon, Philippines. Week-long monsoon rains, which flooded vast expanses of 13 of the 24 provinces of the island of Luzon, killed at least 94 persons; more than one million refugees of the disaster required emergency relief.

Aug. 15

West Bengal State, India. A cyclone killed at least 20 persons and injured about 100 others before moving on to Jamshedpur, where 800 families had to be evacuated.

Aug. 20

Irrawaddy River Valley, Burma. Widespread flooding, brought on by monsoon rains, inundated nearly 2,000 villages and took the lives of at least 12 persons; about 500,000 persons were left homeless.

Sept. 20

Honduras. Hurricane Fifi, battering the northern coast of Honduras with 130-mph winds and torrential rains, brought death to an estimated 5,000 persons and caused extensive damage to crops, buildings, roads, bridges, and communication facilities.

Sept. 29

Medellín, Colombia. A landslide that crashed into a slum settlement on the outskirts of the city took the lives of an estimated 90 persons.

Oct. 3

Peru. A violent earthquake measuring 7.8 on the Richter scale caused extensive damage in Lima and in the coastal cities of Cañete, Pisco, and Ica; reports indicated that the quake killed more than 73 persons, injured about 2,000, and badly damaged or destroyed thousands of homes.

Oct. 3

Chorillos, Peru. An earthquake that demolished numerous buildings killed 44 persons and injured hundreds.

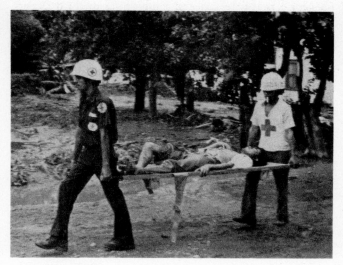

Red Cross workers remove an injured man from the village of Choloma, Honduras, after Hurricane Fifi struck on September 20.

Oct. 23
Sâo Tomé. A landslide that rumbled through a ravine killed at least 30 persons.

Nov. 19
Silopi, Turkey. Floodwaters from a small river swollen by heavy rains trapped members of a nomadic tribe camping nearby; 33 persons lost their lives.

Nov. 29
Off Cox's Bazar, Bangladesh. A 12-foot tidal wave swept over offshore islands in the southeastern Bay of Bengal in the wake of a cyclone that left thousands homeless and killed 20 persons.

Dec. 20
Neskaupstadhur, Iceland. An avalanche of snow and ice roared down on the town, killing 12 persons.

Dec. 25
Darwin, Australia. Cyclone Tracy ripped through the port city of Darwin; 90 percent of the city was destroyed, and the death toll was reported to be more than 50.

Dec. 28
Northern Pakistan. A violent earthquake destroyed at least

nine villages situated at the base of the Karakoram Range; rescue teams placed the death toll at about 5,200 and the number of injured at 15,000.

1975

Early January

Southern Thailand. Unusually heavy rains caused widespread flooding that severely damaged rubber plantations, rice crops, and mining facilities; the disaster also claimed 131 lives.

Early January

Central United States. A blizzard with subzero temperatures and 90-mph winds was responsible for 50 deaths in the midwest and the central plains.

Jan. 10

Mississippi. A tornado that leveled a shopping center killed 12 persons and injured about 200; property damage was estimated in the millions of dollars.

Jan. 19

Himachal Pradesh State, India. A violent earthquake measuring 7 on the Richter scale destroyed numerous dwellings and buried many inhabitants alive under the rubble.

Late January

Philippines. A tropical storm triggered landslides on the island of Mindanao; all told, the storm was blamed for 30 deaths on land and sea.

Feb. 4

Anshan, Liaoning Province, China. A violent earthquake measuring 7.3 on the Richter scale hit Anshan, a major industrial area in northeast China; though no report on casualties or damage was released, at least some of the 830,000 inhabitants were believed to have been killed or injured because of the large number of factories and homes located in the area.

Feb. 20–21

Nile River area, Egypt. In the worst Egyptian flood in 20 years, torrential rains inundated 1,000 acres of land along the Nile River, destroyed 21 villages, and took at least 15 lives.

Mid–March

Nequen Province, Argentina. Rainstorms sweeping in off the Andes caused the deaths of 20 persons; about a dozen others were missing.

Late March

British Columbia, Canada. A violent storm that lashed Vancouver Island and swept some 200 miles inland to Kamloops capsized ships, destroyed aircraft, uprooted trees, downed power lines, and damaged campers, buildings, and stores; 14 fishermen were reported missing and were presumed drowned.

Early April

Alps mountain ranges. In one of the worst series of avalanches on record, huge quantities of snow buried villages, roads, and rail lines; the estimated death toll was 13 in Switzerland, 12 in Italy, and 15 in Austria.

April 21

Northern Iran. Torrential rains in the Damghan area destroyed about 150 villages and took the lives of at least 14 persons.

Mid–June

Pakistan. A searing week-long heat wave that reached 119° F in some areas took at least 14 lives.

July

Northwestern India. Month-long monsoon rains flooded about 400 square miles of crops, damaged or destroyed an estimated 14,000 dwellings, and took the lives of at least 300 persons.

August

Northern Japan. Typhoon Phyllis, which killed 68 persons in Mid-August when it lashed the Japanese island of Shikoku, was followed a week later by Typhoon Rita, which caused extensive damage and claimed 26 lives; 3 others were missing and 52 injured.

Late August

San'a'. Yemen Arab Republic. Floodwaters that swept through the capital of Yemen killed 80 persons, most of whom were women and children.

Aug.–Sept.

Eastern India. Seasonal monsoon rains that caused hundreds of millions of dollars in damage and contributed to the spread of cholera took the lives of at least 450 persons.

Sept. 6

Lice, Turkey. An earthquake that registered 6.8 on the Richter scale leveled the town of Lice and severely affected a wide area in eastern Turkey; tremors continued for several days, collapsing more buildings and bringing the final death toll to 2,312; the number of injured was placed at 3,372.

Early September

Uttar Pradesh State, India. Monsoon rains flooded the town

of Bulandshahr with water up to 10 feet deep and drowned at least 30 persons.

Sept. 16

Puerto Rico. Hurricane Eloise, which packed winds up to 140 mph and dumped torrential rains on Puerto Rico, caused tens of millions of dollars in damage and killed 34 persons before striking the island of Hispaniola, where 25 more persons were killed. After severely battering Haiti and the Dominican Republic, Eloise claimed 12 more lives when it moved into mainland Florida and on to the northeastern part of the United States.

Oct. 22–23

Gujarat State, India. A fierce two-day storm that pounded the west coast of India caused extensive damage to homes and crops and took at least 21 lives.

Oct. 24

Mazatlán, Mexico. Hurricane Olivia hit the peninsula city of Mazatlán on the Gulf of California, bringing death to 29 persons.

Dec. 24

Rhodesia. During a violent storm, 21 persons seeking temporary shelter inside a hut were killed by a bolt of lightning; 14 were children.

The Elbe River in Hamburg, West Germany, rises after severe storms hit northern Europe on January 2–3.

1976

Jan. 2–3

Northern Europe. A violent storm carrying winds in excess of 100 mph struck England with devastating force before moving on to the Continent; there were 26 fatalities reported in Britain, 12 in West Germany, and a total of 17 others in Denmark, Belgium, The Netherlands, Sweden, Austria, France, and Switzerland.

Feb. 4

Guatemala. An earthquake measuring 7.5 on the Richter scale caused extensive damage in Guatemala City and virtually destroyed several other towns and villages; casualties reached an estimated 22,000 to 23,000 dead and at least 75,000 injured.

Feb. 11

Esmeraldas, Ecuador. At least 60 persons were believed to have been killed when a landslide hit a section of Esmeraldas.

Mid–February

Bitlis Province, Turkey. A series of avalanches in eastern Anatolia claimed the lives of 27 persons.

April 9

Esmeraldas, Ecuador. An earthquake that struck the port

Alone, a Guatemalan boy stands among the ruins of his home, which was destroyed by an earthquake on February 4.

city of Esmeraldas claimed at least 10 lives and caused damage estimated at $4 million.

April 10

Faridpur, Bangladesh. A tornado that struck at least a dozen villages in Faridpur District in central Bangladesh killed 19 persons and injured more than 200 others.

May 2

Near Fresno, Colombia. Torrential rains triggered a landslide in the Andes Mountains; 13 persons died and 16 others were injured.

May 6

Northeastern Italy. A major earthquake that struck the northeastern area of Italy caused extensive damage in several towns, killing nearly 1,000 persons.

Mid–May

Luzon, Philippines. Record-breaking rains unleashed on the island of Luzon by Typhoon Olga caused massive flooding that took 215 lives and left at least 600,000 persons homeless; property damage and crop losses were estimated at $150 million.

June 4

Pahire Phedi, Nepal. An early morning landslide took the lives of an estimated 150 villagers.

Mid–June

Bangladesh. Persistent torrential monsoon rains were responsible for the death of at least 143 persons, some of whom were buried under landslides.

June 26

Irian Jaya, Indonesia. A major earthquake that struck this province on the island of New Guinea claimed an estimated 500 to 1,000 lives.

Mid–July

Mexico. After nearly two weeks of almost constant rain, an estimated 120 persons were dead and some 50 others missing as a result of floods in central and eastern Mexico; in addition, hundreds of thousands were homeless and millions of acres of fertile farmland were inundated.

July 14

Bali, Indonesia. An earthquake measuring 5.6 on the Richter scale killed more than 500 persons and injured about 3,400 others; fatalities included schoolchildren who were killed when their building in Seririt collapsed.

July 28

T'angshan, Hopeh Province, China. Two devastating earthquakes measuring 8.2 and 7.9 on the Richter scale struck northeastern China 16 hours apart. Though no official report on damage or casualties was released at the time, it was learned that the industrial city of T'angshan had been virtually leveled and that extensive damage had also taken place in Tientsin and Peking. The death toll was later reliably estimated to be about 700,000, which made the T'angshan disaster the second worst in recorded history. In 1556 an earthquake in three northern provinces of China had claimed about 830,000 lives.

July 31
Big Thompson River canyon, Colorado. A 30-foot-high wall of water raced through the narrow Big Thompson River canyon after more than a foot of rain fell in six hours; rescuers recovered 130 bodies, but many others remained buried beneath the mud and rubble.

Aug. 7
Chonju, South Korea. Torrential rains killed at least 25 persons, 15 of whom were buried by a landslide.

Aug. 10
Northern Pakistan. Heavy rains that caused the Ravi River to overflow its banks caused extensive damage in northern Pakistan; more than 150 persons died in the floodwaters that affected at least 5,000 villages.

Aug. 17
Philippines. A severe earthquake in the Moro Gulf created a 15-to-20-foot-high seismic wave that struck the island of Mindanao and the Sulu Archipelago with devastating force; the death toll was estimated at 8,000, and the damage to property exceeded $100 million.

Aug. 25
Hong Kong. The worst tropical storm to hit Hong Kong in nearly 50 years killed at least 11 persons, injured 62 others, and left about 3,000 persons homeless.

Sept. 5
Baluchistan Province, Pakistan. Floodwaters demolished the 442-foot-high earthen Bolan Dam washing away entire villages and inundating more than 5,000 square miles of land; the death toll was thought to be high.

Sept. 8–13
Southern Japan. Typhoon Fran battered southern Japan with 100-mph winds and deposited 60 inches of rain; 104 persons were killed, 57 were missing, and an estimated 325,000 were made homeless.

Oct. 1

La Paz, Mexico. A 30-foot-high earthen dam burst under the impact of Hurricane Liza, which carried 130-mph winds and dumped 5.5 inches of rain; a 5-foot wall of water swept across part of the city and killed at least 630 persons; tens of thousands of persons were rendered homeless.

Oct. 6

Near Pereira, Colombia. Heavy rains caused a dike to burst, killing at least 47 persons and injuring about 30 others.

Oct. 29

Irian Jaya, Indonesia. A severe earthquake in the Bime, Eipomek, and Nalka areas of New Guinea killed at least 133 persons.

Nov. 6

Trapani, Sicily, Italy. Heavy rains generated floodwaters that took the lives of 10 persons.

Nov. 7

Khorasan Province, Iran. A moderately severe earthquake that struck Vandik and several other villages killed at least 16 persons and inflicted injuries on about 30 others.

Nov. 20

Chameza, Colombia. A landslide that occurred about 190 miles from Bogotá smashed into a cluster of peasant huts and claimed an estimated 20 lives.

Nov. 24

Van Province, Turkey. A major earthquake measuring 7.9 on the Richter scale struck eastern Turkey; heavy snows and rugged terrain impeded the work of rescue teams; the final death toll reached about 4,000.

Late Nov.

Eastern Java, Indonesia. Heavy rains caused extensive property and crop damage and killed at least 136 persons.

Dec. 20

Aceh, Sumatra, Indonesia. Torrential rains caused severe flooding in villages of the district, killing at least 25 persons.

1977

Jan. 10

Goma, Zaire. The Nyiragongo volcano, Africa's second highest active volcano at 11,000 feet, erupted and spewed lava on the town of Goma 8 miles away, killing an estimated total of 2,000 persons.

Jan. 19

Brazil. Heavy rains that caused two rivers to overflow their banks caused extensive damage in the southwest region of Brazil; 60 persons died in the floodwaters and at least 3,500 others were left homeless.

Early Feb.

Madagascar. A cyclone accompanied by heavy rains swept through the island of Madagascar and destroyed 30,000 homes and 38,000 acres of rice fields; 5 persons were injured and 31 were killed.

Feb. 15

Gaza District, Mozambique. The provincial capital of Xai-Xai was flooded under 5 feet of water from the Limpopo River after a safety dike burst; at least 300 persons were killed.

March 4

Svishtov, Veliko Turnovo Province, Bulgaria. An earthquake in the port city of Svishtov injured 164 persons and killed 130.

March 4

Romania. An earthquake measuring 7.2 on the Richter scale devastated the Romanian capital of Bucharest and several major industrial centers; between 7,000 and 11,000 persons were injured, 80,000 were left homeless, and more than 1,400 were killed.

Mid–March

Central United States. A late winter blizzard swept through South Dakota, blocking about 100 miles of interstate highway and killing 9 persons in Colorado, 4 in Nebraska, and 2 in Kansas.

March 22

Southern Iran. A major earthquake measuring approximately 7 on the Richter scale struck near Bandar Abbas where several buildings were severely damaged; at least 60 persons were killed in the adjoining villages of Khvorgu and Qaleh Qazi.

March 25

Eastern Turkey. The fourth major earthquake in four months along the geologic fault running from southern Iran to northern Italy damaged 400 buildings in the town of Palu, rescuers reported 30 fatalities.

April 1

Bangladesh. A tornado that struck the two widely separated areas of Madaripur 80 miles southwest of Dacca and Kishorganj in northern Bangladesh devastated at least three villages, injured 1,500 persons, and claimed the lives of more than 600.

April 4
Southern United States. Tornadoes, heavy rain, and flooding ravaged the southern states of West Virginia, Virginia, Alabama, Mississippi, Georgia, Tennessee, and Kentucky, where the Cumberland River crested 18 feet above its flood stage; property damage was estimated at $275 million and the death toll at 40.

April 6
Central and southwestern Iran. Earth tremors measuring 6.5 on the Richter scale left the villages of Ardal, Borujen, Dow Polan, and Gandoman in ruins; an estimated total of 500 persons lost their lives.

Mid-April
Fagarasului Mountains, Romania. An avalanche claimed the lives of 19 high school students and 4 teachers during a skiing trip.

April 24
Northern Bangladesh. A cyclone accompanied by 100-mph winds ripped through northern Bangladesh, killing 13 persons and injuring nearly 100.

May 20
Moundou, Logone Prefecture, Chad. A tornado that swept through southeastern Chad injured 100 persons and killed 13 others.

May 23
Khorramabad, Iran. A flood following heavy rains claimed the lives of 13 persons, several of whom were children.

June 4
Northwestern Iran. Heavy rains that caused rivers to overflow their banks killed at least 10 persons near the towns of Zanjan and Takestan.

Mid-June
Oman. A tropical cyclone leveled 98 percent of the buildings, injured more than 40, and claimed the lives of 2 persons on the island of Masirah; three days later torrential rains hit Dhofar Province, which suffered even greater destruction when an estimated 15,000 animals were swept away in the floodwaters, large quantities of crops were destroyed, and more than 100 persons were killed.

June 24
Kyushu, Japan. A mud and rock slide estimated at 70,000 tons crashed down a rain-soaked mountain on the Japanese island of Kyushu; 15 homes were demolished and 11 persons were believed dead.

Early July

Southwestern France. Severe flooding following days of torrential rain destroyed nearly 90 percent of the region's cereal and tobacco crops, killed livestock, and contributed to millions of dollars in property damage; 26 persons lost their lives in the worst flooding to engulf southwestern France in the twentieth century.

Early July

Seoul, South Korea. Torrential rains followed by flooding and landslides in Seoul and surrounding areas left 80,000 persons homeless, more than 480 injured, and at least 200 dead.

July 20

Johnstown, Pennsylvania. An overnight 9-inch rainfall caused massive flooding in Johnstown and surrounding areas and left the town accessible only by helicopter; property damage was estimated at $200 million, 30 persons were missing, and at least 70 persons lost their lives in the rampaging waters.

July 25

Kao-hsiung, Taiwan. Typhoon Thelma packing winds of up to 120 mph destroyed nearly 20,000 homes in Kao-hsiung, Taiwan's major seaport and industrial center; 31 persons lost their lives.

July 31

Northern Taiwan. The second typhoon to lash Taiwan in a week struck the towns of Taipei, T'ao-yuan, and Nan-t'ou; at least 38 persons were killed.

Aug. 19

Eastern Indonesia. A major earthquake that struck eastern Indonesia measured betwen 7.7 and 8.7 in various locations on the Richter scale and was one of the strongest ever recorded; 98 persons were injured, 76 were reported missing, and at least 187 were killed.

Sept. 13

Kansas City, Missouri. Flash floods in rivers, creeks, and drainage ditches following 12 inches of torrential rain ravaged Kansas City; the flood damage was estimated at more than $100 million, and at least 26 persons lost their lives in the raging waters.

Sept. 18

Near Kathmandu, Nepal. A landslide destroyed part of a village north of Kathmandu and buried 18 persons alive.

Late September

Taipei, Taiwan. Following 16 consecutive hours of torrential rainfall in Taipei, at least 14 persons were known dead in Taiwan's worst flooding in seven years.

Mid-October

Northwestern Italy. Severe flooding following steady rainfall caused $350 million in damage in Genoa and regions of Piedmont, Liguria, and Lombardy and claimed the lives of 15 persons.

Oct. 22

Gampola, Sri Lanka. A landslide that swept over workers' quarters on a tea plantation flattened rooms that housed nine families; at least 27 persons were killed.

Nov. 2–3

Athens and Piraeus, Greece. Heavy flooding following 15 hours and 2.7 inches of rain caused the normally shallow Kifissos and Ilissos rivers to rise 6.5 feet and overflow their banks; 26 persons were killed, and the damage caused by the river waters was estimated at millions of dollars.

Nov. 6

Toccoa, Georgia. A 35-year-old earthen dam, weakened by several days of heavy rain, collapsed and loosed a 30-foot wall of water that injured 45 and killed at least 39 persons housed on the campus of Toccoa Falls Bible College.

Nov. 8

Palghat, Kerala, India. Flash floods and landslides injured three and claimed the lives of at least 24 persons.

Nov. 10

Northern Italy. Floods and landslides following five days of torrential rain left thousands of people homeless and killed at least 15 persons; the cities of Genoa and Venice were both inundated.

Nov. 12

Southern India. A tropical cyclone that whipped through the southern state of Tamil Nadu claimed the lives of more than 400 persons.

Nov. 14

Northern Philippines. A typhoon that swept through the northern Philippines left nearly 50,000 persons homeless and killed at least 30 persons, most of whom were drowned in swollen rivers or struck by falling trees and flying debris.

Nov. 19

Southern India. A cyclone and tidal wave that devastated the coastal state of Andhra Pradesh left more than 2,000,000 persons homeless and claimed the lives of an estimated 20,-000; 21 villages were totally washed away and 44 others were severely battered in India's worst cyclone disaster of the century.

Nov. 23

Western Argentina. A major earthquake measuring 7 on the Richter scale destroyed thousands of homes, injured hundreds, and killed at least 75 persons; although tremors were felt in Chile, Peru, and Brazil, the greatest damage was reported in San Juan Province, Argentina.

Dec. 20

Kerman Province, Iran. A major earthquake that struck a series of villages in south central Iran in freezing temperatures hit the villages of Babtangal, Gisk, and Sarasiab the hardest; the official death toll was estimated at 521.

Bibliography

The New Encyclopaedia Britannica (15th Edition)

Propaedia: This one-volume Outline of Knowledge is organized as a ten-part Circle of Learning, enabling the reader to carry out an orderly plan of study in any field. Its Table of Contents—consisting of 10 parts, 42 divisions, and 189 sections—is an easy topical guide to the *Macropaedia*.

Micropaedia: If interested in a particular subject, the reader can locate it in this ten-volume, alphabetically arranged Ready Reference of brief entries and Index to the *Macropaedia*, where subjects are treated at greater length or in broader contexts.

Macropaedia: These nineteen volumes of Knowledge in Depth contain extended treatments of all the fields of human learning. For information on *Disaster,* for example, consult: Archaeology; Atmosphere; Atmospheric Sciences; Climate; Climatic Change; Cyclones and Anticyclones; Deserts; Earth, Geological History of; Earth, Gravitational Field of; Earth, Heat Flow in; Earth, Mechanical Properties of; Earth, Structure and Composition of; Earth as a Planet; Earth Movements on Slopes; Earthquakes; Earth Sciences; Etna (Mount); Fluvial Processes; Geological Sciences; Glaciation, Landforms Produced by; Hillslopes; Huang Ho (River); Hurricanes and Typhoons; Hydrologic Cycle; Hydrologic Sciences; Ice Sheets and Glaciers; Igneous Rocks, Extrusive; Igneous Rocks, Pyroclastic; Ionosphere; Irrigation and Drainage; Jet Streams; Jewish Myth and Legend; Landform Evolution; Lightning; Mesopotamian Religious Literature and Mythology; Meteorite Craters; Mississippi River; Monsoons; Mountain-Building Processes; Mountain Ranges and Mountain Belts; Nature Worship; Near Eastern Religions, Ancient; Ocean Currents; Oceanic Ridges; Oceans and Seas; Physiographic Effects of Man; Physiographic Effects of Tectonism; Pompeii and Herculaneum; Rift Valleys; Rivers and River Systems; Rock Deformation; Rocks, Physical Properties of; Sand Sheets and Sand Dunes; Snow and Snowflakes; Thunderstorms; Tides; Tornadoes, Whirlwinds and Waterspouts; Van Allen Radiation Belts; Volcanoes; Water Waves; Weather Forecasting; Weathering; Weather Lore; Weather Modification; Wind Action; Winds and Storms.

Other Publications

Bolt, Bruce A., et al. *Geological Hazards: Earthquakes, Tsunamis, Volcanoes, Avalanches, Landslides, Floods.* Berlin; New York: Springer-Verlag, 1975.

Cornell, James. *The Great International Disaster Book.* New York: Charles Scribner's Sons, 1976.

Holdgate, Martin, et al. *Forces of Nature.* Edited by Vivian Fuchs. London: Thames and Hudson; New York: Holt, Rinehart and Winston, 1977.

Nash, Jay Robert. *Darkest Hours: A Narrative Encyclopedia of Worldwide Disasters from Ancient Times to the Present.* Chicago, Ill.: Nelson-Hall, 1976.

Smithsonian Institution. Center for Short-lived Phenomena. *Annual Report and Review of Events in* . . . . Cambridge, Mass.: The Center, 1969–.

United Nations Educational, Scientific and Cultural Organization. *Annual Summary of Information on Natural Disasters.* Paris: UNESCO, 1966–.

Picture Credits

Index

The Inquisitive Mind

Bantam/Britannica Books were created for those with a desire to learn. Compacted from the vast Britannica files, each book gives an in depth treatment of a particular facet of science, world events, or politics. These accessible, introductory volumes are ideal for the student and for the intellectually curious who want to know more about the world around them.

☐ 12486 **THE ARABS:**
         People and Power $2.50
☐ 12487 **DISASTER:**
         When Nature Strikes Back
                                        $2.50
☐ 12488 **THE OCEAN:**
         Mankind's Last Frontier $2.50
☐ 12485 **THE U.S. GOVERNMENT:**
         How and Why It Works $2.50

The world at your fingertips

Leading historians, sociologists, political scientists, economists, and anthropologists offer personal and political analyses of the world's developing lands.

Bring out the books that bring in the issues.

TEENAGERS FACE LIFE AND LOVE

Choose books filled with fun and adventure, discovery and disenchantment, failure and conquest, triumph and tragedy, life and love.

☐	12033	**THE LATE GREAT ME** Sandra Scoppettone	$1.75
☐	10946	**HOME BEFORE DARK** Sue Ellen Bridgers	$1.50
☐	11961	**THE GOLDEN SHORES OF HEAVEN** Katie Letcher Lyle	$1.50
☐	12501	**PARDON ME, YOU'RE STEPPING ON MY EYEBALL!** Paul Zindel	$1.95
☐	11091	**A HOUSE FOR JONNIE O.** Blossom Elfman	$1.95
☐	12025	**ONE FAT SUMMER** Robert Lipsyte	$1.75
☐	12252	**I KNOW WHY THE CAGED BIRD SINGS** Maya Angelou	$1.95
☐	11800	**ROLL OF THUNDER, HEAR MY CRY** Mildred Taylor	$1.75
☐	11605	**MY DARLING, MY HAMBURGER** Paul Zindel	$1.75
☐	10370	**THE BELL JAR** Sylvia Plath	$1.95
☐	12338	**WHERE THE RED FERN GROWS** Wilson Rawls	$1.75
☐	11829	**CONFESSIONS OF A TEENAGE BABOON** Paul Zindel	$1.95
☐	11632	**MARY WHITE** Caryl Ledner	$1.95
☐	11640	**SOMETHING FOR JOEY** Richard E. Peck	$1.75
☐	12347	**SUMMER OF MY GERMAN SOLDIER** Bette Greene	$1.75
☐	11839	**WINNING** Robin Brancato	$1.75
☐	12057	**IT'S NOT THE END OF THE WORLD** Judy Blume	$1.50

Buy them at your local bookstore or use this handy coupon for ordering: